THE JERUSALEM CENTER
FOR NEAR EASTERN STUDIES
Brigham Young University

Dear Student:

You are on the verge of a great adventure.

The Lord said, "In all places where I record my name I will come unto thee, and I will bless thee....in Jerusalem, which I have chosen... will I put my name for ever." (Ex. 20:24; 2 Kgs. 21:7)

What is so special about this city? What treasures await discovery? What is the best way to start the search? Some ways are more effective and economical than others.

Even frequent visitors need help; a guidebook will prove invaluable. **MICHAEL'S GUIDE JERUSALEM** is one that could accompany your study of the Old and New Testaments plus subsequent history. It is a key which opens doors to greater meaning.

Since we do not always recognize what we see and hear, effective study will also include seeking information from those who have already made valuable discoveries. But remember, the grand master key will always be divine assistance — sincerely ask for it.

Bless you in this great adventure. Open the doors. Make this adventure one of both sight and soul.

JERUSALEM CENTER FOR NEAR EASTERN STUDIES

MICHAEL'S GUIDE SERIES INCLUDES:

MICHAEL'S GUIDE ARGENTINA, CHILE, PARAGUAY & URUGUAY
MICHAEL'S GUIDE BOLIVIA & PERU
MICHAEL'S GUIDE ECUADOR, COLOMBIA & VENEZUELA
MICHAEL'S GUIDE BRAZIL
MICHAEL'S GUIDE SOUTH AMERICA (Continental)

MICHAEL'S GUIDE NORTHERN CALIFORNIA
MICHAEL'S GUIDE SOUTHERN CALIFORNIA
MICHAEL'S GUIDE CALIFORNIA

MICHAEL'S GUIDE SCANDINAVIA
MICHAEL'S GUIDE SCOTLAND
MICHAEL'S GUIDE SWITZERLAND
MICHAEL'S GUIDE HUNGARY
MICHAEL'S GUIDE TURKEY

MICHAEL'S GUIDE NEW YORK CITY
MICHAEL'S GUIDE LONDON
MICHAEL'S GUIDE PARIS
MICHAEL'S GUIDE AMSTERDAM
MICHAEL'S GUIDE BRUSSELS & ANTWERP
MICHAEL'S GUIDE FRANKFURT
MICHAEL'S GUIDE ROME
MICHAEL'S GUIDE MADRID
MICHAEL'S GUIDE BARCELONA
MICHAEL'S GUIDE JERUSALEM

ראש העיריה
رئيس البلدية
MAYOR OF JERUSALEM

Dear Visitor:

A visit to Jerusalem is always a special, often unique, experience.

The Jerusalem experience comprises the city's direct link to history and its spiritual heritage for Judaism, Christianity and Islam. Its antiquities, historical monuments, and architecture all attest to the city's rich traditions.

It is also a city of culture and the arts, of music and painting and theater and film. It is a city of markets and quaint alleys. It is a city of age-old olive trees and wildflowers.

The ideal way to explore this unique city is on foot, which gives you the chance to know the city's streets and hills and unequalled views, to know the city's atmosphere and its people. A travel guide comprising a series of walking tours can open these many opportunities. It allows you to set your own pace while ensuring that you do not miss out on famous landmarks as well as some fascinating, off-the-beaten-track, sites. This guidebook, which leads you through the city in a series of well-planned and geographically oriented tours, is an essential companion for the discerning visitor to our city.

We look forward to welcoming you here!

Teddy Kollek
Mayor of Jerusalem

JERUSALEM

Series editor:
Michael Shichor

INBAL
Travel Information Ltd.

Inbal Travel Information Ltd.
P.O. Box 39090 Tel Aviv Israel 61390

Intl. ISBN 965-288-062-0

Text: Dror Wahrman

CONTENTS

TABLE OF MAPS

Preface

Israel is a tiny country packed with an incredible variety of fascinating sites: Roman amphitheathers and aqueducts, Crusader fortresses, pristine beaches, desert landscapes, sophisticated electronic industries and labyrinthine street markets. In the midst of this, is Jerusalem, a city so complex and fascinating that it requires no less than a guide devoted solely to the city to satisfy the discerning visitor in Israel.

When one prepares a guide to Jerusalem, one is overwhelmed by a feeling of the spiritual and the temporal. On the one hand, Jerusalem is a holy city, a city which has been a symbol of yearning and redemption for thousands of years, a city of religious devotion and emotion, a site of historical importance then, as today. On the other hand, Jerusalem is a city of everyday reality, a city fraught with problems of housing, transportation and inter-religious tensions.

Jerusalem of the past and the present, a city of many faces, many facets, a city in which everyone can find that which he seeks, Jerusalem of Gold. A city which knew splendor and waste, glory and shame. A city of contradictions. Here you find the old and the new intermingled, the modern and the ancient side by side. Jerusalem has no equal.

Much time was spent in the preparation of this Guide. Long months of hard work, collecting, collating, choosing and checking. Weeks of wandering the streets, of visiting the sites, of exploring. Much energy was invested in trying to find the balance between the essential and the redundant. Because of its special character, its importance and the abundance of its sites, a multitude of books have already been written on Jerusalem and there is material enough to write many, many more.

We hope to open to you Jerusalem's multifarious aspects, ranging from archeology to modernization, from Jews through Christians to Moslems, from eternal calm to ceaseless tension, from site to sight. Our aim is not only to introduce to you some of the most impressive sites in the world, but also to reveal them to you in a different way. We want you to know the city not as an outsider, but rather as one who has the experience and insights of in insider, and to make you feel at one with this all-enchanting city.

A whole team, under the leadership of Dror Wahrman, one of the leading young researchers of Jerusalem and a renowned guide, worked on this book. Mr. Wahrmam was responsible for the compilation of the in-depth historical survey and of the tours, while the practical information was compliled by the competent staff of Inbal Travel Information, Ltd. What envolved was not only a travel guide, but also a book quintessential and fascinating, which enfolds in it the whole of Jerusalem in a way which educates the visitor, and which will remain a token of remembrance.

Michael Shichor

Using this Guide

In order to reap maximum benefit from the information concentrated in this Guide, we advise the traveller to carefully read the following advice. The facts contained in this book are meant to help the tourist find his or her way around, and to assure that he see the most, with maximum savings of money, time and effort.

The information contained in the Introduction should be read in its entirety as it has details which will help in making early decisions and arrangements regarding your trip. Reviewing the material thoroughly means that you will be better organized and set for your visit. Upon arrival in Jerusalem, you will already feel familiar and comfortable, more so than otherwise might have been the case.

The basic guideline in all MICHAEL'S GUIDE publications is to survey places in a primarily geographical sequence and not a thematic one. The logic behind it is that a geographical plan not only ensures the most efficient time use, but also contributes dramatically to getting to know an area and its different aspects as well as acquiring a feeling for it.

We now come to the very heart of the Guide — "getting-to-know-the-city." Here we survey the variety of available touring options — and begin our own walking tours around town.

All of our tours are accompanied by a map, each has a numbered index indicating the exact location of the landmarks mentioned in the tour. The maps also indicate the nature of the landmark. On the inside front cover is a colored map which indicates the area covered by each of our tours.

After touring Jerusalem, we turn our attention to the surrounding areas and areas which are relatively close.

Understanding the limitations facing the visitor, who is probably unable to take all of our walks, we have compiled, at the end of our last tour, a list of "musts." It includes only the most fundamental locales, those which really should not be missed. Consult the list when planning your visit.

But there is more to Jerusalem than "musts," and there are other attractions to indulge in — even for someone with very little time to spare. We have therefore compiled information regarding galleries, craft shops and dining in our last chapter,

"Making The Most of Your Stay." The chapter also includes a list of useful addresses and telephone numbers.

To further facilitate the use of this Guide, we have included a detailed index. It includes all the major locations mentioned throughout the book.

Because times and cities do change, an important rule when travelling in general, and when visiting a city like Jerusalem, should be to consult the local sources of information. We have therefore accompanied nearly every place with a phone number for last minute checks and suggest you consult the hotel concierge, *The Jerusalem Post*, the tourist information offices, etc. All of them can advise you of the latest updated information at the specific time of your visit.

As for updating, a guide to a city like Jerusalem cannot afford to march in place, and up to the time that the Guide went to press, we attempted to confirm its relevance. However, it is only natural that due to frequent changes which occur, travellers will find certain time-related facts somewhat less than precise when they arrive at their destination, and for this we apologize in advance.

To this end, cooperation and assistance is necessary and vital from those of you have enjoyed the information contained in this Guide. It ensures, first and foremost, that those who travel in your wake will also enjoy and succeed in their ventures as much as you have. For this purpose, we have included a short questionnaire at the end of this Guide and we will be most grateful to those who complete it and send it to us. A **complimentary copy** of the new edition will be forwarded to those of you who take the time, and whose contribution appears in the updated edition.

During your visit you will see and experience many things — we have therefore left several blank pages at the back of this Guide. These are for you.

Have a pleasant and exciting trip — Bon Voyage!

INTRODUCTION

Part One — An Overview of a Complex City

3000 Years of History

Jerusalem has been settled for more than five millennia. Since its conquest by King David (1000 BC), it has been a site of great importance as focus of the aspirations and prayers of millions worldwide — first of the Jewish People and later of Christians and Muslims. This brief introduction surveys the major phases and significance of Jerusalem's development. A concise chronological chart has been included at the end of the chapter for quick orientation.

Jebus (pre-Davidic Jebusite Jerusalem) was a town of no particular importance, resting between the Judean Desert and the arable Judean Hills. It may have been designed like many other settlements in such locations, to keep shepherds and their flocks off the mountain farmland. Jebus rested at the only spring-fed site in the vicinity — the narrow, pitched slope known today as the "City of David" — between the Valley of Kidron to the east and the Tyropoeon Valley to the west. The steep slope and the nearby desert made Jebus better suited as a place of refuge than a government center. The town was off the main road and on the high mountain ridge, with no evident strategic importance. This may explain why it was not conquered by the twelve Israelite tribes during their conquest of Canaan, but left as a non-Jewish enclave between the tribal domains of Judah to the south and Benjamin to the north.

King David conquered the small, Jebusite enclave around the year 1000 BC and declared it his capital after having ruled for several years from the domain of the Tribe of Judah. By doing so, he avoided tribal preference and attained a neutral capital. The twelve tribes of Israel were thus forged into a single nation under one king. This was the start of the great importance which Jewish tradition attributes to David and Jerusalem.

It was David's son and successor, Solomon, who built the First Temple. This act completed Jerusalem's transformation from a marginal settlement into the religious and governmental center of the kingdom. Solomon built the temple outside the City of David on the adjacent natural acropolis which loomed over it and claimed the backing of Divine authority, a standard practice in the ancient world. The Temple was part of the government complex which Solomon built and during this period it was the major but not the only center where Jewish rites were practiced.

After his death in 925 BC, Solomon's kingdom split in two — Israel to the north and Judah to the south with Jerusalem as its capital. The northern kingdom with its capital at Samaria, lasted for about two centuries until it fell to the Assyrians. This resulted in a stream of refugees which swelled Jerusalem's population.

When Jerusalem was threatened in 701 BC, by Sennacherib the Assyrian, King Hezekiah of Judah prepared the city for the imminent siege. First he constructed a rampart which extended Jerusalem's lines to the 'upper city', the western hill between the Tyropoeon Valley and the Vale of Hinnom. Then he excavated a tunnel to draw water from the Gihon ('Gusher') Spring to the Siloam Pool, which lay inside the city's new walls. After taking 46 cities in Judah, Sennacherib threatened Jerusalem and Hezekiah's defeat seemed imminent, but suddenly Sennacherib folded his tents and returned to Assyria.

That Jerusalem succeeded in overcoming this grave threat, strengthened the belief that it was an unconquerable, mighty and God-favored city. Then belief was shattered when Nebuchadnezzar of Babylon conquered the city in 586 BC. The Temple was sacked and the King and part of the population where exiled to Babylon. This was the end of the First Temple period.

The exile did not last long. The Babylonian Empire was overtaken by the Persians, whose king, Cyrus, issued a decree in 536 BC permitting the restoration of the Jewish community in Judah as well as the rebuilding of the Temple. Within twenty years, the Second Temple, was consecrated though it was smaller and humbler than its predecessor. In the mid-5th century BC, Ezra the Scribe, and Nehemia, who subsequently rebuilt the city wall, arrived in Jerusalem.

In 332 BC, the Persians lost control of Jerusalem to the Greeks under the command of Alexander the Great. The first of Jerusalem's Greek rulers belonged to the Ptolemaic dynasty in Egypt, but during the early second century BC, the Syria-based Seleucids took over. The impact of Hellenistic culture in the country, which had been adopted by many Jews, eventually led to a schism within the Jewish community. This, together with unpopular Seleucid policies — especially those of Antiochus IV

(Epiphanes 'The Wicked') — triggered a revolt led by Mattathias the Hasmonean and his sons, the most famous of whom was Judas Maccabeus. As a result of this successful insurrection, the autonomous Hasmonean Kingdom restored Jerusalem's status as the Jewish people's national and religious center. After three generations of Hasmonean rule, General Pompey of Rome was asked to intervene in an internal struggle for the throne. The resulting infusion of Roman influence ultimately grew into total conquest.

The most important figure in the administration of Roman-satellite Judea was King Herod, who ruled from 37-4 BC. Jewish sources describe this proselyte Idumean Jew with disdain. He wiped out the Hasmonean dynasty on his way to the throne and thereafter ruled by the mercy of Rome. He was nevertheless a vigorous, strong monarch who did much to better his country and subjects. He maneuvered skillfully through convoluted Roman politics to maintain his position of authority and favor.

Herod pursued a policy of extensive development. Apart from Jerusalem, which took on a new image in his lifetime, he built Caesarea (Palestine's great port), reconstructed Sebastia (Samaria), and erected fortresses and palaces in locations such as Massada, Herodion and Jericho. Even the ruins, are impressive and reflect Herod's verve and daring. When he found the Temple Mount unsuitable for the magnificent edifice he was planning to construct, he raised giant retaining walls around the mount and filled them in to create a vast artificial plateau — the world's largest temple compound at the time. Herod's magnificent Temple, an enlargement of the shrine erected by former Babylonian exiles, became central to the city in terms of strength, function and status. It became the destination of hundreds of thousands of Jewish pilgrims from Judea and beyond. Their arrival, mainly during the three 'pilgrimage festivals' (Passover, Shavuot, Succot), dominated life in Jerusalem and did much to define its character.

Jerusalem's status as the religious and national center of Israel grew as never before. At the time, Jews accounted for about 10% of the entire population of the Roman Empire with half of them dwelling in Judea. The centrality of Jerusalem therefore had important economic and political ramifications. Apart from the Temple and the surrounding structures, Herod left an indelible mark on the city by the construction of other impressive edifices. Among them were his palace in the Upper City with its defense towers, as well as typical Roman structures such as the theater, amphitheater and hippodrome. While these and other elements lent Jerusalem something of a Roman profile, important Jewish features, in addition to the Temple, were prominent in Jerusalem. A great number of ritual baths (*mikve*) were built to accommodate the large influx of pilgrims. In compliance with the Jewish doctrine of the time, there was no iconography used to adorn the city.

Jerusalem in Herod's time expanded chiefly towards the north and northwest. The city extended as far as today's Russian Compound and St. George Cathedral, covering an area approximately twice that of today's Old City. Estimates of its population range from 80,000 to 150,000, including Jewish communities of diverse and distant origin. To meet the city's growing water needs, Herod developed a sophisticated conduit system which drew on remarkably distant sources.

Herod's successors were too politically inept to 'toe the line' as Herod had and were unable to keep Judea independent and fulfill Roman desires at the same time. They allowed control of the province to slide into the hands of the Roman procurators. These officials ruled almost uninterruptedly from Caesarea until 66 AD and eradicated Jerusalem's status as the political capital of the country. Jerusalem became a place for occasional visits by procurators, usually on the three 'pilgrimage' festivals, when anti-government agitation and sentiments peaked. It was on such an occasion — Passover of 30 AD — that Procurator Pontius Pilate had Jesus executed by crucifixion.

The only significant interruption in the Procurators' rule occurred in 41 AD, when Herod Agrippas, grandson of his namesake, reigned for three years. During this period the outermost Jerusalem wall, known as the 'Third Wall', was begun.

The Procurators' era was typified by growing ferment among the Jews in Jerusalem and Judea. Political factions emerged which were no less hostile to one another than they were to Roman rule. In 66 AD the Procurator's behavior provoked a riot which escalated into a general revolt. The Roman Governor of Syria was defeated at the Temple gates, and Jerusalem regained independence for three years. The city's Christian community fled and the rebels were torn by internal struggles. Ultimately the situation proved advantageous to Rome and facilitated the subsequent suppression of the revolt. In 70 AD, the Emperor Vespasian sent his son Titus to put an end to the insurrections and to ensure full Roman control of the area. Following a difficult siege, Titus managed to breach Jerusalem's walls in July of that year. Three weeks later — the Ninth of Av according to the Jewish calendar (traditionally the date of the First Temple's destruction), the Second Temple was destroyed. The warfare ended a month later when the rebels' last strongholds in the Upper City were taken. The Great Rebellion, as it came to be known, ended as one of the greatest catastrophes in

Jewish history. The Temple was gone, most of Jerusalem lay in ruins, her population decimated.

Sixty years later, the Emperor Hadrian set out to build a Roman colony on Jerusalem's ruins named *Aelia Capitolina* (after the Emperor's family and the triad of Capitolinic gods). This was one of the factors which led to the uprising led by Simeon Bar-Kokhba. Again Jerusalem enjoyed three years of autonomy (132-135 AD), during which the sacrificial rite was resumed on the Temple Mount. The Romans crushed the revolt, caused immense destruction, and Jerusalem was rebuilt as Aelia Capitolina. A temple to Jupiter was erected atop the Temple ruins and the city was declared off-limits to the circumcised — namely, the Jews. The Roman grid layout of the time is still evident in today's Old City. In order to eliminate any Jewish nationalistic aspirations, Hadrian changed the name of the province from Judea to Syria-Palestina.

A fundamental change in the city's status was caused by Emperor Constantine whose conversion to Christianity in 310 marked the onset of Christian-Roman (Byzantine) rule in Jerusalem. At the Church Council in Nicaea in 325, Bishop Makarios of Jerusalem alerted Constantine to the condition of the holy sites in Jerusalem. The Emperor dispatched his mother Helena to the city in 326, where she uncovered and identified holy places — including the site of Jesus' crucifixion and burial under the Roman Temple of Venus. The pagan shrine was promptly removed and in its place the Church of the Holy Sepulchre was built. Jerusalem became Christianized and the restriction on Jews entering the city was reaffirmed. The only interruption in the process of Christian entrenchment in Jerusalem was the short tenure of Emperor Julian the Apostate who reverted to the ancient Greek religion and favored Judaism. He even permitted reconstruction of the Jewish Temple, but the prior status quo returned upon the premature death of Julian.

Two other figures from the Byzantine period are worthy of mention. The first is Empress Eudocia, who reached Jerusalem in 444 after she separated from her husband, Emperor Theodosius. Dwelling in Jerusalem until 460, she built the wall surrounding Mt. Zion. The second is the Emperor Justinian, who built the massive Nea Church in what was then the southern end of town. This was an active period of construction in Jerusalem and evidence of various projects such as churches and wide thoroughfares is still apparent. A detailed description of the Byzantine city is documented in the sixth century Mosaic Madaba Map, named for the site in present-day Jordan where it was discovered.

In 614 the Persian army captured Jerusalem from the Byzantines, taking the True Cross from the Church of the Holy Sepulchre with them to Persia. The Cross was redeemed by the Emperor Heraclius in 628.

Ten years later, in 638, the Muslim army took the city without opposition. The conquest was part of an extensive campaign whereby the new religion gained control of an area stretching from the Arabian Peninsula to the entire southern Mediterranean Basin.

There are numerous, often confusing, tales surrounding the Muslim conquest of Jerusalem. These accounts differ according to the religious bias of the source. Christians, for example, claim that Caliph Omar refused to enter the Church of the Holy Sepulchre to pray, in hope that other Muslims would take his example and refrain from desecrating their shrine. According to Muslim tradition, the Christians attempted to steer Omar away from the Temple Mount. The Caliph, in fact, did not lead the Muslim army into Jerusalem and the city was taken by a junior officer. At the onset of Muslim rule, Jerusalem was not considered a highly important city and its star rose only when the Damascus-based Umayyad caliphs took control of the Muslim world in 660. They 'rediscovered' the city, holy to Jews and Christians, because of its proximity to their own capital. Jerusalem became especially important to them in light of their competition with Islamic forces in Arabia who dominated the Muslim holy cities of Mecca and Medina. A period of construction began under the Umayyads in which structures were built near and on the Temple Mount. Among them were the Dome of the Rock, the Al-Aksa Mosque and palaces. This led to the increased importance of Jerusalem in Islamic tradition. A literary corpus in its praise subsequently developed (see 'A Holy City to Three Religions'). Nevertheless, the Umayyads established their capital of Palestine not in Jerusalem but in the new town of Ramle.

Beginning in the middle of the eighth century, Islamic dynasties based either in Baghdad or Egypt alternately gained control of Jerusalem. Again the city's importance ebbed. Though Christians were the majority in Jerusalem during the early Islamic era, a local Muslim community developed as well, as did a very small community of Jews (aided by Omar, against the Christians' wishes). Towards the end of the ninth century, the Karaites, a break-away Jewish sect, established a presence in Jerusalem alongside the mainstream Jewish community. In another important pre-Crusader event, Fatimid Caliph al-Hakim persecuted non-Muslims and in 1009 ordered the systematic demolition of all Christian churches, including the Holy Sepulchre, which was partially restored later.

Under the encouragement of Pope Urban II, the First Crusade

set out for the Holy Land and seized Jerusalem on July 15, 1099, and massacred the local population. There were many interesting reasons for the Crusades which set out from Europe to wrest the Holy Land from the Muslims. The immediate pretext for taking Jerusalem involved reports which reached Europe regarding the maltreatment of Christian pilgrims. In many respects the acquisition of Jerusalem was the goal of the Crusaders, who crowned their conquest by designating it capital of the Latin Kingdom of Jerusalem, the only political entity ever to bear Jerusalem's name. This decision imposed problems of defense and administration on the new kingdom. The king's court and administration, religious centers and military and monastic orders (the Templars and the Hospitalers) were established in Jerusalem. Most of the population was of European Christian origin, chiefly from France, but the Eastern Christians were represented as well. Although Jews and Muslims were denied residence rights in Jerusalem, there were exceptions. During this period, Jerusalem attracted thousands of European Christian pilgrims each year.

A building boom characterized the initial Crusader years in Jerusalem. New needs demanded the construction and renovation of Muslim buildings. The Temple Mount mosques, for example, were transfomed into churches. The most important construction project in this period was the Church of the Holy Sepulchre, a unification of existing and new structures. It was consecrated on the 50th anniversary of the Crusader conquest of Jerusalem. In the Upper City, the Crusaders adapted the Citadel to their needs, renaming it *Turris David* (Tower of David) and built the King's palace alongside. Of the many Crusader buildings surviving today, two of the most conspicuous are the Romanesque Church of Saint Anne and the Tomb of Mary near the Brook of Kidron.

The Latin Kingdom of Jerusalem came to an end at the hands of the Muslim Salah-a-din (Saladin) in July 1187. Consequently, European Christians were expelled from the city and Jews were readmitted. Most of the Christian buildings, including original Muslim structures which the Crusaders had 'baptized' upon their arrival, were once again put to Muslim use. An exception was the Church of the Holy Sepulchre which was turned over to non-European Christians. The Muslims also leveled the city's walls so as to deny their protective benefits to returning Crusaders. Until the mid-13th century, military and political instability reigned. The Crusaders, having set up a new kingdom along the coast of Palestine, reclaimed the city and held it for 15 years (1229-1244).

A new period of relative stability under the Mamelukes of

Egypt began in the 1260s. The Mamelukes were a unique society which ruled Egypt. They were ex-slaves, brought from Asia and the Balkans to Egypt, generation after generation, and were converted to Islam and given military training. They later attained the status of free men and joined the ranks of the ruling military aristocracy. The Sultan himself was in fact an ex-slave. While under Mameluke rule Jerusalem was considered neither administratively nor economically important, but religiously, it was very significant. Scores of buildings were erected for religious purposes, primarily scholastic academies (*madrasa*) and convents (*zawiya*). These exotic buildings are among the least-known in the Old City. The proliferation of religious academies in Jerusalem produced a highly influential community of theologians who turned late-medieval Jerusalem into a center of Islamic studies. The religious nature of the city led to hostility toward non-Muslims, which occasionally developed into actual persecution. The major targets were the Franciscan monks who had settled in Jerusalem in 1334. As the Pope's representatives in Jerusalem, they were designated by him as 'guardians of the holy places in the Holy Land'.

In 1517, Palestine and Jerusalem fell to the Turkish Ottoman Empire, the rising power in the eastern Mediterranean, during its campaign against the Mamelukes in Egypt. Shortly thereafter, Suleiman the Magnificent — the last of the ten great Ottoman Sultans, and perhaps the greatest — took the throne in Constantinople and renamed it Istanbul. His reign (1520-1566) was marked by a period of exceptional development and activity in Palestine in general and in Jerusalem in particular. His activities in Jerusalem covered a wide range of areas. He secured the city by erecting the city wall we know today, he fostered the development or resurrection of the Jerusalem market economy, and stimulated commerce and industry with a system of privileges. The water system was restored and expanded, including the installation of public drinking facilities which exist today. In the religious sphere, Suleiman's administration renovated the Dome of the Rock and other parts of the Temple Mount. Jerusalem's population reflected the affluence of this period, exploding from about 5,000 in 1516 to approximately 16,000 by 1550.

The Ottoman Empire, however, began a slow decline which lasted hundreds of years. The city's population ebbed to 9,000-10,000 and stagnated at that level until 1800. No longer politically or economically significant, Jerusalem became a forsaken town at the Empire's fringe, with nothing beyond except Bedouin nomads. The decaying effects of time took over, and the European powers took little interest in the affairs of Jerusalem until their conspicuous change of heart in the early 19th century.

The French did, however, mount several unsuccessful attempts during these two and a half centuries to establish a local consulate. Napoleon, during his Palestine campaign of 1799, took no notice of Jerusalem and even failed to visit it. During these years, the Jews consolidated their presence in Jerusalem.

A dramatic turnabout in status and development of Jerusalem occurred in the 1800s. The first flickerings began at the turn of the 19th century, with both Jewish immigration and European interest in the city. The pivotal event was the insurrection of Egyptian army officer Muhammad Ali who took control of Egypt during the 1830s. Forcing the Ottoman Empire out of Palestine in 1831, he held this province until 1840. Ali's rule was marked by governmental consolidation and great efforts in the general development of the country. He developed a modern, strong army, made roads relatively safe, domesticated many of the nomads, modernized agriculture, introduced new crops, developed industry, instituted centralized government, and improved the workings of administration. Ali had pro-Western leanings and worked to establish relations with European powers and to involve European experts in his military and economic enterprises. In keeping with his overall policy of reform, and in hopes of procuring the support of an educated population, he treated the Christian and Jewish minorities benevolently and repealed many of the restrictions they lived under.

Muhammad Ali's tenure may be seen as the dawn of modern Jerusalem. Hospitable to foreigners and Jews alike, Jerusalem attracted both in growing numbers. For the Jews, the climate of reform made immigration immeasurably easier. The severe earthquake in 1837 which devastated the Jewish community of Galilee, resulted in the migration of Jews to Jerusalem, enhancing the status of the Jewish community there. At this time, after a long wait, Jews were allowed to renovate synagogues and even to build new ones. At the same time, there was an increased non-Jewish European movement to Jerusalem. Though most were pilgrims, a few did come to stay. Muhammad Ali allowed the newcomers to retain their foreign citizenship and to live under the exclusive jurisdiction of their national consuls — a privilege of immeasurable value. In this encouraging environment, the Protestants built their first church in the Middle East and the British opened Jerusalem's first European consulate.

Towards 1840, Muhammad Ali threatened a march on Istanbul, capital of the Ottoman Empire. The question of the crumbling Empire's future — 'the Eastern problem' or 'the fate of the sick man of Europe' — confronted the European powers. Europe, in fact, preferred the easily-manipulated Ottoman Empire to a strong state, and took concerted action to nudge Ali back to

Egypt. Palestine was once again under Turkish rule, but the European powers insisted that the reforms instated by Ali be maintained and extended. To a certain degree, the Ottomans recognized those reforms as advantageous.

Two distinct but interrelated developments emerged in Jerusalem at this time. One was the rapid growth of the Jewish community, from about 2,000 of the city's 9,000 residents in 1800 to a majority of approximately 45,000 of 70,000 in 1914. The second development was the increasing involvement of the European powers in the affairs of Jerusalem and the competition among them for means of influence. This was primarily attained by the construction of massive impressive buildings. These changes coincided with a rapid technological improvement in Palestine which until then had been a backward region. Innovations hitherto unknown appeared — wagons and passenger coaches (wagon wheels, started to furrow the soil of Palestine in 1869), steamships and the telegraph. The Jerusalem townscape changed drastically during the 1800s. Available space within the Old City walls became scarce. The Christians built churches, hospices and other institutions, and the Jews built synagogues and homes. The inevitable expansion beyond the city walls began in the 1850s, a process which quickly turned the walls into functionally worthless ornaments.

While the Jewish community set out to solve its own housing and institutional needs, Christian building was meant to accommodate pilgrims and to attain a position of prominence. The difference outside the walls was conspicuous. Jewish development focused on modest residential quarters, beginning with Mishkenot Sha'anannim and the adjacent windmill (now symbols in Jewish history) and other well-known neighborhoods such as Me'a She'arim. These were pioneer outposts at first; isolated clusters of houses whose residents had to cope with an unfamiliar environment. By World War I, however, the interceding empty areas were filled in, creating an impressive urban area outside the walls. The Old City was relegated to the status of a small suburb. Meanwhile, competing Christian organizations erected scores of public institutions. These were meant to serve the growing numbers of Christian pilgrims, improve the quality of public services (education, health, etc.) and enhance the prestige of the European powers supporting the development enterprise. These buildings — churches, monasteries, schools, hospitals, hostels — account for most of the impressive structures built in Jerusalem during the 19th century. Since each European country incorporated its own architectural styles into its projects, new Jerusalem is eclectic of national styles, including Russian 'onion' churches, a medieval German castle, an English Oxford-style cathedral, and a replica of a medieval

Italian palace of the type found in Florence or Siena.

Rivalry between powers was not confined to design in Jerusalem stone. One of its manifestations was the Crimean War — an international conflict in Asia in 1853, sparked (though not really caused) by disputes between the Russian-supported Greek Orthodox and the French-backed Roman Catholics over rights in the Holy Places in Jerusalem and Bethlehem. Less bloody arenas of competition were the domains of banking, postal services and Holy Land research societies.

Muslim activity during these decades, though less significant, resulted in the development of affluent residences in several neighborhoods in East Jerusalem.

The new city soon became Jerusalem's urban center, with a predominantly Jewish population. The energetic Jewish elements in Jerusalem belonged to the 'Old Yishuv', comprising veteran Jerusalemites and more recent arrivals whose inclinations were religious, rather than nationalistic. The Jewish nationalist movement born in the late 1800s confined most of its activity to the coastal plain and it was only after World War I that the Zionist Movement made its indelible mark on the city.

Four centuries of Ottoman rule in Jerusalem ended in the aftermath of World War I. Although the city was not involved in actual combat, its population experienced serious food shortages, expulsion and poor administration. On December 11, 1917, the city officially surrendered to General Allenby of Great Britain. After three years of military government, a British civil administration was established in 1920, under a High Commissioner who resided in Jerusalem. For the first time since the Crusades, Christians made Jerusalem the capital of Palestine — a decision of great importance to the city's subsequent development. As the British administration settled in, so did the major Zionist institutions (having relocated from Jaffa). In 1923, the League of Nations lent the actions of Great Britain official recognition in the form of a formal Mandate for Palestine.

Jerusalem now developed swiftly, in part because of the orderly, modern administration but mainly because of the accelerated Jewish growth, which was encouraged by the Balfour Declaration of 1917 (compiled by the British Foreign Secretary Balfour), in which the right of the Jewish people to 'a National Home in Palestine' was established. An important event about this time was the opening of the Hebrew University on Mt. Scopus in 1925 in the presence of Lord Balfour and Zionist dignitaries.

During their tenure, the British attempted to create a special, characteristic Jerusalem building style. Outstanding examples from the period are the YMCA building (West Jerusalem), the Rockefeller Museum (East Jerusalem) and the High Commissioner's residence. In addition, Jerusalem's first military Governor, Ronald Storrs, passed a law by which all buildings were required to be either built or faced with Jerusalem stone. This law is still strictly adhered to — except in instances when it entails great expense or impedes absolutely essential construction.

A new phenomenon which dominated the Mandate years was the violent strife between Jews and Arabs owing to Arab opposition to the Zionist designs and actions. Especially bloody disturbances erupted on Passover of 1920, resulting in the loss of lives and destruction of property in Jerusalem's Jewish community. In 1929, tension in the Western Wall area (abutting the Al-Aksa Mosque) sparked riots throughout Palestine causing heavy Jewish casualties including women and children. The years 1936-1939 were marked by a series of Arab strikes, riots and violent disturbances which activist minority factions in the Jewish community met in a similar fashion. The British responded to the escalating discord with a series of investigative committees. The Peel Commission of 1936, the most important of these, was the first to introduce the concept of creating separate Jewish and Arab states by partitioning the country. The tension-torn communities reflected this kind of thinking by taking on a clearer demarcation in areas of residence. The Jewish presence in the Old City, previously evident in most quarters, retreated to the Jewish Quarter. Within a few years, British policy took an anti-Zionist turn which was expressed in restrictions on Jewish immigration and land purchase. This resulted in active Zionist resistance accompanied by acts of terror on the part of underground groups, with occasional collaboration by the main Zionist defense arm, the Haganah. All but the most extreme elements called a 'cease-fire' during World War II, so as not to hamper the British struggle against Nazism, but all political restraints were removed in 1946 when Jewish resistance members blew up a wing of Jerusalem's King David Hotel, which housed British administration and army offices and many people were killed.

On November 29, 1947, the UN General Assembly voted in favor of partitioning Palestine into a Jewish and an Arab state — an act perceived as a victory for the Zionist cause. The resolution assigned municipal Jerusalem an extraterritorial (international) status. The Arab response triggered Israel's War of Independence.

The conflict should be viewed in two phases. Until May 15,

1948, the combatants were Jewish underground and semi-underground groups against Arab partisans and irregulars. The British, though ostensibly in control of the country, were utterly unable — and perhaps at times unwilling — to prevent the warfare. The Arab effort focused on the roads. They attempted to cut off the one narrow road linking Jerusalem with the coast as well as trying to isolate various sections of Jewish Jerusalem. Jerusalem's water supply from the lowlands was also severed. Besieged, Jewish Jerusalem, accounting for one-sixth of Palestine's approximate 600,000 Jews, placed food and water (the latter from its cistern storage) under ration. By early April 1948 the situation was desperate, and an offensive was mounted which temporarily opened the road and renewed supplies to the city. Three months later, the transportation problem was permanently solved when an improvised bypass known as the Burma Road was pushed through from the coastal plain and a new water pipe was laid.

In town, however, every street corner had seemingly become a battle front with the neighborhood fabric a chessboard of partial or total siege. The Jewish forces had one objective, namely to achieve territorial continuity between the Jewish neighborhoods.

The last of the British left Jerusalem on May 15, 1948. The State of Israel was declared and Jewish forces took over the British Government buildings in the center of the city. Phase two of the War of Independence began the same day when five Arab countries invaded the country. Egyptian and Iraqi forces reached Jerusalem city lines, in addition to the Jordanian Legion which had been operating there even before the British pulled out. The new Israel Defense Forces succeeded in uniting the Jewish quarters on the city's west side. The besieged Jewish Quarter in the Old City, however, defied all rescue attempts and finally surrendered. The Jordanian Legion moved into the Quarter on May 28 and immediately leveled many of its buildings. When a cease-fire was declared in June, Jerusalem's partitioning into an Israeli West and a Jordanian East was by then a fact.

To a certain extent, the aftermath of the war brought a decline in Jerusalem's status on both sides. The eastern sector was annexed by Jordan and ruled from Amman. It was cut off from the Mediterranean and detached from Bethlehem and Hebron until a lengthy, winding detour was pushed through in place of the original road held by Israel. Some major municipal services were on the Israeli side. Thus, for several years East Jerusalem lacked a regular supply of electricity. The Jordanian military presence at times led to tension and clashes with the local civilian population. Jordanian Jerusalem developed slowly and by 1967 its population stood at 65,000 — roughly equal to the number of Muslims and Christians in Jerusalem in 1948.

Israeli Jerusalem resided at the tip of a dead-end 'corridor' with hostile Arabs on three sides. Most of the young country's economic and political activity took place in Tel Aviv. When the UN moved ahead with its internationalization plan in December 1949, Israel responded by declaring Jerusalem its eternal capital and swiftly moved its Parliament (the Knesset) and government ministries there. As in the rest of the country, the city absorbed large-scale immigration after the fighting ended. The newcomers were settled in abandoned Arab neighborhoods as well as in newly-built areas mainly to the south, south west and along the armistice line. New public institutions were constructed, among them Government Ministries, the Knesset and the Israel Museum. The Hebrew University reopened on Giv'at Ram because the original Mt. Scopus site, though in Israeli hands, was inaccessible. Hadassah Hospital relocated to Ein Karem for the same reason.

Construction bustle notwithstanding, Jerusalem up to 1967 was a quiet city on the fringes of Israeli economic and cultural activity. One reason for this, as we have noted, was its location. Another was the nature of its population. A third reason was the fact that most of the world withheld recognition of Jerusalem as Israel's capital, locating their diplomatic representatives in Tel Aviv.

The artificially-fixed 1948 border ran for about five miles in a general north-south direction. The so-called 'city line' often split residential neighborhoods and, in several instances, individual houses. Complex relations took shape between the two sides. Jordanian sniping was a commonplace occurrence which precipitated Israeli reaction. Nevertheless the two sides had to coexist, maintain a dialog and solve the various problems which arose from this unnatural state of affairs. In Jewish Jerusalem, concrete walls were built to protect pedestrians from sniping. Though incidents grew serious on occasion, the Jordanians usually tried to keep things quiet. The demilitarized enclave on Mt. Scopus (an Israeli island in Jordanian territory) posed a special problem. Members of a garrison force of Israeli police were relieved in a convoy every two weeks. They had to pass through Jordanian territory, which was a constant point of friction. The most trivial occurrences in routine life along the armistice line immediately escalated into international incidents and became topics for UN deliberation. One day, for example, a Jewish family built a latrine alongside its house on the border. The Jordanians claimed that the bathroom crossed the border and the incident was debated at length in the UN...

One event worth noting was Pope Paul VI's 1964 visit to both sides of the city — the first and only Papal appearance in Jerusalem to date.

In June 1967, the Six Day War broke out when Jordan joined Egyptian and Syrian forces in war against Israel, disregarding explicit Israeli warnings. On the Jerusalem front it was a three-day war, in which Israel enveloped and occupied the Jordanian sector, including the Old City. The spearheads were the Israeli paratroopers (though they 'landed' in Jerusalem not from the air but by bus). The city was reunified and in a quick decision on June 28th, the Israel Government declared the reunification official — that is, East Jerusalem was annexed, unlike the other occupied territories which were placed under military administration.

Activity in Jerusalem developed with unprecedented momentum. The Jewish Quarter in the Old City was rebuilt, as were other sites damaged under Jordanian rule, such as the Jewish Cemetery on the Mount of Olives. New Jewish neighborhoods were built around the city with the intention of making re-partition physically impossible. A large, modern university campus arose on Mt. Scopus and an abundance of hotels went up for the throngs of tourists who began to frequent the united city. The presence of government ministries grew. Archeologists began digging in the Old City, changing the face of research and the extent of knowledge regarding ancient Jerusalem. Traces of the division are, however, still apparent: there are two university campuses, two Hadassah hospitals, two electricity grids and two central bus stations. Modern Jerusalem presents a host of new problems which are described in more detail in 'Jerusalem Today — A Political, Ethnic and Urban Maze'.

Chronological Chart

BC

Late Israelite Period
1000 — King David conquers Jerusalem from Jebusites.
967-928 — Reign of King Solomon.

Kingdom of Judah Period
925 — Solomon's kingdom splits; Jerusalem becomes capital of Judah.
701 — Sennacherib's siege of Hezekia's Jerusalem is unsuccessful.
597 — Nebuchadnezzar of Babylon marches on Judah; King of Judah is exiled.
586 — Nebuchadnezzar pillages Jerusalem and levels the First Temple.

INTRODUCTION

Persian Period
538 — First Babylonian exiles return to Jerusalem.
520-515 — Former Babylonian exiles erect Second Temple.
444 — Jerusalem's walls are rebuilt under Nehemia.

Hellenistic Period
332 — Alexander the Great conquers Jerusalem.
301 — Beginning of the rule of the Ptolemy dynasty in Jerusalem.
198 — The Seleucids take Jerusalem.
167 — Antiochus IV (Epiphanes) desecrates the Temple; Hasmonean revolt begins.
164 — Judas Maccabeus takes Jerusalem, reconsecrating the Temple.
164-63 — Jewish Hasmonean dynasty rules Jerusalem.

Roman Period
63 — Pompey of Rome is summoned to Jerusalem in wake of dispute between two Hasmonean brothers; Roman conquest ensues.
37-4 — Reign of King Herod.

AD
6-66 — Roman procurators rule (with brief interruptions).
30 — Crucifixion of Jesus.
41-44 — Reign of Agrippas I.
66 — Jewish insurrection against Rome begins.
70 — Jerusalem and Second Temple are destroyed under Titus.
132-135 — Bar-Kokhba Jewish Revolt, defeated by Rome.
136 — Aelia Capitolina, a Roman colony, is erected on Jerusalem's ruins.

Byzantine Period
326 — Helena, mother of Constantine the Great, visits Jerusalem after Nicaea Council; Christian rule in Jerusalem commences.
335 — Basilica of Constantine is dedicated at site of Jesus' burial.
361-363 — Julian the Apostate permits Jews to settle in Jerusalem and rebuild the Temple.
614 — The Sassanid Persians invade Jerusalem.

The Early Muslim Period
638 — The Muslims conquer Jerusalem.
691 — Dome of the Rock is built.
705 — Al-Aksa Mosque is built.
750 — Rule of Jerusalem shifts from Umayyad to Abassid caliphs.
969 — Jerusalem falls under Fatimid rule.
1009 — Fatimid Caliph Al-Hakim orders non-Muslim houses of prayer including Church of the Holy Sepulchre razed.

INTRODUCTION

Crusader Period
1099 — Crusaders capture Jerusalem.
1149 — Crusaders celebrate 50 years of Crusader rule in Jerusalem by consecrating new Church of the Holy Sepulchre.
1187 — Salah-ed-Din (Saladin) defeats the Crusaders, conquers Jerusalem, and levels city walls.
1229-1244 — Crusaders temporarily regain control of Jerusalem.

Mameluke Period
1260 — Mameluke rule begins.
1267 — Jerusalem's Jewish community is reborn under Nahmanides.

Ottoman Period
1517 — Ottoman King Saleim I conquers Jerusalem.
1520-1566 — The reign of Suleiman the Magnificent — an era of prosperity and growth.
1537-1541 — Old City walls are constructed as seen today.
1700 — Rabbi Judah ha-Hasid ('the Pious') settles in Jerusalem.
1832-1840 — Muhammad Ali of Egypt rules Jerusalem.
1839 — Britain opens Jerusalem's first European consulate.
1850s — First attempts at settlement outside the walls are undertaken by Christians.
1860 — Mishkenot Sha'anannim is founded — first Jewish residence outside the walls.
1870 — The Jews become the majority in Jerusalem's population.
1898 — Kaiser Wilhelm II of Germany pays Jerusalem a visit.

British Period
1917 (Dec. 11) — General Allenby enters Jerusalem to accept Turkish surrender.
1920 — Arab riots in the city and elsewhere.
1925 — Hebrew University opens.
1929 — Arab riots.
1937 — Following more riots, Peel Commission recommends the partition of Palestine.
1946 (Jul. 22) — King David Hotel is blown up by Jewish terror group.
1947 (Nov. 29) — UN General Assembly resolution calls for partition of Palestine into Jewish and Arab states; Israel's War of Independence ensues.

Israeli Period
1948 (May 15) — British Mandate in Palestine ends; State of Israel is declared and invaded by five Arab armies.
1948 (May 28) — Jewish Quarter in Old City falls to Jordanian Legion.

1949 (Dec. 13) — Israel declares Jerusalem its capital.
1948-1967 — Israel-Jordan border splits the city.
1965 — Teddy Kollek elected mayor.
1967 (June) — Jerusalem reunited under Israeli rule in the Six Day War.
1980 — Enactment of the 'Jerusalem Law', reaffirming Israeli sovereignty over East Jerusalem; foreign embassies move to Tel Aviv.

A Holy City to Three Religions

There are few cities whose name is as familiar to hundreds of millions of people worldwide as Jerusalem. It would be hard to find anyone schooled in even the rudiments of Judaism, Christianity or Islam — who has not heard of Jerusalem. Each of these three faiths assigns Jerusalem a symbolic significance far beyond its physical manifestation as a city.

Judaism

The source of Jerusalem's sanctity in Judaism is primarily the Temple. When the First Temple stood, it marked Jerusalem as an Eternal City in the timeless Kingdom of David and the abode of the Deity. In the Bible, Jerusalem plays an important role in the End of Days and the Last Judgment. To Isaiah it is the 'city of Justice', where the absolute perfection of the final judgment will come to pass. Biblical Jerusalem also symbolizes the entire Jewish people: its destruction denoting exile and in its future, resurrection. During the Second Temple period, pilgrimage to Jerusalem attained an unprecedented importance as the clearest indications of Jewish identity throughout the Diaspora. The significance of Jerusalem matched the blow absorbed by the Jewish People upon the city's destruction in 70 AD. Jerusalem in ruins became a symbol of the exiled and oppressed Jewish people. The day the Temple fell — the Ninth of Av, or *Tisha B'Av* — is still marked by fasting and lamentation. Expressions such as 'Next Year in Jerusalem!' or 'Build Jerusalem, the Holy City, speedily and in our days!' are integral in Jewish prayer and liturgy (the latter is incorporated into the daily *Grace after Meals*). Every Jew encounters mention of Jerusalem and its destruction throughout the day, every day. Throughout the world, Jews yearn for this city. As Rabbi Judah Halevi said: *"Though I am in the West, my heart is in the East."* And Rabbi Nahman of Bratslav said: *"Wherever I go, I am going towards Eretz Israel — The Land of Israel."*

Jerusalem's position in Zionism, the Jewish national movement of the past hundred years, presents an interesting ambivalence.

The movement takes its name from Zion, a synonym for Jerusalem, thereby hinting at its goal of making the 'dream of return (to Israel) come true'. The first Zionists in the late 1800s, however, were a generation of social visionaries who considered Jerusalem and the community of their time as the epitome of all they had rejected — a black-clothed mini-theocracy which lived off charity and congregated around synagogues and other religious institutions. Early Zionism, for the most part, avoided Jerusalem. It was only after World War I and toward Israel's War of Independence (1948) that the city became a major factor in Zionism and a symbol of the entire Zionist enterprise.

Christianity

Jerusalem has a special significance in Christianity as the spot where history began and where it will reach its apocalyptic end. Nevertheless, Jerusalem arouses ambivalent and complicated attitudes in Christianity. On one hand, it is the city where Jesus was afflicted, crucified and buried, and whose destruction he prophesied, evoking a negative Christian attitude. On the other hand, it is the Holy City intimately associated with the End of Days. Christianity thus maintains a constant tension between the allegorical Heavenly Jerusalem and the literal reality. As far back as the time of Origen (one of the Fathers of the Church), Church leaders have claimed that New Jerusalem was meant for Christians only and that the Jewish city could never again rise. Nevertheless, difficult questions were left unanswered. Why was Jerusalem leveled only some four decades after Jesus' death? And why, if the cataclysm were preordained, did Jesus bewail it?

Christian attachment to earthly Jerusalem grew stronger in the wake of Byzantine development of the city and its churches. In 451, the Patriarchate of Jerusalem was recognized in the Church Council of Chalcedon. The city of Jerusalem became a center for pilgrims from all Christendom who came in search of physical contact with Biblical sites and with the mystical world of miracles — especially cures. Jerusalem also turned into a source for holy relics — "genuine relics" from the Holy Places have found their way to various locales the world over. During the Crusades, Jerusalem (particularly the Church of the Holy Sepulchre) became a major symbol invoked to inflame the bearers of the Cross. Crusader ideologues perceived the city in both its physical and symbolic manifestations. The religious significance has continued to accompany political events in Jerusalem. In our own century, for example, many viewed General Allenby's conquest of the city as the fulfillment of prophecy, if not as a new Crusade.

The State of Israel, by rebuilding Jerusalem as a Jewish city, has brought about a paradox in Christian attitudes. One approach views a Jewish Jerusalem as anachronistic while the other sees this as the first step toward the fulfillment of prophecy. Vatican action regarding Jerusalem has consisted primarily of efforts to secure political guarantees concerning the right to hold rituals and to maintain free access to the Holy Places.

To understand the Christians in Jerusalem, one should also consider the numerous Christian denominations and sects. Most churches are represented in Jerusalem; their current status is the outcome of a lengthy historical process. Though we can neither list them in detail nor explore the differences between them here, distinctions among major groupings of churches are worth noting. These are the Roman Catholic Church (also known in Jerusalem as the 'Latin Church'), officially represented by the Franciscan Order until the 19th century; the Protestant churches which arrived in Jerusalem in the 1800s; the Eastern churches such as the Greek Orthodox, the Armenians, the Pravoslavs, the Copts, the Syrians and the Abyssinians; and the Uniate Eastern churches (those who ultimately recognized the Papacy) such as the Greek Catholics (the Melchites), the Armenian Catholics, etc. Complicated? Wander through narrow lanes of the Old City and you will see it all in the buildings and people.

Islam

One prayer in Mecca is equal to ten thousand elsewhere; one prayer in Medina equals one thousand; and one prayer in Jerusalem equals five hundred. This Muslim saying encapsulates the hierarchy of holy places in Islamic tradition. The importance of Jerusalem in early Islam is debatable. The city was mentioned explicitly on one occasion during this period, when Muhammad established it as the *qibla* — the direction believers face during prayer — as part of his efforts to attract Jewish tribes. When this unsuccessful endeavor was dropped less than a year and a half later, the *qibla* was reassigned to Mecca.

It was only in the late seventh century that Jerusalem began to claim an important place in Islamic theology. The Damascus-based Umayyad dynasty fostered Jerusalem as a Muslim center close to the seat of government and as a counterweight both to the Muslim center in Arabia and to the impressive Christian churches in Jerusalem. *Hadith* literature (the oral law and tradition of Islam) contains a large accumulation of new material known as *In Praise of Jerusalem* — an amalgam of sayings glorifying the city. Various traditions were adopted from the Jews with the help of Christian and Jewish converts to the new faith. Islamic perceptions of Creation and the End of Days in their Jerusalem contexts, for example, reflect Jewish origins. Thus, the world originated in the holy stone in the center of the Temple Mount (the foundation stone); and Jerusalem is intimately associated with the End of Days as venue of the future Resurrection of the Dead and Last Judgment. According to the Islamic version, this will all happen when the *Kaaba* stone of Mecca will be transfered to the Temple Mount. Jerusalem has a special role in Islamic mysticism, too — perhaps under the inspiration of Christian asceticism. Jerusalem's sanctity and importance in Islam solidified and became universal during the Crusader period when it was no longer under Muslim control. Its liberation became a pan-Islamic goal which, when fulfilled in 1187, sent reverberations throughout the Muslim world.

Today, the holiness of Jerusalem is reflected in the background of the Arab-Israeli conflict. Muslim spokesmen occasionally call for a *jihad* — a holy war — in which millions of believers will ascend to liberate Jerusalem from the Zionists.

Jerusalem Today: A Political, Ethnic and Urban Maze

Jerusalem today is entangled in acute and complex political, religious, ethnic and urban conflicts. When Teddy Kollek, Mayor of Jerusalem, was once asked what good wishes he held for his city, he replied that he hoped Jerusalem and her problems would not appear in newspaper headlines even once.

Unfortunately, this hope has never been fulfilled so far. And worse — the Palestinian uprising, known as the *Intifada*, which at its first days stayed away from Jerusalem, becomes more and more part of the daily life. A lot of military and semi-military forces are to be seen in the conflict areas, like the Old City, where the once colorful market has lost most of its glory.

Modern Jerusalem dates from June 1967, following the Six Day War and the conquest of Arab-populated East Jerusalem. The sector was promptly annexed by the Israeli government, whereas the other territories taken in the war — adjacent Judea and Samaria (West Bank) — remained under military government. The question of Jerusalem's political status evolved into one of the harshest points of controversy in the Arab-Israel dispute. Jerusalem's unification forced two populations — an Arab minority in East Jerusalem (appr. 65,000 in 1967) and a large Jewish majority in the West (appr. 200,000 at the time) to maintain an uneasy coexistence.

The Arabs of Jerusalem were a new phenomenon in Israel, completely distinct from the pre-1967 Arab population. They were an urban community with economic potential, a relatively high level of education and a tradition of participation in Jordanian political institutions. These Arabs were now confronted with unfamiliar modes of government. One example is Israel's welfare state which is characterized by high taxation and a broad array of social services. Under Jordanian rule, they had been accustomed to low taxes and few services. The disparities between the two populations evolved against a backdrop of mutual suspicion. Some Israeli Jews considered the Arabs a hostile population to be kept at arm's length, while some of the Arabs viewed the Jews of Jerusalem as occupiers who threatened to dispossess them. On the practical level, the Arabs felt it necessary to oppose any initiative liable to be interpreted as recognition of what they regarded as an illegal annexation.

All this notwithstanding, Jews and Arabs in Jerusalem have developed a *modus vivendi* of sorts; a reasonable coexistence marked by cooperation in certain areas, segregation in others and crackling tensions at times. The Arabs of Jerusalem stress that most terrorist incidents in the city are the work of outsiders. Cooperation occurs chiefly in industry and business. Thousands of Arabs work for Jewish employers. At one time, the Old City markets were thriving commercial centers packed with Israeli shoppers, though, now, the waters are not so calm. The vast majority of Arabs employed in Jewish Jerusalem are blue-collar workers at the bottom of the wage and promotion scales. Even in the absence of a political conflict, this situation would engender ethnic tension and is considered unsatisfactory by many Israelis. To a certain extent, 'unified Jerusalem' has proved to be a superficial cover for a city which essentially remains divided. The respective populations lead separate lives both physically and socially. The city has two distinct central business districts, two bus systems, two electricity grids and different criteria for taxation, for land and for development values.

The Temple Mount is one of Jerusalem's hottest trouble spots. The element of religion in an otherwise political dispute is especially conspicuous here. The Mount, once the site of the Jewish Temples, has, for the last thousand years, housed two buildings holy to Islam — Al-Aksa Mosque and the Dome of the Rock. The Mount is the third holiest site in the Muslim world following Mecca and Medina in Saudi Arabia. In order to prevent friction, the Israeli Government decided after the Six Day War to leave the Mount under exclusively Muslim control. Only the Western Wall at its foot (a remnant of the Mount's retaining wall in the Jewish Temple days) was developed as a Jewish place of prayer. Right-wing and Orthodox Israeli groups, noting that the Mount is the holiest of sites in Judaism, object to this decision and insist on the right to pray there as well.

Small extremist factions go so far as to demand the mosques' demolition and a restoration of the Mount to Jewish hands. The Arab world, in turn, invokes the Mount for purposes of symbolism and solidarity in its struggle against Israel. Periodic exhortations by Muslim leaders for 'a march of millions for the liberation of holy Jerusalem from the Zionists' should be understood in this light, and so the violent demonstrations of Palestinians after Fridays' prayers.

Another point of tension is the settlement of Jews within the Old City's Muslim Quarter. The buildings involved had belonged to and were inhabited by Jews until they were abandoned during the Jewish-Arab struggle in the 1920s and 1930s. The discord surrounding this movement originates in the deeper controversy in Israel regarding the settlement of the territories occupied in the 1967 war. The Muslim Quarter's Jewish settlers, a group which includes both political extremists and Messianic ideologues, claim a legitimate right to settle in these buildings. The Arabs of the area fear dispropriation and the penetration of a radical Israeli element.

Israeli sovereignty in East Jerusalem has been highly controversial and often not accepted, even by Israel's friends. Many nations, including the United States, do not recognize unified Jerusalem as Israel's capital. Israel reaffirmed its stance in 1980 with the enactment of the 'Jerusalem Law', a restatement of its standard position. Ratification of the new statute precipitated an exodus of the last friendly embassies in Jerusalem to new quarters in Tel Aviv, the country's de facto diplomatic capital.

In the shaping of Jerusalem's physical character too, politics have played no small role. Town planning decisions are frequently taken at the national level, and not by Jerusalem's own engineers. The factor of greatest importance in post-1967 Jerusalem development was Israel's desire to forestall any possibility of a repartitioning, especially in light of its 1948-67 experience. The result has been the design and construction of large Jewish neighborhoods in concentric circles around the city core. Ramot Eshkol, French Hill and Ma'alot Dafna were among the first neighborhoods to go up on what had previously been the the Jordanian side of the border. They were followed by four large projects: Gilo, Ramot, Neve Ya'akov and East Talpiot. The Hebrew University reopened on Mt. Scopus, previously a demilitarized Israeli-held enclave across the cease-fire line during the partition period. These have resulted in a significant and irreversible change in Jerusalem's profile.

The Israel-Arab conflict is not the only point of discord which has left its imprint on the city and its development. Within the Jewish population, tension runs high between its ultra-Orthodox and secular communities. The ultra-Orthodox sects are attempting to establish their own unbroken urban space where they may practice their special way of life. Some reject Jewish national awakening on theological grounds. The struggle surfaces chiefly in disputes regarding the Sabbath (Saturday), the Jewish holy day on which a great many activities are restricted. The extreme Orthodox elements push for the closure of streets and entertainment spots on the Sabbath, and they resort to violence at times. Such strife has become an integral part of Jerusalem's character today, affecting the allocation of various areas adjacent to ultra-Orthodox neighborhoods (see 'A Unique Ethnic Experience - Me'a She'arim).

A simpler, though no less important, issue revolves around Jerusalem's struggle to maintain the special ambience of the Holy City. On the surface, it appears less dramatic. Its protagonists are neither historic nor political rivals but rather buildings and streets which strive to keep that special nature and atmosphere alive. Their allies are a devoted handful who stand firm against every pressure affecting the planning processes.

Since the 1967 reunification, Jerusalem has become Israel's largest city in size and in population alike. The city's current dimensions and their implications clash with its traditional character. The small, intimate Jerusalem of before 1967 — a mosaic of small, ethnically distinct neighborhoods — has fallen victim to the massive, concentric neighborhood layout prevailing today. Jerusalem's urban infrastructure, too, creaks under the strain. Pre-1967 downtown was a small area with very few cross streets and a few of its buildings exceeded three stories in height. The effects of rapid post-1967 development are obvious. The burgeoning tourist industry has greatly contributed toward this change and the scores of new hotels, which punctuate the city's profile, are some of the most conspicuous features of today's Jerusalem skyline — for better or worse. During the past 20 years, Jerusalem has changed radically, continuing to evolve toward a destination as yet unknown. Jerusalemites often complain that Jerusalem is Israel's capital only in the institutional sense, and that Tel Aviv still claims primacy in the economic, commercial, entertainment and diplomatic realms. On the other hand, it may be due to these 'losses' that Jerusalem still retains her unique character.

Part Two — Setting Out

How to get to Israel

By air: Ben-Gurion Airport, about 35 miles from Jerusalem, is Israel's major international airport. Many flights from all over the United States and major cities in Western Europe arrive daily. In addition, South African Airlines (SAA) and Israel's El Al fly to Israel from South Africa and Kenya. There is a wide range of flights at different fares, including charter arrangements offered by many companies. Special cut-rate package deals, including plane fare, lodging and car rental, are often available as well. An organized tour is possible too, of course. Thorough comparison shopping should precede any selection.

By sea: Sol Lines operates a regular ferry from Piraeus, Greece to Israel's Haifa port (two hours from Jerusalem), with departures every Thursday all year round. Other lines travel this route during the summer.

By land: Israel is accessible by land from Egypt and Jordan only. A direct bus to Tel Aviv sets out every day from Cairo, the Egyptian capital. A port tax of about $15 is collected en route at the border crossing at Rafiah in the Gaza strip or Taba in Sinai. From Tel Aviv, Jerusalem is less than an hour away on a highway served by very frequent bus and taxi service. From Jordan, cross the Jordan River at Allenby Bridge and catch a bus to Jerusalem.

Documents and customs

Tourists from all Western European countries and the United States need only a valid passport to enter Israel. Passengers receive entry forms on the plane, which are filled out and handed in at passport control. An entry visa good for a stay of three months is issued at the border.

Israel's customs laws resemble those of most Western countries. Tourists may import personal effects in unlimited quantites, but must declare valuables. According to Israeli law, visitors may bring in 400 cigarettes, one liter of liquor, and two liters of wine. Duty-free shops accept foreign currency only.

Visitors who wish to drive in Israel must have an International Driver's License. An International Student Card is good for reduced admission to quite a few museums and sites, including guided tours and entertainment in certain cases, you can try your luck on the buses too. A brochure called *Tourist Passport*, is available at immigration control at the airport, and provides handy information and vouchers good for reduced admission to various attractions.

Insurance

Jerusalem, the holy city, does not abound with muggers and thieves. Nevertheless, it has been known to harbor types who might covet your belongings. Theft of uninsured gear may be a considerable financial setback. The situation is more serious if one needs hospitalization or medical care of any kind, which is very expensive. One should **not** leave home without appropriate insurance.

When to visit

Jerusalem weather is good for touring almost all year round. The low humidity makes an otherwise hot summer easy to bear. The hottest months are July and August when temperatures range between 25-30 degrees Celsius (74-86 degrees Fahrenheit). Winter sets in December-February. It is often cold and rainy, and a few snowy days occur some years, but nevertheless most winter days reach 10 degrees Celsius (50 degrees Fahrenheit) or so, and summery sunny days are not infrequent. The nicest months are April-May and October-November, when Jerusalem's mountain air is 'clear as wine', as in the famous song, *Jerusalem of Gold*.

Jerusalem's peak tourist periods are the summer vacation months, Jewish holidays (especially *Rosh Hashana* — New Year, and Passover) and the Christian holidays — Easter, Christmas and New Year's Day. For these occasions, reservations for flights and lodging are recommended.

Bear in mind that all institutions and shops, and most museums, are closed on the Sabbath (Saturday) and Jewish holidays. Entertainment and cultural events are almost never held on days preceding holidays. This is not true of the Arab part of town, which is as active then as on any other day.

What to wear

In the hot summer, dress as lightly as possible, preferably in cottons. In the evening, you will need a light jacket or even a sweater. A winter visit calls for warm clothing and a heavy jacket. During the in-between seasons, light clothing is fine for the day, but the evenings are rather chilly. An umbrella or raincoat is worth packing, too.

A swimsuit will come in handy for a refreshing dip in a pool or an outing to the Dead Sea, The Sea of Galilee (*Kinneret*) or a beach on the Mediterranean Sea.

How long to stay

However long one spends in Jerusalem it is unlikely that you will be able to see everything in the city, for the possibilities here are endless. The tourist in Israel should devote three days to a week in Jerusalem. Because of the concentration of many sites in a small area, one can see and experience a lot in a relatively short amount of time. Two to three days for the Old city, one to two days for the modern city and one more day for excursions in the area, shopping or rest.

How much will it cost

A visit to Jerusalem should be no more expensive than to anywhere else in Israel. The most expensive part of one's stay is the accommodation (with the exception of a guided tour in a limousine). Hotels offer attractive prices — especially if the booking is done through any travel agency throughout the world. It is therefore recommended to book a room in advance or get a package deal with your air ticket.

Generally the entrance fee to sites is low, as are the other expenses which are incurred by tourists. There are restaurants of various standards, but inexpensive ones are plentiful and good, so eating should not be much of a burden on one's budget.

Part Three — Getting Around

Transportation

Airports

Ben-Gurion International Airport is situated 35 miles from Jerusalem, on the main Jerusalem-Tel Aviv highway. The passenger terminal, though not large, usually handles the flow of passengers satisfactorily. From there it's about a 45 minute drive to Jerusalem, through lovely scenery.

Egged (public transportation) buses depart every 45 minutes between 7am and 9:30pm from the airport. The last stop on the line is Jerusalem's Central Bus Station, at the entrance to town. Buses back to the airport depart from there. The fare is about $3.00.

A gaggle of taxis await passengers at the airport's taxi stand. They run day and night, and seem to 'swallow up the road'. Fixed fares to various destinations in Israel (about $30 to Jerusalem) are listed on a sign at the taxi stand. Make sure the driver does not overcharge. The Nesher Tours taxi company has its Jerusalem office at 21 King George St., downtown, and the taxis will drop you either there or at your hotel. Return to the airport either from the Nesher office or from your hotel (tel. 227-227 to reserve a seat).

Jerusalem is also served by the **Atarot Airport** which is primarily for internal flights. There are regular flights here from Eilat, Tel Aviv and Haifa. Transport to the city should present no problem as there are both taxis and buses from the airport.

Public Transport

Buses and *sheruts* (fixed-route taxis) connect Jerusalem with all other cities in Israel. The fare is inexpensive ($4-$5) and the buses are comfortable, air-conditioned and fast. Public transport does not run on Saturdays and on Jewish holidays. The *sherut* service is slightly more expensive than the bus and is relatively quicker.

In-Town Transportation

Car rental: All car rental companies have airport branches and arrangements can be made there. Cars rented elsewhere can be returned at the airport by prior arrangement.

All the large firms have Jerusalem branches. Smaller companies may offer slightly lower prices, but are usually less reliable. Most companies set a minimum age of 21 for car rental, and sometimes insist on a year's driving experience. An International Driver's License is necessary, of course, as is a credit card. The minimum rental period is 24 hours. The charge is based either on a predetermined price for unlimited mileage, or on the number of miles actually driven. Some companies, mainly the large ones, deliver the car to your hotel, and, by prior arrangement, allow you to return it to any of their offices in Israel.

Car rental companies with offices in Jerusalem are:
Hertz: 18 King David St., tel. 231-351. A large reliable company which offers good service.
Eldan: 30 Keren Hayesod St., tel. 636-183. A fast-growing Israeli company.
Avis: 22 King David St., tel. 249-001.
Budget: 14 King David St., tel. 248-991.
Europcar: 22 King David St., tel. 248-464.

Two smaller companies also deserve mention:
Orli: 2 Hillel St., tel. 240-213.
Splendid: 3 Ben-Sira St., tel. 242-556.
Other companies may not be as reliable.

Driving in Jerusalem is no simple matter. Its streets make orientation complicated, and many are one-way. It is best to stay off the central roads during rush hours. Bear in mind, too, that the Israeli driver is not noted for excessive road courtesy. On top of all this, downtown Jerusalem has acute parking problems. Regular parking lots are hard to find, and the few which exist are frequently filled to the brim. Any would-be Jerusalem driver should take these points into consideration.

Several streets, most in or around the ultra-Orthodox neighborhoods, are closed to traffic on the Sabbath and Jewish holidays. They are identified by blue police roadblocks.

Be aware that buses do not run on the Sabbath and Jewish holidays. Fixed-route taxis (*sherut*) do operate on those occasions, picking up passengers along a restricted number of fixed routes. The fare is only a little higher than the bus fare.

Taxi: Jerusalem taxis swarm all over town, and can be hailed at any time of day (including the Sabbath) with no difficulty. Taxis do not come in any standard model or color, but all have 'Taxi' signs on the roof. The fare is set by the meter only. Do not be tempted into negotiating a rate with the driver before setting out; you will be the loser. Fare no. 1 on the meter is the standard; fare no. 2 (25% higher) is in effect after 9pm, and on the Sabbath and holidays. Local custom is not to tip, but you may round the fare up.

You can hail a taxi in the street or order one by phone. Major taxi stations are:

Ben-Yehuda: Herbert Samuel St., Zion Square, tel. 222-111, or 225-555.
Hapalmach: 42 Hapalmach St., tel. 667-777.
David Hamelech: King David St., tel. 222-510.
Habira: 234 Jaffa Rd., tel. 534-444.
Merkaz Habira: 1 Harav Kook St., tel. 224-545.
Rehavia: next to the Plaza Hotel, tel. 224-444.

Bus: The bus service in Jerusalem is very efficient. The many winding routes reach most corners of the city and run quite frequently. Bus stops have route numbers, though route descriptions are rarely provided. Within the city itself one inexpensive fare applies to all routes and distances. A 25-ticket ride (*kartisiyya*) is available, and gives you 5 free rides. People over 60 and children (under 18), have a lower priced *kartisiyya*.

Jerusalem's Central Bus Station is at the western entrance to town. All intercity lines begin and end here, and many in-town lines pass through it as well, serving all parts of town. The baggage check department is open Sun.-Thurs. 7am-5pm, Fri. till 3pm, and the lost-and-found department is open Sun.-Thurs. 7am-3pm (tel. 551-725).

Most bus lines start up before 6am, and the last buses set out at 11:45pm. Since certain lines stop earlier, make sure in each case that the bus you are waiting for is still running. **Important:** Service stops about half an hour before sunset on Fri. or eve of Jewish holidays. Service resumes the following evening.

Intercity transport

Taxi: Fixed-route taxis (*sherut*) connect Jerusalem with Israel's other major cities at highly frequent intervals, and the fare is slightly higher than for the bus. They set out the moment they're full. One can also order a special taxi, of course, but this is rather costly.

Several inter-city taxi stands are mentioned below:

Ha-Uma: 234 Jaffa Rd., tel. 533-333. *Sherut* to Tel Aviv (also operates on Sat. and holidays).
Habira: 1 Harav Kook St., tel. 232-320. *Sherut* to Tel Aviv (also

operates on Sat. and holidays).
Aviv: 12 Shammai St., tel. 224-034 or 227-366. *Sherut* to Tel Aviv; to Haifa and Beersheva by reservation.
Yael Daroma: 12 Shammai St., tel. 226-985. *Sherut* to Beersheva every half-hour.

Bus: As stated, buses leave for all parts of Israel from the Jerusalem Central Bus Station at the beginning of Jaffa Rd. Buses to Tel Aviv and Haifa depart very frequently, and schedules for the other lines are available at the information window (tel. 528-231, 523-456 or 551-703). Intercity buses operate at roughly the same hours as do in-town lines.

There is no need to buy a ticket in advance. The only exception is the much in demand Eilat line, for which tickets should be purchased at least one day ahead of travel.

All the buses are modern, comfortable and air-conditioned. Travel time is less than an hour to Tel-Aviv, about two hours to Haifa and Beersheva, and approximately 5-6 hours to Eilat.

In addition to the Egged network, there is an Arab-owned bus system, which can be used though it is not recommended. Arab buses head for Judea and Samaria (West Bank) from their own central bus terminal, on Suleiman St. opposite Damascus Gate. The vehicles are old, uncomfortable and crowded, and the fares are only slightly lower than Egged's. However, certain destinations in Judea and Samaria are served only by them.

Train: The only passenger train out of Jerusalem departs for Haifa Sun.-Thurs. at 4pm. It follows a lovely route through the Jerusalem Hills, but the trip takes about 3.5 hours — almost twice as long as the bus. The Jerusalem railroad station is on Hebron road, and is served by buses 5, 6, 7, 8, 21 and 48.

Hitchhiking: This is common in Israel, and one seldom has to wait very long, but women are not advised to hitchhike alone. Major out-of-town intersections have hitchhiking shelters, meant mainly for soldiers. Since drivers usually pick up soldiers first in any case, try not to hitchhike on Friday afternoon or Sunday morning, when throngs of soldiers are heading for home and back to base.

By the same token, intercity travel of any kind is inadvisable on those occasions. The bus terminals and roads are packed, making travel difficult and uncomfortable.

Accommodation

Jerusalem accommodation covers the whole range — from deluxe five-star establishments to small, inexpensive hotels, and youth hostels. Quite a few hotels are new and modern. They are subject to Ministry of Tourism control, and their standards are set by their 'star' ranking. All good hotels accept credit cards.

Reservations are highly recommended during peak tourist periods (see 'When to come').

Jerusalem has three hotel districts: near the western entrance to town, downtown, and East Jerusalem. The downtown hotels are almost all within walking distance of entertainment spots, shopping centers and business areas. East Jerusalem hotels are far from downtown but are less expensive. Various communities just out of town, in the hills surrounding Jerusalem, offer pleasant places to stay. The disadvantage, of course, is their distance.

Rules and regulations

Hotels must post their nightly rates clearly on a display at the reception desk. The prices shown do not include VAT, a 15% tax from which tourists are exempt if they pay in foreign currency.

The rate usually includes a rich and nutritious 'Israeli breakfast'. Fees for related hotel services such as phone calls and laundry, however, are high.

All hotels in West Jerusalem have kosher kitchens. Hot meals are not served on Sabbath (Sat.) afternoons, though quality hotels offer inexpensive salad bars with a satisfying, delicious selection.

It is important to note that prices vary dramatically during the year. During the high season prices can be double or more than if the booking was made through a travel agency in your country of origin. Be sure to inquire first.

Out of the many hotels in Jerusalem we have selected to list only those of exceptional value or which have particularly attractive locations and views. Below are a number of hotels in different price categories.

Very Expensive (five-star)

The King David: 23 King David St., tel. 221-111. A remnant of British colonial grandeur, with traditional decor, is close to downtown and the Old City. The favorite of world leaders and celebrities.
The Jerusalem Hilton: Giv'at Ram, tel. 536-151. A modern hotel, it hosts many international conferences. Views in all directions.
The King Solomon: 32 King David St., tel. 241-433. Comfortable and modern.
The Jerusalem Plaza-Sheraton: 47 King George St., tel. 228-133. Convenient and centrally located.

The Seven Arches: Mount of Olives, tel. 894-455. East Jerusalem's finest hotel, offering splendid views from rooms facing the Old City.
Mount Scopus: Sheikh Jarrah, tel. 828-192. With only 65 rooms, it is the smallest of Jerusalem's prestige hotels.
Laromme Jerusalem Hotel: 3 Jabotinsky St., near Liberty Bell Gardens, tel. 697-777. Very nice hotel in nice location.
St. George International: 8 Salah-Ed-Din St., tel. 282-571.

Expensive (four-star)

Hyatt Regency Jerusalem: 32 Lehi St. Mount Scopus, tel. 821-333. A new, modern, beautifully-designed hotel, near the Hebrew University at Mount Scopus.
Kings: 60 King George St., tel. 247-133. A centrally located hotel with classical decor.
Moriah Jerusalem: 39 Keren Hayesod St., tel. 232-232. Offering 301 rooms, it is centrally located and comfortable.
Central: 6 Piness St., tel. 223-111. This hotel caters especially to the Ultra-Orthodox.
Holyland: Bayit Vegan, tel. 630-201. A popular, quiet hotel located far from downtown.
American Colony: Nablus Rd. (Derech Shechem), tel. 282-421. An historic site, this hotel offers a special ambience and decor in East Jerusalem.

Moderate (three-star)

Windmill: 3 Mendele Mocher Sfarim St., tel. 663-111. Highly recommended.
Jerusalem Tower: 23 Hillel St., tel. 222-161. Centrally located.
YMCA: 26 King David St., tel. 227-111. Reasonable price and quality.
Eilon Tower: 34 Ben-Yehuda St., tel. 233-281. Centrally located.
Sonesta Jerusalem: 2 Wolfsonn St., tel. 528-221. At the western entrance to town.
Tirat Bat Sheva: 42 King George St., tel. 232-121. Downtown, Orthodox.
Scottish Hospice: tel. 717-701. Located near train station, on British Consulate territory, it has a pleasant, special atmosphere.
Gloria: Jaffa (Yaffo) Gate, tel. 282-431.

Inexpensive (two-one-star)

Palatine: 4 Agrippas St., tel. 231-141.
Ron: 42 Jaffa Rd., tel. 223-471.
Astoria: en route to the Mount of Olives, tel. 284-965.
Lawrence: 18 Salah-ed-Din St., East Jerusalem, tel. 282-585.
Metropole: 6 Salah-ed-Din St., East Jerusalem, tel. 282-507.
New Imperial: Jaffa Gate, tel. 272-400.

Har Aviv: 16a Beit-Hakerem St., quite near city center, tel. 521-515.
Rivoli: 3 Salah-ed-Din St., East Jerusalem, tel. 284-871.

Youth Hostels

Jerusalem has four main youth hostels.
Beit Bernstein: 1 Keren Hayesod St., tel. 228-286. Most centrally located.
Moreshet Hayahadut: The Jewish Quarter, tel. 288-611. A new and comfortable hostel at a convenient location.
Ein Kerem: Ein Kerem, tel. 416-282. Offers a unique atmosphere. Recommended despite its distance from downtown.
L. Wetterman-Weiss: 8 Hapisga St., tel.423-366. Located in Bayit Vegan, it is far from town and not as pleasant as Ein Kerem.

Out-of-town accommodation

Various hostels are at hand in communities in the hills surrounding Jerusalem. Visitors with their own (or rented) cars may take advantage of them, while those without may enjoy them as weekend resorts or whenever you want to enjoy the crisp air and beautiful scenery. All the resorts mentioned here are accessible from Jerusalem by bus at least once an hour.

The best-known resort is in Kibbutz Ma'ale Hahamisha (tel. 342-591). It offers a swimming pool (in the summer), tennis courts, cafeteria, and outings in the area. Kibbutz Ramat Rahel hosts the Mitzpe Rahel Tourist and Sports Center (tel. 715-712) — gorgeous scenery, guest house and restaurant, camping grounds, year-round swimming pool, tennis courts and sports facilities. Other recommended resorts are Kibbutz Kiryat Anavim (tel. 348-999), Moshav Neve Ilan (tel. 341-241) and Moshav Shoresh (tel.341-172).

Practical tips for getting around

Business hours

Government offices are open to the public Sun.-Thurs., 7:30am-3pm and Fri. 8am-1pm, but it is always best to phone first and check for a particular day. Phone 144 to find out the number of whatever office you need and if you can, get someone to ask for you in Hebrew.

Shops and businesses are usually open Sun.-Thurs. 8am-1pm and re-open 4-7pm after a siesta. They are closed Tues. afternoons, and usually shut down at 2pm on Fri. and on eve of holidays. Some shops open and close an hour later or so; many downtown shops stay open throughout the day.

On Saturday, the Jewish Sabbath, all West Jerusalem offices and shops are closed. Most East Jerusalem establishments, by contrast, are closed on Friday, the Muslim Sabbath. Everything is open on Sunday.

Communication

The **Central Post Office**, 23 Jaffa Rd., is open Sun.-Thurs 7am-7pm, and Fri. 7am-2pm. Apart from regular postal services, this office offers telex, facsimile, and parcel delivery services at the following times: Sun., Tues. and Thurs. 7:45am-12:30pm and 3:30-6pm; Mon. and Wed. 7:45am-2pm; and Fri. 7:45am-1pm. The telegraph service shuts down on Fri. at 2pm and re-opens Sat. at 8pm. On the Sabbath and holidays, telegrams can be sent from the East Jerusalem Post Office, 2 Salah-ed-Din St., open 8am-2pm.

Branch post offices around town are open Sun., Tues. and Thurs. 7:45am-12:30pm and 3:30-6pm; Mon. and Wed. mornings only; and till 1pm on Fri. Branches can be found at the Hebrew University on Mt. Scopus (Administration Building), at the Jaffa Gate, 8 Shammai St., and 8 Keren Kayemet St. in Rehavia.

International phone communication is good in Israel and most countries can be dialed directly. Not only is there no need to go through an international operator, it is also the least expensive way to call abroad. The tariff for calls to North America and parts of Europe is 50% lower every day between 1-7am. Because the charge is calculated by the number of call units, there is no minimum time on the line. Payment is for the exact duration of the call.

The telephone office, on Coresh St., next to the Central Post Office, is open Sun.-Thurs. 7am-9pm and Fri. 7am-2pm. Direct overseas calls can be made from hotels, but this service is expensive.

Collect calls from Israel to countries which support this service can be made from public phones. Dial 188 for the international operator, which puts the call through.

Public phones proliferate in Jerusalem. Insert a token (*asimon*) before dialing. Tokens can be purchased at any post office, sometimes at vending machines in public places, and at peddlars' stalls. The Jerusalem area code, 02, is dialed only when calling from outside the city.

Currency

The Israeli currency is the new shekel (NS or NIS), divided into 100 *agorot* (*1 agora*). In recent years Israel's economy and currency was noted for its instability, but the new shekel, introduced in 1986, has held its value.

Money can be changed at any bank and in large hotels, though the hotel exchange rate is slightly under the official one. The banks accept cash, travelers' checks and credit cards. International bank transfers, too, are easily handled in Israel, and the money is provided either in foreign currency or in shekels. One can also change money on the black market — around Damascus Gate, for example — or with private moneychangers. Since the Israeli economy stabilized, however, there is little to gain by taking that route.

Most hotels, restaurants and businesses honor credit cards; the most common are Visa, American Express and Master charge.

Banks

All Israeli banks have downtown branches, particularly in the vicinity of Jaffa, Ben-Yehuda, King George, Shamai and Hillel Sts. Banks are open Sun., Tues. and Thurs. 8:30am-12:30pm and 4-5:30pm; Mon., Wed., and Fri mornings only. Closed on Sat. and holidays.

Measurements, electricity and time

Israel uses the metric system. While clothing and footwear are measured by the European method, many salespeople are familiar with the American equivalents.

Temperatures are recorded in Celsius.

Israeli electricity runs on 220V, and the appliances on sale in Israel use this current. You will need a 2-pin adaptor for any electrical goods you bring.

The time in Israel is +2, or +1 when daylight saving time is in effect.

Tourist information

The **Government Tourist Information Office**, 24 King George St. (tel. 241-281), provides detailed and up-to-date information. Open Sun.-Thurs. 8:30am-6:30pm in the summer (Apr.-Nov.); 8:30am-5pm in the winter; and 8:30am-2pm on Fri. all year round. A branch tourist office is located at Jaffa Gate (tel. 282-295/6).

The **Jerusalem Municipal Tourist Information Office**, 17 Jaffa Rd. (tel. 228-844), keeps visitors posted about everything in Jerusalem from hotels to laundry services to out-of-town excursions. A guidance center in the office provides written and photographic material on Jerusalem. At times, too, lectures are given here in Hebrew, English, French, Spanish and German.

Inside Jaffa Gate, opposite the Citadel, is the **Christian Information Center**. Here one can get an update on information about Christian sites, schedules for mass in the various churches, etc. Open Mon.-Fri. 8:30am-12:30pm and 3-6pm (till 5:30pm in winter). Sat. mornings only. Closed Sun. and Christian holidays, tel. 287-647.

A tourist bulletin called *This Week in Jerusalem* is published weekly and has details on entertainment and cultural performances, sales, and special events in Jerusalem each week. It is available free at tourist offices and hotels.

Another recommended source of information is *The Jerusalem Post*, the English-language daily newspaper of Israel. The Friday weekend edition is larger, with supplements, including one on entertainment. The Monday edition has a supplement of the New York Times.

Manners and conduct

Israel's rules of conduct are no different from those in any Western country. The 'dress code', too, is similar. Evening suits are worn at official events, concerts or elegant dinners. By day, however — especially in the summer — light and informal dress is accepted. A visitor can feel quite at home even in shorts and sandals. One important exception is holy places, where entry in shorts is forbidden. Ultra-Orthodox quarters, such as Mea She'arim, can be visited only in modest dress. This is especially pertinent for women. In general, dress appropriately when exploring the city.

Jerusalem is safe at night. Nevertheless, do not stroll down outlying streets at very late hours, especially in East Jerusalem and the Old City. At this hour, these areas are desolate, even if there is no actual danger, the feeling is unpleasant.

Restaurant bills sometimes include a service charge. If not, a tip of 10%-15% of the bill is customary. Hotel service personnel should be given small tips. While taxi drivers do not expect tips, passengers should 'round' the meter fare upward.

From the observation point of Mount of Olives to the west

JERUSALEM

Getting to Know the City

Touring the city independently

Bus line 99, Jerusalem's "round line", links 36 city sites. The special tourist line uses luxury coaches with commentary in both Hebrew and English. One can take the line from end to end for a first-hand acquaintance with the city, but it's better to buy special tickets, good for a day or two, which allow one to get off anywhere on the route, stop somewhere, and board the next bus to move on. Fares: $1.00 for the round trip, $4.00 for one day, $5.00 for two days. The round line leaves every 2 hours, Sun.-Thurs. 10am, 12pm, 2pm and 4pm, till 2pm on Fri. and eve of holidays, from the Egged parking lot next to Jaffa Gate.

Group tours

If only for an initial acquaintance with the city, many visitors prefer a guided tour of various sites around town. Many travel agencies and companies organize such outings. They are either by coach or on foot, and are conducted by professional guides, usually in English.

Three large companies offer regular tours in Jerusalem and throughout Israel:

Egged Tours: 44a Jaffa Rd. Zion Sq., tel. 224-198 or 223-454. This is the tourist branch of Israel's largest public transport cooperative.
United Tours: King David Hotel., tel. 222-187 or 225-013.
Galilee Tours: Center One (Near Central Bus Station), tel. 383-460. A small selection of outings by a good and reliable company.

All companies offer a similar itinerary on similar routes at similar prices. Egged has a pick-up system which enables you to be fetched from your hotel.

Several examples of the offerings follow:

Old City tour, approximately four hours, mostly on foot. Enter the Old City at Jaffa Gate and cross the Armenian and Jewish Quarters to the Western Wall, the Temple Mount, Via Dolorosa, and the Church of the Holy Sepulchre. Price: $12 per person.

Night time tour of the Old City — a walk on the wall from

Zion Gate to Jaffa Gate; sound-and-light show at the Citadel of David; tour of the Armenian Quarter, the Jewish Quarter and the Western Wall. Offered only by United Tours. Price: $12 per person.

Half-day tour of synagogues of various Jewish ethnic communities, with explanation of Jewish religion, customs and beliefs. Price: $9.00 per person.

One-day tour of the Old and New Cities: the Knesset, the Second Temple Jerusalem model at the Holyland Hotel, the President's Residence and the Jerusalem Theater, the Hebrew University on Mount Scopus, the Old City via Jaffa Gate, and the rest as described above. Price: $23 per person.

Other tours explore Jerusalem's immediate surroundings. Attractions include the Stalactite Cave, the Dead Sea, Masada, Jericho, Bethlehem, Hebron and more. Most of these are one-day outings. Price up to $35 per person.

Eshkolot Tours is an exclusive travel agency which offers limousine service. The drivers, professional tour guides, take you anywhere you want in Israel. Prices per day: $145 for up to four people, $175 up to seven. The price includes up to eight hours' guiding and 130 miles travel. Eshkolot Tours is at 36 Keren Hayesod St. tel. 635-555, 665-555.

Sightseeing airplanes

Egged Tours offers flights over Jerusalem. The Egged office at 44a Jaffa Rd. (tel. 223-454) is open Sun.-Thurs. 7am-7pm, Fri. 7am-12.30pm. There are flights in the morning on Mon., Wed. and Fri. and on Sun., Tues. and Thurs. in the afternoon. The light plane stays aloft nearly an hour, and the tour is followed by the sound-and-light show at the Citadel of David. Price $33 per person.

Nesher Company also arranges flights over Jerusalem by request. One must arrange the flights in advance. Their office hours are Sun.-Thurs. 8:30am-4pm. tel. 851-345.

Jerusalem — Area by Area

The best way to get to know this unique city is to walk through the different neighborhoods. Our walking tours will lead you to many fascinating discoveries.

The walking tours include the surroundings of the Old City (Mt. of Olives to Hezekiah's Tunnel), the Old City itself (several tours in a circular route) and the more modern parts of the city. Certain of the routes end near the starting point of the next tour, so that they can be done in sequence.

The walking tours are suitable for everyone and do not demand much physical effort. However, the tours are designed for those who have the time to follow all the routes, acquiring an intimate knowledge of Jerusalem in the process. For travelers whose time is limited, we have included a list of 'Musts' in the Guide, so that in planning your itinerary you do not miss any important sites.

Before beginning the walking tours, we recommend a preliminary visit to a few observation points around the city. This will give you a good idea of the general layout of the city.

Observation Points — A Preliminary Tour

This tour provides an initial acquaintance with Jerusalem. We have selected the most spectacular views, to give you a taste of the city's landscapes and an architectural, historical and religious impression of Jerusalem. The finest of all is the Mount of Olives. You may wish to do the Mount of Olives tour, which begins at the observation point. (see 'History and Beauty — from the Mount of Olives to the City of David'). The most convenient way to visit all the observation points is by car. It is difficult to do these sites in sequence by bus because there are no connecting lines.

Hill of Evil Council — towards the Old City, Temple Mount and Kidron Valley

Buses 8 and 48, Kiryat Moriah stop, reach this point.

Armon Hanatziv was on the Hill of Evil Council, the residence used by the British High Commissioner in Palestine between 1931 and 1948 and since then, by the UN as its headquarters.

During the Six Day War, the Jerusalem front opened here when the Jordanian Legion invaded the UN-held site. We, however, have come here to enjoy its splendid view from the promenade, facing the valley to the south of the Old City. The promenade is by the access road, leading toward the grove. The building itself, at the end of the road, is not open to visitors. The promenade has been hugely extended recently and now provides a very pleasant walk overlooking the **Peace Forest** all the way to the neighborhood of Abu-Tor.

Armon Hanatziv is a good place to begin exploring Jerusalem. The view gives an appreciation of the landscape of ancient Jerusalem and its impact on the city's development. First identify the **Temple Mount**, protruding above the wall. Note the Dome of the Rock (the gold dome) and **Al-Aksa Mosque** (the grey dome). Below Al-Aksa, outside the wall, a low hill slopes toward us. This is the **City of David**, or **Jebus**, where Jerusalem first began to develop. From here, the Temple Mount may be clearly seen, relative to the City of David, as an acropolis. Over time, the city spread to the west (to the left). Since the hills in that direction reached greater heights, the Temple Mount was no longer the highest point in Jerusalem.

Ancient Jerusalem was demarcated by steep valleys. To the east (right) of the Temple Mount and the City of David is the **Brook of Kidron**, known in part as the **Valley of Jehoshaphat**. It separates the city from the Mount of Olives, which rises to its right. West (left) of the City of David was another deep watercourse - the **Tyropoeon Valley** (Heb. *hagai*, or simply 'the valley'). Because great quantities of debris accumulated in this valley each time Jerusalem was sacked, it is hardly visible today. With an effort, you can make it out in the indentation which seems to slope from Al-Aksa Mosaue in our direction, to the left of the modern road. Although difficult to see from here, a third deep watercourse — the **Vale of Himmom** or **Gehenna** - demarcated Jerusalem further to the west.

In the course of its development, Jerusalem spread across the Tyropoeon Valley and on to the hill to the west (the Upper City); which is also inside today's Old City. It was not until the 19th century that the city expanded beyond the Brook of Kidron to the east and the Vale of Hinnom further to the west. Until then this V-shaped landscape restricted Jerusalem's development to the more gentle terrain in the north. The steep valleys and rugged slopes protected the city from every direction but the north.

The little houses on the Mount of Olives on your right belong to the village of **Silwan** (Siloam or Shiloah). The Mount of Olives borders the Judea Desert which is visible to the right. On the slopes, notice the large Jewish cemetery.

Across the road is the memorial to the soldiers who died fighting in this area in the Six-Day War. From here we have a view south and east. Right underneath us there is a tunnel of an aqueduct, built in the Second Temple Era, to supply Jerusalem with water.

From here we can see the new neighborhood of East Talpiot, built after the Six-Day War. Nestling on the further hill are the houses of the Arab village Tzur Bahr. The barren hills of the Judea Desert spread to the east, and protruding from it is the cone shaped mountain of Herodion, built by King Herod.

Visitors traveling by car can stop at another viewpoint, offering an even clearer view. Return to Derech Hebron, turn right, and take another right on to Na'omi St. (you can walk from here to Armon Hanatziv if you like. At the end of the monastery wall is the other end of the promenade.) Follow the road to the left, drive through the village of Abu Tor until you reach a turn in the road then stop and cross. The neighborhood we pass through was partitioned between Israel and Jordan from 1948-1967. The bullet marks in many of its houses testify to those tense years. From here we can see the Vale of Hinnom below and Mt. Zion beyond it. Mt. Zion is part of the western slope on which Jerusalem developed after crossing the Tyropoeon Valley. Note the **Church of the Dormition** with its black pyramidal roof and belfry. Though the Tyropoeon Valley itself has almost vanished, it reappears to the left of the road, which seems to descend from the Al-Aksa Mosque. Follow the road around to take you back to Derech Hebron.

The Mount of Olives — towards the Temple Mount, Kidron Vallley and beyond

Take bus line 99 or taxi to reach this site.

This is a 'must' — the most impressive view of all. Our tours of the Mount of Olives and the Brook of Kidron begin here. There is a detailed description of the view in the chapter 'History and Beauty'.

From the Mount of Olives we head north to Mt. Scopus. Passing through the Arab village of **Et-Tur**, to the right we see the turret of the white Russian **Church of the Ascension**, the site where Jesus rose to heaven. Continuing our ride, notice to the right, a building conspicuous by its massive tower — **Augusta Victoria**, a turn-of-the-century German edifice. Originally a hospice, it is now a hospital. Lovely scenes of the Judea Desert open up to the right.

Mount Scopus — towards Eastern Jerusalem

Take buses No. 4, 9, 28, or 26 to reach this site.

Mt. Scopus with its modern Hebrew University campus and tower, can be spotted from miles away. **The Hebrew University** was originally established here after World War I. The official opening held on April 1, 1925 was one of the most important and impressive events in Zionist history. Participants in the inauguration ceremony, which symbolized the renewal of Jewish spiritual life, included Lord Balfour (whose 1917 Declaration concerning a National Home for the Jewish people in Palestine was a cornerstone in realizing the Zionist dream), General Allenby (who conquered Jerusalem for the English in 1917), Sir Herbert Samuel (the Jewish-born first British High Commissioner for Palestine), and much of the Zionist elite — such as Chaim Weizmann (Israel's first president) and Chaim Nachman Bialik (the Jewish poet and disseminator of Jewish enlightment). The ceremony was held in the University's amphitheater, which today is accessible from the campus itself. A visit to the amphitheater affords a highly impressive view (especially in the afternoon) of the **Judea Desert** and the **Dead Sea**. A new Israeli settlement, **Ma'ale Adumim**, stands out in the desert.

Mt. Scopus was cut off from Jewish Jerusalem during the 1948 War of Independence. Postwar arrangements demilitarized the mountain and left it as an Israeli enclave in Jordanian territory. An Israeli convoy climbed the mountain under UN escort every two weeks to relieve the garrison force of Israeli police. The University and the Hadassah Hospital (est. 1939), were re-established at other locations in the Israeli sector. This situation lasted until the Six-Day War when the entire region was restored to Israeli control. A renovated and expanded Hebrew University campus houses the Administration, the Faculties of the Humanities, Social Sciences and Law, and part of the Bezal'el Academy for Arts and Design. The hospital too, has reopened here.

Having climbed Mt. Scopus to gaze upon Jerusalem, we step off the road which circles the University. The mountain's name — a derivative of the Greek *skopein*, means observation and study. For a fantastic view climb to the well preserved ruins of the Roman amphitheater. On a clear day you can see the Dead Sea.

The City Tower — a bustling center

Our final observation point gives a glimpse into the heart of the city. The **triangle** bordered by Ben Yehuda St., King George

From the Mount of Olives

The Western City from Mount Scopus

St. and Jaffa Rd. is always bustling and the ambience of traditional downtown Jerusalem has been preserved. A stroll along Ben Yehuda St. is especially worthwhile. Since it became a pedestrian mall several years ago it has become the site of several cafes and performances by street theater groups and musicians. Climb the **City Tower** (King George St. corner Ben Yehuda St.) to the rooftop restaurant, **The Jerusalem Delight**, for an unsurpassed view of the center of New Jerusalem. Open Sun.-Thurs. 12:30pm-midnight, Sat. after sundown, closed Fri.

History and Beauty — From the Mount of Olives to the City of David

The Mount of Olives

We begin our tour at Jerusalem's most spectacular observation point — the **Mount of Olives**, near the Seven Arches Hotel. There is almost always an Arab here who makes his living by encouraging tourists to sit on and photograph his camel. Since we recommend this as a **hiking route**, leave your car behind and take a taxi (direct from Damascus Gate) or Bus 99 to the mountaintop.

From the top of the mountain, look west toward the eastern wall of the Old City. Between the wall and this observation point is the **Brook of Kidron** (or the **Valley of Jehoshaphat**), one of the three watercourses that determined the development, of ancient Jerusalem. The valley is so deep and steep that Jerusalem has never crossed it, and always developed to its west. Opposite us is the **Temple Mount,** which, despite its name, is utterly flat. This unique platform among the Judean Hills owes its shape to King Herod (1st century BC) who expanded and leveled its top for the construction of his Temple. Nothing remains of Herod's Temple. The structures seen on the Mount today are Muslim. The Mount is one of the three holiest sites in Islam. The two major buildings are the gold-crowned **Dome of the Rock**, which shelters the holy Foundation Stone, and the **Al-Aksa Mosque** with the dark dome. These and the ancillary structures at their flanks are jewels of Muslim architecture and art. Ruins relating to Herod's Temple were unearthed in archeological digs, which you can see to the left of the Al-Aksa dome. To their left is the slope of a low hill where the **City of David**, the most ancient nucleus of Jerusalem, once stood. To complete the panorama, do not forget that Jerusalem lies on the edge of the **Judea Desert**. It begins east of where we're standing, on the other side of the Mount of Olives (to our left).

The **Jehoshaphat Valley** before you, between the Mount of Olives and the Temple Mount, has been the subject of numerous Jewish traditions which found their way into Christianity and Islam. For example in Joel 4:1-2 *'For, behold, in those days, and in that time, when I shall bring back the captivity of Judah and Jerusalem, I will gather all nations, and will bring them down into the valley of Jehoshaphat; and I will enter into judgment with them there...'*

FROM MOUNT OF OLIVES TO THE CITY OF DAVID

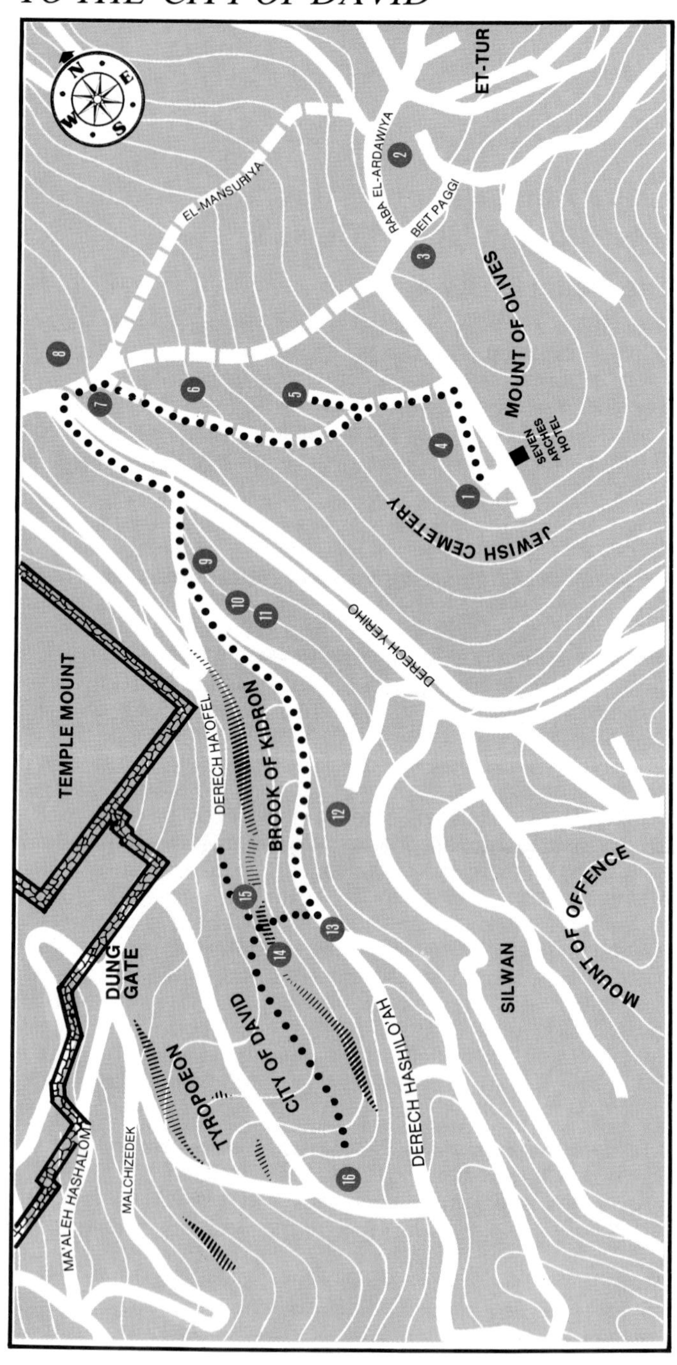

Dome of the Rock — a view from the Mount of Olives

Index

1. Observation Point
2. Church of Pater Noster
3. Chapel of Ascension
4. The Prophets' Graves
5. Dominus Flevit
6. The Russian Church of Mary Magdalene
7. Church of All Nations
8. Church of the Tomb of the Virgin
9. Tomb of Absalom
10. Tomb of Bnei Hezir
11. Tomb of Zechariah
12. Tomb of the Daughter of Pharaoh
13. Gihon Spring — Entrance to Hezekiah's Tunnel
14. Warren's Shaft
15. Area G
16. Siloam Pool

An important role in these traditions is reserved for the **Gate of Repentance** or the **Golden Gate**, a sealed double aperture in the wall facing us. According to all three faiths, it is here that the Messiah will enter Jerusalem. The New Testament account, by which Jesus reached Jerusalem from the Mount of Olives, lends credence to these traditions. Jewish legend relates that two bridges will be thrown over the Valley of Jehoshaphat in the End of Days — one of iron and one of paper. All of humanity will have to cross it to reach the court where God will sit in judgment. The wicked, trusting only in the present world and its attributes, will choose the bridge of iron, which will collapse, plunging into the abyss. The righteous, trusting in God, will chose the bridge of paper... and cross safely.

Several of the new neighborhoods built around Jerusalem since its 1967 unification may be seen from here. To the right, far on the horizon, is **French Hill** (Giv'at Shapira). To its left, farther away still, is **Ramot** (slightly out of view, next to the minaret at Nebi Samuel). At the far left of our view is **Gilo**, the largest of these new neighborhoods. Looking back to the Old City, we may point out another two structures. The white tower with the pyramidal top (itself one of Jerusalem's finest observation points) belongs to the German Lutheran Church. To its right are two grey domes belonging to **The Church of the Holy Sepulchre**, Jerusalem's most important Christian building. Left of the Old City wall is a prominent building with a pointed black dome and an adjacent belfry: the Catholic **Church of the Dormition**, where Mary fell into eternal rest.

A more thorough exploration of the Mount of Olives calls for a visit to several of the churches here. The most immediate is the Catholic Church of **Pater Noster**. (open 8:30-11:45am, 3-4:45pm, closed Sunday.) To reach it, return to the street on which you arrived and turn right. It is worth noting for its lovely cloister on whose walls the *Lord's Prayer* is engraved in some 60 languages. This structure, the property of the Carmelite Sisters, was built in 1868 by Princess de la Tour d'Auvergne of France. She is buried here in a crypt embellished with a life-size statue of her. Visit the court for a view of the ruins of the **Eleona Church** (*Eleona* is Greek for the Mount of Olives), an opulent church built under patronage of Queen Helena, mother of the Emperor Constantine, in the fourth century AD. It was demolished by the Persians, rebuilt by the Crusaders and pillaged once again at the end of their rule. Jesus is said to have prophesied the End of Days and the Last Judgment from the cave in the yard, at the burial crypt. Another traditional belief is that he taught his disciples the Lord's Prayer here. The walls above the cave are parts of the **Church of the Holy Heart**, whose construction began in 1920, and is yet to be finished.

Another important institution nearby is the **Chapel of the Ascension**. (There are no special visiting hours — just ring the bell to enter.) This small chapel, set in the middle of an open octagonal court, marks the spot from which Jesus ascended to heaven 40 days after his resurrection. Inside the chapel, which functions today as a mosque, is his footprint. The first church on this site was built in the fourth century. The ancient section of the chapel dates back to Crusader times. Notice the column capitals and their rich display of floral embellishments and griffins (mythological beast with the body of a lion and the head and wings of an eagle). The dome which marks Jesus' ascent heavenward was open during the Crusader period. The Muslims converted the church into a mosque after recapturing Jerusalem in 1187 and built the closed dome seen today. Although a mosque, the various Christian denominations are permitted to celebrate the Feast of the Ascension (40 days after Easter) here and their altars may be seen in the courtyard.

According to Russian tradition, the precise spot of Jesus' ascent is inside the adjacent **Russian Monastery**, a structure conspicuous for its high pointed steeple (usually closed to visitors). To the immediate south of the Chapel of the Ascension is a burial grotto — of Hulda the Prophetess according to the Jews, of Pelagia the Ascetic of Antioch (5th century) according to the Christians, and of the mystic Rabi'a al-Adawiyya (8th century) in Muslim tradition. This site too is usually closed to visitors.

The Brook of Kidron

We now descend from the Mount of Olives to the Brook of Kidron. The path, originating at the observation area next to the Seven Arches Hotel (note the orange sign) follows the **Jewish cemetery**. Though the Mount of Olives was first used as a burial ground during the First Temple period, the tombstones seen today date from the 16th century to the present day. The site was chosen for several reasons: Jews always bury outside the Old City walls, and the Mount of Olives looks onto the Temple, thus enhancing its value. In addition, tradition says that the End of Days and Resurrection of the Dead will commence here, making those buried here the first in line...

For centuries Jews have come to Jerusalem so that they can be buried here when they die. Jordan, after taking the cemetery area with the rest of East Jerusalem in 1948, used many of its stones as building material. A Jordan Legion camp, built in part with Jewish gravestones, still stands beside the road to Jericho. One of the graves will attract your attention (note the orange sign): a large, square **mass grave** with 48 markers. Here

The Jewish cemetery on Mount of Olives

lie the last defenders of the Old City's Jewish Quarter who were killed just before Israel's surrender of that area to Jordan. Until 1967 they were buried in a secret location within the conquered Jewish Quarter but after the unification were reinterred here with military honors.

Nearby there is a burial chamber, traditionally called '*The*

The Russian Church of Mary Magdalene

The splendid mosaic facade of the Church of All Nations

Prophets Graves', stating it as the burial site of the prophets Hagai and Malachi. In fact the cave dates to the Byzantine era and contains 26 graves (visiting hours Sun.-Fri. 9am-3.30pm).

Continue going down and turn right. You have reached **Dominus Flevit**. (open daily 8-11:45am, 3-5pm.) This Franciscan church, whose name means 'The Lord Wept', marks the place where Jesus, arriving in Jerusalem before his crucifixion, wept for the city's future destruction: *'And when he was come near, he beheld the city, and wept over it, saying... for the days shall come upon thee, that thine enemies shall cast a trench about thee, and compass thee round, and keep thee on every side; and shall lay thee even with the ground, and thy children within thee; and they shall not leave in thee one stone upon another...'* (Luke 19:41-44). The prophecy came true in 70 AD — when the opulent Jerusalem of the late Second Temple period was leveled by the Romans.

The tiny church was built in 1954 by the Italian architect Antonio Barluzzi. Its tear-like shape recalls Jesus' tears. While most of the churches here face east, this one faces west. Its large front window provides a view of Jerusalem as Jesus saw it. The ornamentation over the window includes Jesus' cup of tears and crown of thorns. Inside, to the left of the entrance, are ancient Byzantine (5th century) mosaic floors, remnants of an earlier church at this site. Burial caves from the First and Second Temple periods were discovered in the courtyard and some, uphill from the path, may be viewed *in situ*. The findings include stone burial vaults, or ossuaries. As their size indicates, bodies were not buried in an ossuary in one piece; they had initially been buried elsewhere, and were later disinterred and their bones reinterred in this container. Some of the ossuaries have inscriptions in Hebrew, Aramaic and Greek.

The Russian Church of Mary Magdalene is the next stop on our steep descent from the Mount of Olives. (open Mon.-Thurs. 9am-noon, 2-4pm.) Its major distinction is its exterior which stands out even from the path for its seven Russian-style 'onion' domes. These are an imitation of the Russian style of the 16th and 17th centuries and are reminiscent of those of the Great Church in Moscow. The Russian Church was founded in 1886 by Czar Alexander II in memory of his mother, Maria Alexandrovna. This was the period when the world powers vied for footholds in the Middle East in general, and in Jerusalem in particular. One manner of expressing their influence was the construction of buildings in the respective homeland's representative style. The remains of Grand Duchess Elizabeth Feodrovna, who was brutally murdered during the Bolshevik Revolution, were smuggled to China and ultimately buried here.

At the foot of the Mount of Olives is **Gethsemane** (Heb. *Gat Shemanim* — lit. 'olive oil press'). Here, according to tradition, Jesus prayed for the last time before being betrayed by Judas Iscariot. To the left of the path is the **Basilica of the Agony** or the **Church of All Nations**, a Catholic institution completed in 1924 by means of donations solicited from the entire Catholic world (hence one of its names). (open daily 8am-noon, 2:30-5pm; summer 2:30-6pm.) The court is graced with ancient and lovely olive trees which, tradition claims, stood during Jesus' time. The most impressive element in this church is the splendid mosaic facade above the main entrance, which stands out when viewed from the hill across the valley. The mosaic depicts Jesus mediating between God and the people. Inside the church is the 'rock of agony', where Jesus uttered his last prayer. The rock is enclosed in a grating shaped like a crown of thorns. Remains of a fifth century Byzantine church at this site have survived, including sections of the mosaic floor which are visible under the modern flooring. Today's church, also designed by Barluzzi, preserves the lines of the Byzantine church in a general sense, especially in the pattern of its mosaic floor. The mosaics on the walls portrayed Jesus' last moments before and after his betrayal.

At the brook, to the right of the road, is the **Church of the Tomb of the Virgin**. (open every day 6:30am-noon; 2-5pm.) In Christian tradition, Mary, mother of Jesus, did not die but rather went into an eternal slumber and ascended to the heavens — an event known as the Assumption. This church was built in two major stages, remnants of which are visible today. During the late fourth century a cross-shaped church was built around the Tomb of Mary. The Crusaders extended the staircase and added a large basilica and adjacent monastery. During the Moslem conquest the Crusader buildings were destroyed and all that remains from this period is the impressive doorway and the staircase by which we enter the site.

Look to your right as you go down the stairs. The 14th century chapel, though dedicated to Anne and Joachim, Mary's parents, is really the **burial place of the Crusaders' Queen Melisanda**, a major figure in Crusader Jerusalem, who died in 1161. The chapel to the left of the stairs bears the name of Joseph, Mary's husband. The lower section of the church dates from the fourth century. The tomb chapel itself is to the right; note the two entrances with their ornate Crusader lintels. The tomb itself is a bench-sized structure of stone, enclosed in a marble slab with three apertures through which pilgrims might touch the tomb itself. All around are altars belonging to various Eastern Christian denominations which have controlled the church since the 18th century — the Greek-Orthodox, the Armenians, the

Copts and the Syrians. A structure comprising four pillars and a small dome stands beside the path leading to the church courtyard, at the side of the road. It is the grave of Mujir-ed-Din, a judge in 15th century Jerusalem who became famous as the author of a book on Jerusalem and Hebron of his time.

To the right of the plaza in front of Mary's tomb is the **Grotto of Gethsemane**. (open daily 8:30am-noon, 2:30-5pm.) It is a natural cave which, tradition claims, was visited by Jesus and the 12 Apostles before he parted with them for his last prayer. The cave, converted into a chapel as early as the fourth century, is administered by the Franciscans today. The ruins and wall murals belong to the Crusader era.

Cross the road and look back at the mosaic facade of the Basilica of the Agony and the Russian Church above it. We are about to enter another world, a voyage into the archeology of Jerusalem at its pinnacle — the First and Second Temple periods. We follow the path from the bus stop to the right, toward the Brook of Kidron (which ultimately spills into the Dead Sea). On the slope to your left (east) there are many ancient graves. The first of these — a striking feature — is the **Pillar** (or **Tomb**) **of Absalom**. It consists largely of a monolithic stone which was hewn right out of the mountainside. Only the rounded cylinder at its top was built in the conventional manner, as is easily discerned. The monument displays various building styles: the half-columns beside the monolith bear Ionic capitals crowned by a Doric frieze and an Egyptian-style upper rim.

The Pillar dates from the first century AD, and is one of the few monuments in Jerusalem which has survived almost intact from that period. It is traditionally associated with Absalom, the son of King David who launched an insurrection against his father and died when he was caught by the hair on an overhanging terebinth branch while riding his mule. Samuel II 18:18 relates: *'Now Absalom in his life-time had taken and reared up for himself the pillar, which is in the king's dale for he said: 'I have no son to keep my name in remembrance;' and he called the pillar after his own name; and it is called Absalom's monument unto this day.'* The monument in front of us was identified as the one mentioned here, even though the events happened a millenium (1,000 yrs) before the pillar was erected. It was an entrenched Jerusalem custom that anyone passing the grave would throw a stone at it, befitting a son who rebels against his father. Unless the pile of stones was cleared away, from time to time, the grave would have vanished long ago. During the Byzantine period a monk chopped an opening in the stone (the gaping hole in its facade) and took up residence there.

Behind the Pillar of Absalom is a burial grotto known as the **Cave**

Absalom's Tomb

of Jehoshaphat. The name stems from identification of the Kidron Valley as the Valley of Jehoshaphat mentioned in the Book of Joel. The broad opening at its top is graced with a gable decorated with floral motifs.

We head away from the Pillar of Absalom and come upon an elevated cave hewn out of the rock — **The Tomb of Bnei Hezir**. Note the two Doric stone pillars carved in the facade. Of all the tombs in this cluster, only in this case is it known who is actually buried here. A barely-perceptible inscription between the two columns includes the names of *Bnei Hezir* — offspring of the Hezir family known from Chronicles I, 24:15 as the 17th Order of Temple Priests. The site's appearance, too, gives one the impression of aristocracy: priests, confidants of the royal court, or dignitaries of some other sort. The three line inscription, dating from the first century BC, is one of the longest known from the Second Temple period. According to the Greek style of the cave facade, it is presumed to predate the first century BC, and that the inscription is a later addition.

Now we proceed to another monument quarried out of the hillside. This monolithic tomb, crowned with a pyramid and 'supported' by Ionic columns, is the **Tomb of Zechariah**. Tradition identifies it with the Prophet Zechariah who was active in Jerusalem during the reign of King Joash and was stoned to death because of his harsh reproaches. This monument too, appears to date from the first century BC. Note the proliferation of Hebrew inscriptions, if the sunshine enables you to see them.

Another grave — the **Tomb of the daughter of Pharaoh** — should be mentioned as well. It is farther down the slope at the same elevation and is hard to identify due to its natural camouflage. This grave indeed belongs to the First Temple period, predating those already described by several centuries. This square structure was originally crowned with a stone pyramid which no longer exists and bore an inscription which has since been erased. Other First Temple tombs have been found in the village of Siloam which we notice to our left as we continue down the valley.

Continue down the stream to a large parking lot. Behind it to the right are the stairs which lead to the Spring of Gihon.

Gihon Spring and Hezekiah's Tunnel

(Open Sun.-Thurs. 9am-4pm and Fri. 9am-1pm.) From its earliest days up to Israel's War of Independence in 1948, Jerusalem has always been plagued by a scarcity of water. We are about to visit Jerusalem's only spring, which was outside the confines of the ancient city. Originating in the nearby Kidron watercourse, it determined the site of the town in the pre-Israelite (Canaanite) and Davidic periods. This spring, called **Gihon** ('Gusher'), is at a level lower than the Kidron today because of the great quantities of debris and city ruins which have been washed into the valley.

In ancient Jerusalem, perched on the hill over the spring, various attempts were made at securing its waters although their source lay outside the city walls (sections of these walls, from different periods, are still visible today on the slopes of the hill above you). During the Canaanite and early Israelite period, the problem was solved by sinking a vertical underground shaft from a position inside the city to the spring. Known today as Warren's Shaft, it has survived intact and we shall return to it at the end of this tour. Some accounts identify it with the 'gutter' mentioned during David's conquest of Jerusalem from the Jebusites (II Sam. 5:8). The Biblical account asserts that reaching and gaining control of that 'gutter' or water channel (perhaps damaging it or penetrating the city through it) would bring the siege to a decisive end. Various waterworks were built around the spring as time passed. The most audacious of these was **Hezekiah's Tunnel**. Most of it has survived intact, allowing us to assess the ample engineering talents available 2,700 years ago.

When Hezekiah assumed the throne (727 BC) Jerusalem comprised of the City of David area and the Temple Mount. The city began to develop beyond those borders during his reign (727-698 BC), expanding to the hill to the west as it encircled the Tyropeon Valley which had thus far served as its western boundary. Hezekiah's engineers were able to perform a remarkable feat, because the western Tyropean stream lay inside the city walls and because parts of it were lower in elevation than the Spring of Gihon. The Spring of Gihon was rechanneled from the Kidron Valley east of the walls to a pool in the watercourse west of the City of David — inside the walls. The engineers were far from idle during peacetime. Sennacherib, King of Assyria, had begun a campaign of conquest in Judah (701 BC) and was about to march on Jerusalem. Chronicles II 32:2-4 and 30 (cf. Kings II 20:20 and Isaiah 22:11) describe the response as follows: *"And when Hezekiah saw that Sennacherib was come, and that he was purposed to fight against Jerusalem, he took counsel with his princes and his mighty men to stop the waters of the fountains which were without the city; and they helped him. So there was gathered much people together, and they stopped all the fountains, and the brook that flowed through the midst of the land, saying: 'Why should the kings of Assyria come, and find much water?' This same Hezekiah also stopped the upper spring of the waters of Gihon, and brought them straight down on the west side of the city of David."*

The account was corroborated in greater detail in 1880 when a child discovered an inscription on the wall of the tunnel while at play. The inscription, the longest known from the Biblical period in Israel, commemorates in the ancient Hebrew alphabet (Paleo-Hebraic) the dramatic moment when the two groups of quarrymen met, each having begun on opposite ends of the tunnel. The inscription is kept in Istanbul today, a replica is on display in the Israel Museum. The tunnel is still an impressive piece of engineering: almost 2000 feet long, with a total downward slope of only seven feet — a 0.4% gradient! Once completed, the spring in the Valley of Kidron was stopped up — and the Siloam Pool (Heb. *Shiloah*) became Jerusalem's water source.

It is not known for sure whether this was really the reason for Hezekiah's victory over Sennacherib. One way or another, Biblical and Assyrian writings account that Sennacherib, after having taken 46 armed cities in Judah, besieged Jerusalem, but failed to bring it down. He retreated and Jerusalem continued to use the pool. The Spring of Gihon was subsequently forgotten until the 15th century when it was rediscovered following an earthquake. In the meantime, the pool was thought of as a 'spring', explaining why some call it 'the spring of Siloam'. The Arab village of Silwan, alongside the Mount of Olives, derives its name from the same source. The village and the escarpment are pocked with burial grottoes and graves from the First Temple period, some of which may be seen from afar.

Access to the tunnel: Visit only on warm days and aim for the warmest hours at that. You'll need a flashlight or candle (the shop next to the entrance sells candles). It involves about 20 minutes of hiking through water which is usually knee-high and can reach three feet in depth at certain points. The tunnel is about 1.5 feet wide and one can walk erect for about half its length (its lowest point is five feet, and its highest point is 15 feet).

To the right of the entrance, inside, is the spring. Several feet further on, when the tunnel's ceiling gets lower from the ends, it bears to the right — the linkup with the bottom of Warren's Shaft. The tunnel's ceiling gets lower from the ends towards the middle, possibly attesting to hasty digging under the threat of Sennacherib's approach. The tunnel follows an S shape: it is not known why, but perhaps the workers followed a vein of soft stone, natural cavities or a weak trickle of water. At several points, mainly near the junction of the two workers' groups, are the beginnings of subsequently abandoned tunnels, probably indicating errors in orientation. The meeting point itself may be identified if the digging marks are carefully traced in the tunnel walls — which suddenly reverse direction. Here, too, a lintel of sorts protrudes from the ceiling.

The tunnel exits at the **Siloam Pool**. Today's pool is part of a larger, colonnaded reservoir dating from Byzantine times (5th century) and fragments of the columns are still visible. It was built here in remembrance of Jesus' miracle in restoring sight to the blind, as described in the New Testament. A modern mosque looms over the pool.

The City of David

Hezekiah's Tunnel is the most interesting remnant of First Temple Jerusalem. The destruction was aggravated by severe erosion along the steep slopes and the ravages of time have left little of special interest besides the tunnel. The most impressive remnant is part of the underground water system which is also associated with the Gihon Spring. This installation is known today as **Warren's Shaft**. (open seven days a week. 9am-4pm; Fri. 9am-2pm.) To reach its entrance, climb the stairs from Hezekiah's Tunnel entrance area and follow the signs. If coming from the road connecting the exit of Hezekiah's Tunnel with the Dung Gate — face uphill and turn right on the path at the top part of the hill, until you reach the paved lane with the steps. From here, follow the signs. A third way of reaching the shaft is from the path which begins at the Old City peripheral road under the Southern Wall excavations.

Warren's Shaft gave the population of Israelite Jerusalem access to the waters of the Gihon Spring, secure from discovery by an enemy. The water project included a sloping tunnel from the center of the City of David to a vertical shaft which, plunging to the level of the Gihon Spring, served as a well of sorts. A special 70 foot tunnel led the water from the spring to the bottom of the shaft. The City of David shaft was discovered by Charles Warren, a British officer who reached Jerusalem in 1867 (and later served as the fortifications engineer in Gibraltar). Researchers once attributed the pit to the Jebusites or the Canaanites, i.e., to periods preceding David's conquest of Jerusalem. This hypothesis resolved an obscure biblical account in Samuel II 5:8 of David's feat: *'On that occasion David said, 'Those who attack the Jebusites shall reach the gutter''*. That 'gutter', the scholars said, could only be the shaft which brought water to the city and the Israelites succeeded in taking Jerusalem by finding it during their siege. Today's scholars, reconsidering the matter, date Warren's Shaft (and other similar waterworks found in Palestine) from the time of the Israelite kings.

As you enter the site, notice to the right an illuminated picture which reconstructs the City of David as it appeared in its prime: walls, houses, royal palace and — above them to the right — the Temple Mount. Also displayed here is an illuminated model which explains the structure and function of the shaft. From here we go down a spiral staircase to a passageway leading to the shaft. **Note:** several dozen steep stairs must be navigated. The entrance to the tunnel is through a vaulted room built over the original entrance and is of later (Second Temple period) construction. To the right is the horizontal tunnel (an alternative exit today) with a lovely stone roof also dating from the Second Temple era.

We spend a few minutes walking through the First-Temple period tunnel, noting its varying degrees of graduation. It ends at the top of the vertical shaft to the bottom of which the Gihon Spring waters were fed. The sound of flowing water below comes from Hezekiah's Tunnel which ultimately made Warren's Shaft unnecessary. If just the thought of climbing back up makes you apprehensive, remember that anyone who drew water here nearly 3,000 years ago went just the same way — lugging full pitchers of water!

Area G: Along the road to the Dung Gate are some of the City of David excavation areas, among them the one known as 'Area G.' The excavations here during the early 1980s provoked a bitter dispute between professional archeologists and ultra-Orthodox Jewish groups in Jerusalem. The ultra-Orthodox claimed that bones discovered during the digs proved the presence of a Jewish cemetery at the site. If so, digging up the area and disturbing the dead was wholly out of the question. Counterclaims — that one might dig up bones anywhere in a city thousands of years old and that the 'Area G' findings did not demonstrate the presence of a Jewish graveyard failed to convince those opposed to the excavations. However, despite objections and even violence on the part of the ultra-Orthodox, the majority of Jerusalem residents, together with the authorities, sided with the archeologists. Thus the excavations progressed, but in an atmosphere of great difficulty and an ocean of newspaper headlines.

The area may be something of a letdown. A footpath has been pushed through; follow it to the lowest point of the area, the 'eastern observation' point (it is marked and numbered for your convenience). From here the major elements unearthed during the digs may be observed. The wall overhead does not belong to our story; it is 'new' (dating from the Second Temple and Byzantine years) and has two towers which demarcate the site. A terraced stone structure 50 feet high appears under the wall, dated at the 10th-6th century BC, (Judah's kings). Its location at the forefront of the city and its massive strength suggest that it may be a remnant of the 'Citadel of David', that is the citadel of the city. Below and to the left are earlier ruins belonging to a pre-Davidic Canaanite fortress (14th-13th centuries BC). In the center of the site, over the Canaanite ruins, stands a partial reconstruction of a typical Israelite house found here — *Beit Ahiel* or the Ahiel's house. Another interesting house is presently hidden under the path: scholars call it 'the seal house' for the 51 clay seal impressions they found here. One bears the inscription *"Gemaryahu son of Shaphan"*, a scribe under King Yehoyakhin, mentioned in Jeremiah. This is one of the rare instances in which archeologists have actually identified someone from the Bible! The Babylonian takeover of 586 BC destroyed the City of David as well as the First Temple. One house here, "the Burnt Room", testifies to this devastation.

We follow the path and go up to the high ('northern') observation point. From here you can encircle the entire site, and return to the entrance gate to the road, parallel to the City of David. Alternatively exit by the gate on the flank of the hill, next to the northern observation point, for a lovely view of the Kidron Valley. Before going, look behind at the terraced structure unearthed during the excavations, it is particularly impressive from this angle.

The path follows a flat route along the flank of the hill and finally joins up with the road which runs alongside the Old City walls below the excavations of the southern wall of the Temple Mount. This route gives an excellent view of the Kidron Valley and the village of Silwan. Notice the openings of the burial caves in the cliff under the village buildings. Take another look, too, at the First Temple grave traditionally identified with Pharaoh's daughter: the tomb, hewn out of the rock, is conspicuous for its black opening and prominent rim and is inset a little way from the left edge of the lower row of village houses. From here, we find ourselves back on the road, only a few minutes' walk away from the Dung Gate and the Western Wall.

The Via Dolorosa

Buses 1 and 99 reach this point.

This route begins at the eastern gate of the Old City wall — the **Lions' Gate.** The name of the gate comes from the two pairs of 'lions' fixed outside the wall on either side of the gate. These 'lions' are in fact panthers which once served as a symbol of a 13th century Mamluk sultan and were transfered here after the wall was built. Popular tradition explains the name differently, ascribing it to a legend about the Ottoman Sultan, Suleiman the Magnificent, who dreamt that lions were standing over him and ripping him apart. He consulted seers who explained that the Lion of Judah was angry at him because no wall had been built for the Holy City of Jerusalem after it had been conquered by his father. The wall was erected and legend relates that Suleiman ordered two pairs of lions placed at the point where the project began, commemorating his dream. The portal is also known as St. Stephen's Gate in honor of the Stephen the Martyr who was stoned to death near the gate. (Damascus Gate is also referred to as St. Stephen's Gate due to a similar legend.) In recent Jewish history, the Lions' Gate has acquired a special distinction as the point where Israeli paratroopers first entered the Old City on June 7, 1967. This was the first time that Jerusalem was taken from the east.

We pass through the gate, which has been widened for vehicles. For this purpose, the L-shaped turn, which was meant to slow down a charging enemy, was removed. The Temple Mount wall appears to the left. The car park area occupies the site of the ancient **Israel Pool** (*Birkat Yisrael*) that was filled in by the British. We follow the road as far as **St. Anne's Church.** (open daily

---

Index

1. Lion's Gate
2. St. Anne's Church
3. Beit Hisda Pool
4. First Station — Omariyya School
5. Second Station — Franciscan Biblical School
6. Lithostrotos
7. Convent of the Sisters of Zion
8. Austrian Hospice
9. Third Station — Polish Catholic Chapel
10. Fourth Station — Church of Our Lady of the Spasm
11. Fifth Station — Franciscan Church
12. Sixth Station — St. Veronica's Church
13. Seventh Station
14. Eighth Station

VIA DOLOROSA

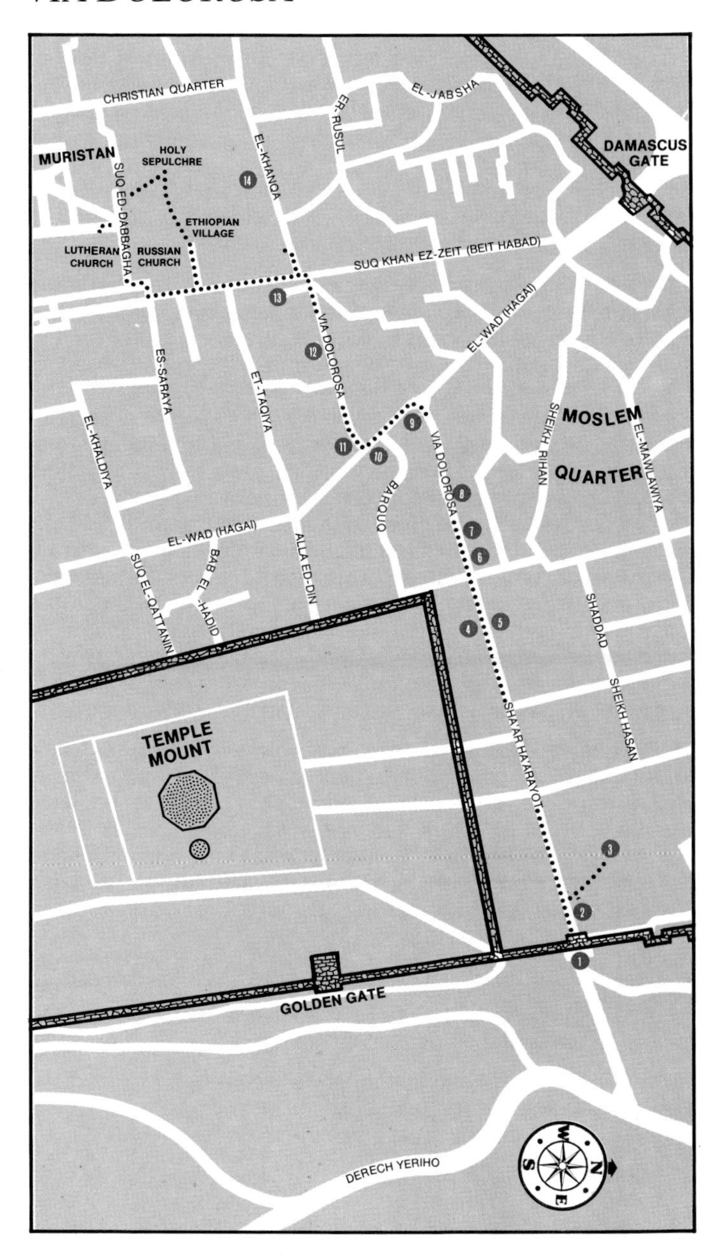

8am-noon, 2-5pm; in summer 2-6pm.) This Crusader church is a heavy, impressive but sparsely adorned building and is one of the loveliest examples of Romanesque building style in Israel. The church is dedicated to St. Anne, who in Christian tradition lived here when she gave birth to Mary. It was built in 1140 with the support of representatives of the ruling Crusader family, on the foundation of what was a Byzantine church. After the Muslim Salah-ed-Din vanquished the Crusaders in 1187, the church became an important *madrasa* (Muslim religious academy). A five-line inscription which attests to this is affixed over the middle entrance to the church.

Over the years the building was neglected. In the wake of the Crimean War of 1856, when Ottoman relations with France improved, the Sultan consented to the request of the French Consul in Jerusalem that the church be given to France. The church was renovated, and since 1878 has been in the possession of the Order of the White Fathers (*Les Peres Blancs*). Here, as was frequently the case during the Crusader era, European and local building traditions have been integrated. The structure is built in the early 12th-century French style, but its builders added a few foreign features, such as pointed arches. The church facade once had three openings, but one no longer exists. When examining the detail of the church facade, note the 'pillow' pattern which appears in the arch above the uppermost window. This pattern is characteristic of Crusader buildings in Jerusalem and apparently originated in the Orient. In accordance with Crusader tradition each of the column capitals is different. The crypt under the church marks Mary's birthplace.

In the church courtyard is a pool of water identified as that of **Beit Hisda** (Bethesda) where, according to Christian tradition, Jesus cured the ill, the blind and the lame. This pool may have served as a place of worship of Asclepius, god of medicine. The sizeable pool (40 x 150 x 400 ft) belonged to the complex water system which existed in Jerusalem at the time of the Second Temple. During that period, the expanding city had to contend with complicated problems of storing and transporting water. The pool served mainly the Temple Mount area where great quantities of water were required for the daily rites. A large church was built over the previous pool in Byzantine times, and a smaller one in the time of the Crusaders.

We leave St. Anne's and turn right. Before taking the walk down the Via Dolorosa, let us summarize the last events in Jesus' life, as described in the four gospels of the New Testament.

In approximately 30AD, Jesus entered Jerusalem triumphantly from the Mount of Olives, to celebrate Passover with thousands of other Jews. Passover marked the peak of pilgrimage to the Temple. The Roman rulers feared an intensification of anti-government ferment in a religious event of this type. The Roman Procurator used to relocate his seat from Caesarea, the permanent capital, to Jerusalem at this time of year, to crack down on any suspected insurrection. Jesus' appearance and his sermons were perceived as suspicious activities. After sharing the Last Supper (apparently the *seder* — the Jewish Passover feast) with his twelve disciples, Jesus was arrested in Gethsemane. The Gospels indicate that Jesus was betrayed by his disciple Judas Iscariot. He was tried first by Jewish priests, and later by Romans in the presence of the Roman Procurator Pontius Pilate, and found guilty by both. The first station of Via Dolorosa, according to tradition, was the site of the second trial, in which he was condemned to crucifixion. The historical authenticity of the 14 Via Dolorosa stations is dubious, as the tradition developed only in the late Middle Ages. An earlier tradition places the site of Jesus' trial on Mt. Zion, in the Upper City.

The first station of the Via Dolorosa, left of the street, is the site of the **Antonia Citadel**. The citadel dominated the Temple Mount to the north during the Second Temple period. In the 14th century, a Muslim *madrasa* was erected here, which today is the **Omariyya School**. If open, peek through the school's grilled windows for an interesting view of the Temple Mount.

Every Friday at 3pm a procession sets out from this point along the entire Via Dolorosa, led by the Franciscans. The participants, carrying a large wooden cross, include monks, priests and pilgrims. Joining them may offer an interesting and colorful though cursory look at the various sites. It is especially colorful on the Friday of Easter week (Good Friday).

Continue on the right of the street to the **second station** — the **Chapels of the Condemnation and the Flagellation** (open daily 8am-noon, 1-5pm; summer 2-6pm). These are small structures located in the courtyard of the **Franciscan Biblical School**. The Church of the Flagellation (right of the entrance to the court) was built in the 1920s in medieval style. It marks the place where Jesus was whipped and beaten by Roman soldiers and where a crown of thorns was placed on his head after the verdict was handed down. The crown of thorns appears in a ceiling mosaic, and the event is described in the central stained glass window. The New Testament account, portrayed in the other two windows, stresses the part played by the Jews in decreeing Jesus' execution, and plays down that of the Romans. According to this account, Pilate wanted to free Jesus under the custom of pardoning one prisoner at holiday time. The Jews insisted on having Jesus put to death and a different prisoner — Barabbas

— was released. In the right window Barabbas is portrayed celebrating his liberation. The left-hand window commemorates the moment Pontius Pilate rose to his feet and informed the crowd which had demanded Jesus' crucifixion, '*I am clean of the blood of this righteous man*' (Matthew 27:24); to which the crowd replied, '*His blood is upon us and upon our sons.*' Hence the source of the accusation against the Jews for Jesus' death — a charge of which the Jews were finally cleared only under 20th-century Catholic Church decisions.

The second church, left of the courtyard, is the Church of the Condemnation. Here, the **second station** of the Via Dolorosa, Jesus received the cross after his condemnation. Note the stone paving on the righthand side of the church. It is Roman and dates from the 2nd century. We will follow it later.

The **Franciscan Biblical School** houses a museum which exhibits mainly those archeological findings collected by the Franciscans in the course of their excavations throughout Israel. Interesting objects include a volume given by Henry IV of England to the Mt. Zion Franciscan Monastery in the 15th century, a 17th century shell and olive-wood model of the Church of the Holy Sepulchre, and receptacles produced for the Franciscan pharmacy in Jerusalem during the 18th century and thereafter. The museum is normally closed, and a visit must be arranged in advance, tel. 282-936.

One of the most interesting sites in this area, though not an "official" station on the Via Dolorosa, is the **Convent of the Sisters of Zion** down the street, on the right. Notice the arch which rises above the road at the entrance to the convent. This ancient arch shall be discussed at greater length once we enter the convent's church. (open daily 8:30am-12:30pm, 2-4pm. Closed Sundays and holidays.) The heart of the church is an ancient arch built of small stones (in constructing the church in the 1860s, an effort was made to imitate this style). We are, in fact, observing more than a single arch. You can discern a small arch and the beginning of a larger one whose continuation is the one seen outside above the road. The niche between the two arches was originally meant for a statue. These remnants constitute part of a triple Roman triumphal arch which had a high portal in the middle flanked by smaller openings (one of which is seen in the church). The arch, discovered during construction of the church, was believed to be the gate where Pontius Pilate took Jesus out and proclaimed *"Ecce homo"* ('This is the man'). Therefore, this church is named the Basilica of Ecce Homo. The convent was built by the Catholic Order of the Sisters of Zion, it was founded by a Jewish convert, Alphonse Ratisbonne of Strasbourg. Archaeologists date the arch to the second century

A.D., and believe that it was built by the Emperor Hadrian.

When you leave the church turn right, and immediately to your left you will find a door which leads to the **lithostrotos** — a name originating in the New Testament meaning 'stone floor'. Go down the stairs where a surprise awaits you: steps which descend to an underground pool of water. It is cut in part into the rock, and a row of arches divides it into two pools. During Second Temple days the pool (known then as Strotion's Pool) was part of the city's complex water system. According to Josephus' descriptions of Jerusalem, the pool was uncovered at that time. Today, the only source of water here is drainage from the immediate area. The pool's ceiling was built by the Romans after the city's fall in 70 AD. This fact helps to date the lithostrotos (which we will see in a few minutes) which was laid atop the pool's ceiling and therefore must be of later construction. Complicated? Perhaps, yet a good example of archeological inference. Follow the arrows and explore the pool and other findings, finally emerging at a plaza paved in a manner similar to that previously seen in the Church of the Condemnation. Various pavement games are chiseled into this section of the stone paving, as well as surface drainage channels, and slots to keep horses from slipping. You are now over the pool, which can be seen through the peepholes. You will find a souvenir shop on the way out, if you feel the need to spend some money.

We continue down the street to the main north-south artery of the Old City, Hagai St. En route on the right, is a Greek Orthodox monastery, the site where Jesus was imprisoned. At the corner of Hagai St., is the **Austrian Hospice** built in 1856, Austria's main contribution to the 19th-century power struggle in Jerusalem. The building served as a hospice until World War II and then as a hospital, which closed only recently.

Hagai St. runs from Damascus Gate on our right to the Western Wall on our left. If we follow it only a little way to our left we notice the sections of ancient pavement, which were found under the street during construction and integrated into the modern pavement. To the left of the road, is a **Polish Catholic Chapel** — the **third station** of the Via Dolorosa which marks the point where Jesus fell for the first time under the weight of the cross. The chapel was built from contributions of Polish Catholic soldiers in 1947, and today it belongs to the Catholic Armenians. The **fourth station** immediately follows. Here, according to tradition, Jesus encountered his mother. Beside it is an Armenian Catholic church, **Our Lady of the Spasm**, built on the ruins of a Byzantine church. A sixth-century mosaic shows the outline of a pair of sandals at the spot where the anguished Mary stood as Jesus passed her with the cross on his back. The site is held by the Armenian Catholic Church; a Uniate church, ie. an Eastern Church which accepts the supremacy of the Pope.

Nearby, you can stop for a taste of *Abu-Shukri's* famous hummus. Opposite the continuation of Via Dolorosa which turns right, on the left side of Hagai St., Abu-Shukri is identifiable, at least on Saturdays, by a long queue. Especially recommended is *hummus* with *tznobar* — pine seeds. (If you join the Friday procession, don't worry: Abu-Shukri's will wait for you until it's over...)

We turn right on Via Dolorosa to a small **Franciscan Church**. This is the **fifth station**, marking the place where the Roman soldiers ordered Simon of Cyrene to help Jesus bear his cross. A little farther up the street to the right is a ceramics workshop run by two Armenian brothers. Some of the most beautiful and delicate examples of Armenian ceramic painting — tiles, dishes and other implements are displayed and for sale here.

To reach the **sixth station**, continue on to **St. Veronica's Church** (Greek Catholic). Here tradition places the home of St. Veronica, who dried the brow of Jesus with a cloth when he passed, whereupon the features of his face were miraculously imprinted on it.

At the intersection with Beit Habad St. (or Khan ez-Zeit St., known in Crusader times as Malcuisinat St., meaning 'bad cooking') is the **seventh station**. This is where Jesus fell for the second time under the weight of the cross. The chapel belongs to the Franciscans, and is used by the Catholic Copts (also a Uniate denomination). The column which stands here dates from Roman-Byzantine times, and was originally part of the colonnade which lined the Cardo.

To reach the **eighth station** follow Khanqa St. to a stone-engraved cross which bears a Latin inscription. Here tradition has Jesus speaking to the daughters of Jerusalem. We return to Beit Habad St. and turn right (south). From here we can climb the steps to Deir es-Sultan and the Ethiopian settlement on the roof of the Church of the Holy Sepulchre. Beside it is the **ninth station** where Jesus fell for the third time. Deir es-Sultan and the remaining stations, 10-14, which are inside the Church of the Holy Sepulchre are described in the following tour.

For a welcome treat after this tour, try the Ayub Brothers, experts on Oriental sweets. Even if this is not normally your taste, we recommend trying *k'nafe*, an unforgettable combination of noodles, cheese and honey.

The Church of the Holy Sepulchre

From Jaffa Gate: walk down David St. and turn left at Hanotzrim (Christians) St.; continuing beyond the Greek Church of John the Baptist until Saint Helena St. Here turn right, following the street until you come to the Holy Sepulchre plaza. Buses 3, 13, 19, 20 or 30 reach Jaffa Gate. (open daily 4:30am-7pm; summer till 8pm).

The Church of the Holy Sepulchre is the holiest Christian site in Jerusalem and one of the most important places in the world for hundreds of millions of Christians — in particular Catholics and adherents of the Eastern denominations. This site, identified by non-Protestant Christians as Jesus' burial place, has attracted thousands of pilgrims during its 2,000 years of history. Then, as now, interdenominational disputes spill over into the realm of politics.

Architecturally, the building is a multi-layered complex, with a long, complicated and often baffling history. It is rich in numerous holy associations. We shall try to clarify the picture as we proceed.

History

The Gospel of John (19:17-18, 20, 41) relates: *'And Jesus bearing his cross went forth into a place called the place of a skull, which is called in the Hebrew Golgotha: where they crucified him, and two other with him, on either side one, and Jesus in their midst.'* John describes Golgotha as *'the place where he was crucified there was a garden; and in the garden a new sepulchre, wherein was never man yet laid.'* Jesus was resurrected on the third day following the crucifixion. These occurrences took place outside Jerusalem on the hill of **Golgotha** (Calvary), an area which had been used as a quarry in ancient times (traces still exist). In the second century AD, the Romans built a city atop the ruins of Jerusalem, installed a temple to Aphrodite at the sepulchre site, and erected a civil basilica — a large structure for public gatherings — to its immediate east. At the Ecumenical Council of Nicaea (325), the Bishop of Jerusalem asked Emperor Constantine, who had converted to Christianity not long before, to uncover the sepulchre site. As a result, Constantine's mother Helena came to Jerusalem, identified the place and, according to tradition, discovered the true cross there. Aphrodite's temple was cleared away and, during the fourth century, two churches

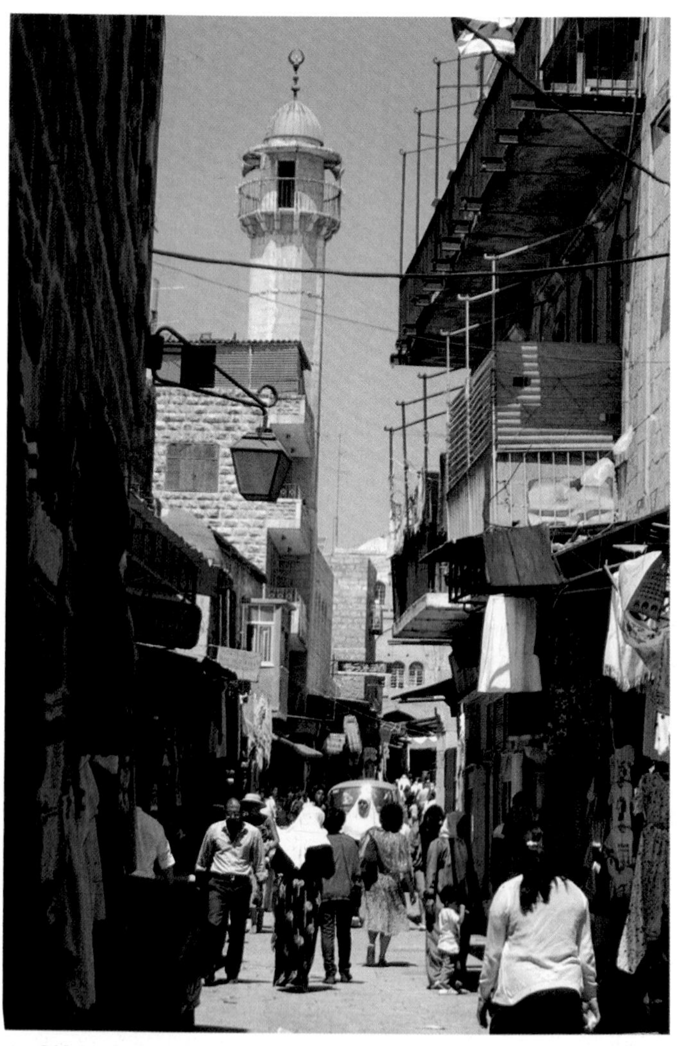

An Old City street

were built. One was a great basilica, much longer than today's structure; the other was a round church at the sepulchre site — the Church of Anastasis, or the Resurrection.

In 614, the Persians invaded Palestine, burned the Holy Sepulchre and captured the true cross. The Byzantine Emperor Heraclius, routing the Persians 14 years later, restored the cross to Jerusalem and had the church renovated. In 638, the Muslims took Jerusalem — but left the church and the city's Christians unharmed. Christian tradition explains that Caliph Omar refused to pray in the church 'so as to deny Muslim believers a pretext for demanding its conversion into a mosque.' This account, like many traditions concerning Omar in Jerusalem, is of course of dubious authenticity. In any case, the Muslims' attitude towards the Christians of Jerusalem changed in the early 11th century when the Church incurred the wrath of Islam. The ruler at the time was Caliph Al-Hakim Be-Ammar Allah ('he who rules by God's word'), an extreme anti-Christian religious zealot. The church was razed to the ground in 1009 by his personal command, thus ending the first chapter of its history.

Reconstruction of the Holy Sepulchre, the building we know today, occurred in two stages. Between 1030 and 1048, Byzantine-style structures were erected at the site by the Byzantine Emperor Constantine Monomachus of Constantinople. These included the rotunda, a circular building enveloping the sepulchre and an open arcaded courtyard adjacent to it from the east (today's center of the church). A number of chapels ringed the court, such as the one which marked the crucifixion site at Golgotha, and one where the Cross was found. The church underwent the second phase of construction when the Crusaders captured Jerusalem in 1099, and immediately began expanding the church. They succeeded in integrating Monomachus' rotunda and chapels into a unified Romanesque structure around the open courtyard. They also constructed a dome over the area they had enclosed — in addition to the rotunda dome — and added a belfry and an impressive southern facade. The new church, consecrated on July 15, 1149 — exactly 50 years after the Crusader conquest of Jerusalem — has, basically, survived to this day.

The church has been damaged during the intervening centuries by earthquakes, fires and by man, resulting in periodic repair work. The great fire of 1808 was especially grievous, undermining the structure itself and underscoring the urgent need for thorough renovation. Interdenominational disputes concerning control of various parts of the building delayed this endeavor until the mid-20th century. In 1955, after an international conference devoted to the subject, work began under a technical bureau shared by the Greek Orthodox, the Catholics and the Armenians. Serious progress commenced in 1960 and work continues today.

The authenticity of the Holy Sepulchre

The question of the Holy Sepulchre's authenticity — namely, was Jesus truly crucified and buried here? — is a major issue in Jerusalemite archeology. Since by Jewish law he must have been interred outside of town, a fact attested by the Gospel, a crucial point of contention concerns the route of Jerusalem's circumferential wall, the so-called Second Wall, at the time of events. Though the wall's approximate course is known (from today's Damascus Gate to Jaffa Gate), its precise route remains a mystery. Compounding the dilemma is the fact that Jerusalem's original Christian community left during the destruction of 70 AD and no Christian presence is recorded until the arrival of Helena in 326. Thus, a gap of some 250 years is left in the tradition. The account does find some support in the form of a burial crypt dating from Second Temple days discovered inside the church, proof that the site did serve as a burial ground. If the crypt predates construction of the Second Wall, however, it solves nothing. Attempts were made in the 19th century to identify other sites as the sepulchre of Jesus. The most famous of these is General Charles Gordon's Garden Tomb, which is accepted by the Protestants.

Christian denominations and their holdings in the Church of the Holy Sepulchre

Six Christian churches share control of the Church of the Holy Sepulchre. Of these, three dominate: the Greek Orthodox, the Catholics (represented by the Franciscan Order) and the Armenians. Three have lesser rights: the Copts, the Ethiopians and the Syrians. A 'claim' to part of the church usually entails responsibility for its maintenance, cleanliness and, when necessary, renovation. The latter has caused much controversy during the recent renovation projects. Interdenominational disputes over unresolved points have lengthy histories and occasionally become violent. The Ottoman Turks made an initial effort to stabilize the situation in 1757 by means of an order fixing a status quo. Disputes between the Greek Orthodox and the Catholics, concerning this church and the Church of the Nativity in Bethlehem, so intensified during the 1800s that they served as a pretext for the Crimean War. As part of ongoing efforts to preserve a viable status quo, the church keys were deposited with two respected Muslim families. Such problems persist to this day; one example, which we discuss below, is the rift in Ethiopian-Coptic relations.

Before entering the church, one can make an interesting and relevant one hour detour to the adjacent **Russian Alexander Niyevski Church** and the **Ethiopian Village**. This 'village' is on the roof of part of the Holy Sepulchre (through which the Via Dolorosa enters the Holy Sepulchre). To reach the Russian Church, leave the Holy Sepulchre plaza through the arched eastern opening (opposite the steps from which you came) to the door on your left.

This church and the adjacent convent were erected by the Russians in 1887. (open Mon.-Thurs. 9am-3pm, and occasionally at other hours.) The church is interesting mainly for the archeological findings discovered on the premises. The sixth-century mosaic map of Jerusalem found in Madaba (Jordan) depicts the Byzantine Church of the Holy Sepulchre as a round structure — the rotunda which encircles the sepulchre itself — and an elongated basilica with a front courtyard (atrium) and three openings onto the Cardo, the city's main street. Remains of these buildings can be seen inside.

Enter the Russian Church, follow the corridor to its end, turn right and go down the stairs. You'll find yourself beside a reconstructed arch, evidently part of a second-century Roman forum. Now cross to your left and enter the second hall. Part of a wall belonging to Constantine's original basilica can be seen here. Note the southernmost of the three gates which open onto the Byzantine street. The basilica was much larger than the present-day church. It began here and ended inside today's Holy Sepulchre. This is essentially all that remains of the original Church of the Holy Sepulchre which was pillaged in 1009. A small room to the right houses a few black columns *in situ*; these belonged to the Cardo colonnade (the basilica's steps descended to this main street of Byzantine Jerusalem). Christian tradition identifies the glass-covered stone doorsill demarcating the room (where the basilica door was found) as the city gate through which Jesus passed en route to his crucifixion.

Deir es-Sultan and the Ethiopian Village

Exit the Russian Church, turn left, and left again on the street encircling the church from the outside. Pass through the teeming market as far as a wide staircase rising to the left along the outer wall of the Russian Church. Here Via Dolorosa enters the Church of the Holy Sepulchre. Follow the path as it ascends, turn right (don't go through the open gate facing you), then left. You have reached the entrance to the **Coptic Monastery, Church and Patriarchate** — the Copts' Jerusalem center and the seat of their Bishop. There is an interesting cistern underneath the building, but admittance to the Coptic compound is rarely permitted. Look into the small anteroom, (the guard may deign to turn the lights on for you) and look into a lovely little room preserved intact from a Crusader structure described below. A marble column embedded in the wall to the left of the entrance to the Coptic compound marks the **ninth station** of the Via Dolorosa. Here Jesus buckled under the weight of the cross for the third time.

An Ethiopian priest with an Amharic prayer book

Pass through the opening to the left of this column into a broad courtyard with a dome in its center: **Deir es-Sultan**. In Byzantine times, this area was part of the interior of the great basilica whose entrance we viewed in the Russian Church. During the Crusader period, when the Church of the Holy

Sepulchre was rebuilt in smaller dimensions, an Augustine monastery was located here. It consisted of a cloister encircled with colonnaded porticos which opened on to the court center. Parts of these portico rooms are preserved; one example is the Coptic anteroom. In the wall opposite the courtyard entrance, traces of the ceiling of the monastery's refectory (dining hall) are clearly visible. The courtyard is open today, and the dome of the **Chapel of St. Helena** (inside the Holy Sepulchre) protrudes from its center. Presently it is controlled by the Ethiopian Church. The Ethiopians are engaged in bitter and violent dispute with their cousin churchmen, the Copts, over title to the courtyard itself and control of the passage of the Via Dolorosa from here to the Holy Sepulchre plaza. The intractable feud is a topic for recurrent debate in various public and political forums, including diplomatic talks between Israel and Egypt (the Copts' homeland).

The most interesting phenomenon here is the **Ethiopian Village**, a cluster of African village type huts which house members of this community, chiefly monks. To view this amazing site from up close, cross the court, pass under the low lintel to your left, and walk over to the great mulberry tree. Accommodation in this mini-neighborhood consists of airless, waterless cubbyholes which appear unfit for human habitation. The Ethiopians cannot replace these shacks since new construction in this area, under the status quo, requires the consent of all denominations, including that of the Copts. Neither can they abandon the huts, as this would undermine their claims to the only part of the Holy Sepulchre complex in their possesion. But don't just look: talk with the Ethiopian monks who will be delighted to describe their side of the dispute with the Copts.

To climb down, head for an opening in the wall adjacent to the Holy Sepulchre (ask for directions) and proceed through it to two small chapels which lead into the Holy Sepulchre plaza. The first of these is worth noting for a painting on a wall to your left which depicts the Ethiopians' legendary ancestors, King Solomon and the Queen of Sheba, in their historic encounter. Note, in the painting, the anachronistic depiction of the Jews who escort the King. They have *peot* and *streimelach* — the traditional sidecurls and fur hats which were only worn by some European Jews in the last few centuries.

As you exit the lower chapel into the Holy Sepulchre plaza, look up and to the right for a glimpse of part of a lovely sculptured pair of lions. One is headless. Legend tells that these lions roared whenever a Jew passed the church front, until a certain Jew exploited the opportunity afforded by the Muslim conquest, and beheaded one of the beasts...

Church of the Holy Sepulchre — entrance plaza and facade

The facade of this church, perhaps the structure's most impressive element, is almost entirely of Crusader vintage and actually overlays an older wall. The best way to appraise it is to step back and then to approach it for examination of its detail. One of the doorways leading to the church was permanently sealed during the Muslim conquest. The entrance design — two doors on the south — departs from European tradition of the time, typified by three apertures on the west. The reason, of course, is the constraints imposed by the site, since the Crusaders were adding to an existing Byzantine structure. The facade presents a combination of Romanesque architecture and indigenous Byzantine Eastern elements. An example of the latter is the 'pillow' motif carved inside the arches over both the doorways and the windows. Some of these Oriental devices were subsequently exported to Europe by returning Crusaders. According to one hypothesis, the European Gothic pointed arch originated in part in the gently pointed Oriental arches incorporated into this otherwise Romanesque Crusader church. The lintels above the doors, now unadorned, were originally graced with lovely reliefs. These were transferred to the Rockefeller Museum during the 1930s, where they are on display today.

The square Crusader belfry is to the left of the church facade (it was originally higher than it is today). The wall leading to it, left of the plaza, displays three trapezoidal protrusions — the apses of three Greek chapels. At the left edge of this wall is a column with a 'basket' shaped capital and the beginning of an arch. These elements belong to the arcade built in 1048 by pre-Crusader Byzantine Emperor Constantine Monomachus. The several buildings around the courtyard belong to various Christian denominations. One worth noting is the dome-shaped arcaded structure to the right of the church entrance. It is the **Chapel of Our Lady of Dolours**, commemorating Mary's agony during the crucifixion. Note the grapevine and bird ornamentation in its arches. Since the chapel is under Catholic control, while the entire plaza is held by the Greeks, a problem arises: who cleans the first low step leading to the chapel? It leads to Catholic territory, after all ... but it rests on Greek holdings! In 1901, this dilemma grew into such an altercation that the Turkish Sultan had to intervene.

Inside the Church of the Holy Sepulchre

As you enter the church, notice the numerous crosses carved into the doorway columns by Christian pilgrims. Turn right as you enter and head up the stairs which obstruct the eastern (sealed) church entrance. This takes us to **Golgotha**, the stony hill which, since Jesus' crucifixion, has been so extensively developed that it is barely discernible. The site is divided into two distinct areas, one Catholic (to the right) and the other Greek Orthodox (to the left). The two are distinguishable by the different alphabets and languages in the wall ornamentation. Four stations of Via Dolorosa are located here: Jesus was undressed in the right-hand (Catholic) room **(10th station)**, and nailed to the cross as seen in the wall mosaic beyond the altar **(11th station)**. The left-hand (Greek) room marks the site of the crucifixion itself; kneel and feel the indentation where the cross stood **(12th station).** Between the two rooms is a statue of Mary, a diamond-studded gold crown on her head, marking the spot where she took Jesus' body into her arms **(13th station).** The mosaics here are modern, excluding one handsome 12th century portrait of Jesus on the ceiling of the Catholic room.

Leave Golgotha by the stairs at the edge of the Greek room. At the bottom notice a flat pink stone affixed in the floor to your left. As the picture on the wall shows, Jesus' body was laid here, anointed with oil and wrapped in shrouds. The pink stone is in fact a marble cover which protects the real stone underneath; this became necessary after fervent pilgrims broke off bits of the original unction stone as holy relics. The pink wall near it, where the picture hangs, is a product of the recent renovations. Now we turn left to the great round colonnaded hall — the rotunda.

The rotunda and the sepulchre of Jesus

On the way to the rotunda, we pass the Armenian wing on the left. It is recognizable as Armenian by the wall mosaic, embellished with inscriptions in Armenian, of Jesus with his mother Mary and Mary Magdalene. Another indication is the balustrade leading to the Armenian galleries, ornamented with pairs of peacocks — reminiscent of Noah's Ark, which settled to earth on Mt. Ararat (located in Armenia, of course). The round metal grille in front of the mosaic denotes 'the Stone of the Three Marys' where, according to tradition, Mary, mother of Jesus, Mary Magdalene, and Mary, mother of James the Apostle all stood.

The rotunda is a round two story structure encasing Jesus' sepulchre. The dome overhead is new, one of the main achievements of the renovations of recent years. The ancient pillars have also been replaced, and the present ones are modern replicas. Since Jesus was entombed in a grotto, one might wonder momentarily how his sepulchre came to be

THE HOLY SEPULCHRE

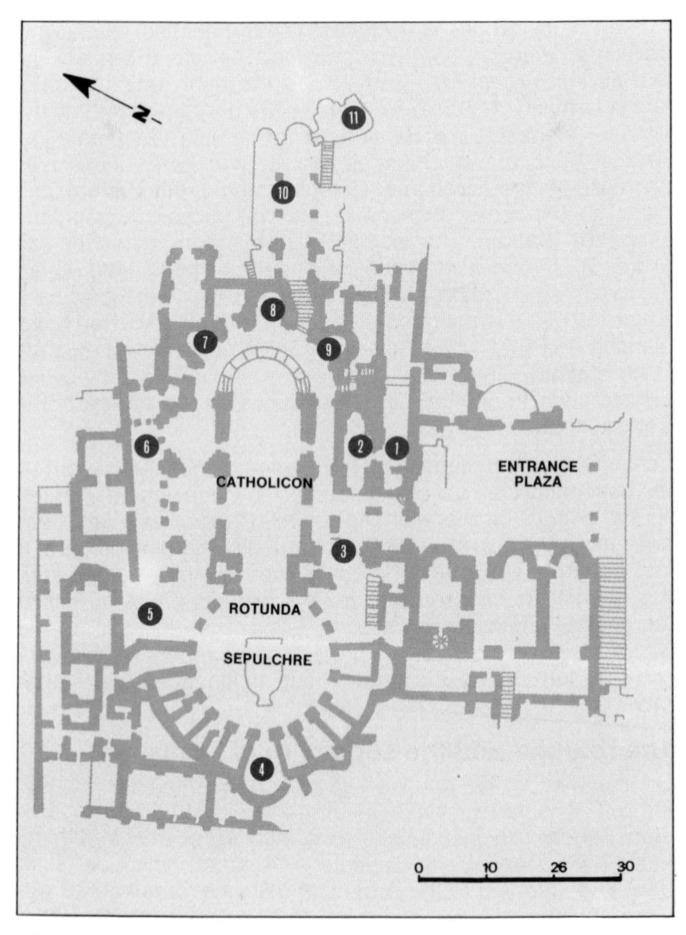

Index

1. Golgotha
2. Site of the Crucifixion
3. Anointment Stone
4. Chapel of Joseph of Arimathaea and Nicodemus
5. Latin (Catholic) Area
6. Chapel of the Binding
7. Chapel of St. Longinus
8. Chapel of the Division of the Raiment
9. Chapel of the Mocking
10. Chapel of St. Helena
11. Chapel of the Finding of the Cross

The Church of the Holy Sepulchre

inside the structure sheltered by the rotunda. The answer is simple: when Constantine built the original Church of the Holy Sepulchre, he dug the hillside around the grotto and left it, with its covering, as a free-standing structure. The candle sticks and lamps beside the sepulchre entrance belong to the various denominations.

The sepulchre itself comprises two small rooms. The first is the **Angel's Chapel**, where, according to tradition, Mary Magdalene visited the grave the first Sunday after the crucifixion, found Jesus' body gone, and saw an angel in white sitting on the stone altar. From here we pass through a low aperture into a small room with a stone slab which marks the tomb itself. The sepulchre structure is marked with several round, sooty holes; through which, it is said, holy fire, kindled by no man, emanates during a special ceremony during Easter. Thousands have tried to trap and preserve the miraculous flame without success.

The large hall opposite the sepulchre entrance (usually closed off with a golden chain) is the **Catholicon**, the major hall belonging to the Greek Orthodox. The most conspicuous element here is the huge chandelier suspended by an iron chain from the domed roof. The hall is demarcated on either side by walls of pink stone. They were built in the course of renovations during the latter half of the 20th century, in order to separate the Greek prayer area from the rest of the church, and to prevent possible interruptions. The construction caused great opposition since the great Crusader achievement of unifying the various parts of the church into a single architectural entity was lost. To get the job done, the Greeks even had to replace a bishop who resisted the project too strenuously. The remodeling did detract from the architectural quality of the church by fracturing its unity, and today the structure can no longer be viewed from end to end at once. In the front of the hall on the altar side is the iconostasis, a partition embellished with icons which stands between the congregation and the apse. The priest performs his rites somewhat removed from his congregation, a standard practice in Eastern churches. According to Greek Orthodox tradition, the large chalice (stone receptacle) in the middle of the hall marks the 'navel' or center of the world.

As you walk around the sepulchre itself, you will see a small chapel behind it. This is the only part of the Church of the Holy Sepulchre owned by the Copts. The Copts believe that Jesus was indeed buried in the tomb belonging to all, but they own the spot where his head rested. A doorway in the rotunda wall opposite the Coptic chapel leads to another chapel. A neglected, sooty chamber, it belongs to the Syrians, a fact disputed by the Armenians. An agreement about its renovation could not be reached, and so it remains. This chapel is important for the ancient burial crypt which opens onto it, a cavern which may be evidence in the dispute over the authenticity of Jesus' tomb. It is named the **Chapel of Joseph of Arimathaea and Nicodemus**, after those who took Jesus off the cross and buried him (according to tradition, they, too, are buried here). Its outer wall is part of the ancient Byzantine fourth century rotunda wall — one of the few prominent remains from this period.

As we complete our clockwise progression around the rotunda, we reach the Latin (Catholic) part, identifiable by the black and white checked floor and the organ. This chamber is named for Mary Magdalene and commemorates her discovery of Jesus' body, as depicted in the relief to the right. From here a doorway leads to the **Chapel of the Apparition** where, according to tradition, Jesus was revealed to his mother. The artifacts preserved in the Catholic wing include a sword, prods and a crucifix attributed to Godfrey de Bouillon, a king of Crusader Jerusalem. A procession of Franciscan monks sets out from the Catholic wing every day at 4pm and parades through the entire church in prayer, song and burning of incense.

The ambulatorium

Derived from the Latin for 'to walk', an *ambulatorium* is a processional concourse — usually circular — which encircles a church or a holy site in a church. The ambulatorium takes us past the sanctified sites traditionally associated with Jesus' last pre-crucifixion moments. We begin at the Catholic wing at the rotunda.

Before looking into the various chapels along the *ambulatorium*, we devote a moment to the architectural history of the Church of the Holy Sepulchre. There is a clear view of the Church from the exit which leads from the Catholic room to the *ambulatorium* beyond the arch. Notice the two independent rows of pillars to the left of the corridor. They incorporate two Crusader supports, and, behind them, eight lower, thinner pillars. The latter belong to a Byzantine structure erected after the church was destroyed in 1009 and before the Crusaders arrived in 1099. The Byzantine pillars are recognizable by the 'basket' shaped capitals. In the rear section of the church, the Crusaders were not as careful about closing the 'seam' between their own structure and the earlier Byzantine structure. The Byzantines had left an open courtyard in the center of their church, and these pillars belonged to its peripheral arcade. The Crusaders built the central dome and linked the various parts of this holy site into an architectural whole. Do not forget that the wall to our right, which obstructs our view of the heart of the church, is a modern, 20th century Greek innovation.

We now survey the chapels along the *ambulatorium*. Behind the Byzantine arcade, off the main passage are two Greek Orthodox chapels. The **Chapel of the Binding** marks the binding of Jesus (the Greeks display his footprints); the other commemorates the prison where Jesus was kept while the cross was being prepared. The leftmost column is crowned with an interesting (if somewhat blurred) capital in 11th century French style: two lions eating a bull, the head of a man above; a bird perched on a lion to the left; a dove (emblematic of the Holy Spirit) next to a bull on the right; and an angel over the lion; all this on one capital!

The *ambulatorium* passes three chapels at the section which rounds the Catholicon apse. The first is the Greek **Chapel of St. Longinus,** the soldier who stabbed Jesus with his spear to confirm his death (or, according to a different tradition, the centurion who acknowledged Jesus as Son of God while standing near the cross). The **Chapel of the Division of the Raiment** marks the handing out of Jesus' clothes by Roman soliders; it belongs to the Armenians. The third is the **Chapel of the Mocking,** held by the Greeks. It marks the spot where, by tradition, Jesus was bound to a pillar (a fragment of which is displayed here) and suffered the soldiers' ridicule.

A staircase between the Chapels of the Division of the Raiment and the Mocking leads to the last significant wing of the church. Note the crosses in the staircase walls, especially the elaborate specimens affixed in the stone to the right at the beginning of the descent; these are *katchkars*, typical Armenian elements. The steps lead to two important chapels. The first is the Armenian **Chapel of St. Helena**, mother of Constantine, who found the true cross nearby. The presence here of a column with 'basket' capitals under the Crusader capitals attests to the building's Byzantine origin. The dome of this chapel is the protrusion which rises in the middle of Deir es-Sultan, the Ethiopian rooftop compound. The truly conspicuous element here, however, is the **modern mosaic floor** commemorating the Armenian genocide — the annihilation of millions of Armenians by the Turks during World War I. The mosaic shows major Armenian churches worldwide, surrounded by pairs of animals descending from Noah's Ark. Excavations next to the chapel (closed to the public) unearthed a unique find: an interesting painting of a ship with its mast broken, apparently a pilgrims' vessel, and a Latin inscription underneath. It is dated 330 AD — that is, the very first years of the rediscovery of Jesus' burial place.

The lower chapel, a cave to be exact, is the **Chapel of the Finding of the Cross.** Here Helena, mother of Constantine, found the true cross. Note the signs of quarrying in the grotto and recall that the Golgotha area had been a quarry during the First Temple period. Tradition tells that Helena found three crosses when she reached this spot — one which had been used for the crucification of Jesus, and the other two for the execution of two thieves. To identify the true cross, Helena found an infant who had died that day and touched it with each cross in turn. The true cross brought the baby back to life. A different tradition relates that the crosses were brought to a woman on her deathbed and tested similarly; the true cross produced the same result, while the others aggravated her condition. In any event, this cross was kept in the Church of the Holy Sepulchre until its capture by the Persians in 614. The Byzantines recovered it in 628 and brought it shortly thereafter to Constantinople in apprehension of the approaching Muslims. It was later cut into many fragments; today, every church in the world named *Santa Cruz* boasts of owning one. The **Chapel of the Finding of the Cross** has two altars — a Greek altar to the right and a Latin (Catholic) one to the left. The latter, donated in the 19th century by Duke Maximilian of Austria, bears a statue of Helena holding the cross she discovered.

We retrace our steps back to the *ambulatorium* and turn left, completing our round of the church and returning to the entrance. On the way, we pass one more chapel — the **Chapel of Adam**. According to a tradition which originated in Byzantine times, Adam, too, is buried at Golgotha. The name of the site (Aramaic for skull), in fact, is said to refer to Adam's skull, on to

The Lutheran Church of the Redeemer

which Jesus' blood dripped during the crucifixion thus absolving him from the original sin (crucifixion paintings frequently portray a skull at Jesus' feet). Behind the chapel, we see the **Rock of Golgotha** itself. Its fissure, according to tradition, opened the moment Jesus died. Greek tradition associates this site with the grave of Melchizedek King of Salem as well.

The Lutheran Church of the Redeemer

Energy permitting, the Lutheran Church of the Redeemer — particularly the unique view from its belfry — is worth a visit as well. (open Tues.-Sat. 9am-12:45pm, 2-4:45pm; Mon. 9am-12:45pm. Closed Sun.) To reach the church, leave the plaza of the Church of the Holy Sepulchre through the left-hand gate (facing away from the church facade), and go to a doorway of a conspicuous white building. Before entering, glance at the northern wall of the Lutheran Church at the side facing the Russian Church. An ornate Crusader arch is integrated into the modern building. The names of the 12 months and depictions of their characteristic labors are engraved into the gate. Today, the building is entered from the west.

The Church of the Redeemer is a German Lutheran institution

which was consecrated in 1898 during one of the most impressive events of 19th century Jerusalem — the visit of Kaiser Wilhelm II. It was built on the ruins of the Crusader Church of Santa Maria Parva. In addition to the exterior arch seen earlier, the two lions at the entrance south of the church and the entire cloister (usually closed to the public) survive from the Crusader period. The interior column capitals are replicas of a single original specimen located in the southern wall. This is an obvious mistake in the reconstruction, since the capitals in Romanesque churches were seldom identical to one another. The major attraction here, again, is the excellent observation point from the top of the belfry — the best Old City view open to the public.

Other sites of interest

The Christian Quarter abounds with churches and monasteries which await the inquisitive tourist. One recommended attraction is the **Greek-Orthodox Patriarchate Museum.** Leave the plaza of the Church of the Holy Sepulchre via the steps which rise to Hanotzrim St. and take the first turn left. About 250 feet farther on, there is an orange sign on the left which directs you to the museum. (open daily 9am-1pm, 3-5pm.) The museum, itself part of a Crusader structure, includes various archeological finds and Greek Church objects; the latter are but a small part of the treasures of this wealthy patriarchate. The archeological exhibits include lead and stone sarcophagi, Greek-Christian burial markers from the fifth through the seventh centuries, pottery and glass artifacts, oil lamps and architectural fragments. Of particular interest is a famous 12th century Crusader capital from Nazareth, embellished with carved likenesses of Moses and Aaron. The Greek-Orthodox exhibit also includes historical documents — *firmans* (Turkish governmental edicts) in lovely Arabic calligraphy which were issued to the church in various periods. One of these is particularly worth noting: a copy of a *firman* allegedly given to the Patriarch of Jerusalem in 638 by Caliph Omar, conqueror of Jerusalem, which acknowledges Greek rights in the holy places. Also on display are carved wooden crosses, ritual objects, woven artifacts, and various manuscripts including rare books.

If you've seen enough of what others have unearthed in their diggings, try being your own archeologist among the buried treasures of **Rittas the Greek's Shop,** to the right of the Greek museum at the end of the street. If it's open, you can hunt for old cards, ancient Christian souvenirs, various holy artifacts and sundry bargains. Enjoy yourself. To leave the Old City, head for Jaffa Gate (left) or the New Gate (right, via Casa Nova St.). On the way there are many more churches. Examples are the Greek Catholic Church (an interesting complex) on the way to Jaffa Gate, and the Catholic church in the Franciscan San Salvador Monastery on the way to the New Gate. It is recognizable by its pointed, towering belfry, which is closed to visitors.

The Temple Mount

The Temple Mount is more than one of the most attractive places in the Jerusalem cityscape. It is a site of decisive importance in Jerusalem and in its history. The Jewish Temple stood here, for about 1000 years (though not consecutively). Though the structure has long since been destroyed (an event Jews have never stopped lamenting), the mount has remained a focus for the prayers and aspirations of Jews. In Islam, the Temple Mount is the third holiest site in the world, surpassed only by Mecca and Medina in Saudi Arabia. The buildings atop the Mount today, among the most ancient of all Muslim edifices, are prominent in the annals of Muslim architecture. (Usually open Sat.-Thurs. 8-11am and noon-3pm, but these hours change on Muslim holidays and should be checked first, tel. 272-358.)

Today too, the Temple Mount is caught in the religious and political dispute between Israel and the Arab world — one of the most difficult obstacles in resolving the prolonged conflict in the Middle East. In a decision taken by the Government of Israel, the Temple Mount was placed under control of the Muslim Religious Trust (Arabic: *Wakf*), and indeed its Muslim character has been painstakingly preserved. Right-wing Israeli groups challenge these decisions and insist that Jews be permitted to pray on the mount. Some extremist factions aspire to replace the Dome of the Rock with a Jewish Temple.

History

The Temple Mount became sacred to Jews when Solomon built the First Temple on the site which had been, according to Biblical tradition, '*the threshing floor of Araunah the Jebusite*' (Samuel II, 24:16). Jewish tradition associates this spot with Mt. Moriah, where Abraham was to sacrifice Isaac. To understand the selection of this acropolis as site of the Temple, it should be observed from the City of David (south) where Jerusalem stood at the time. It was standard practice in the ancient world to situate a temple at the highest location. In Jerusalem, this rounded hill (unlike the flat Temple Mount of our time) over the adjacent City of David was the natural choice. Admittedly, this was not true later on when the city developed to the west (toward today's Jaffa Gate) and the Temple Mount was found to be lower than the western sections of town. In choosing Jerusalem as site of the Temple, Solomon was also following the conventions

Magnificent mosaic and golden dome

of the ancient world. Jerusalem was the new capital of a new dynasty and the construction of a new religious center here lent the regime divine legitimacy. Solomon's Temple Mount was also the seat of government, the royal palace and other public buildings. The Babylonians leveled the First Temple in 586 BC; no traces of it remain.

The Second Temple, consecrated in 515 BC, was built by Jews who had returned from exile in Babylon. Its pinnacle of glory was attained during the latter half of the first century BC, following the expansion and rebuilding under Herod. The current shape of the mount — a vast, flat surface — was created artificially by Herod's builders. Support walls were raised on all sides of the original round hill (the Western Wall is one of these) and the resulting spaces were filled in with earth or left in the form of chambers under the paved Mount surface. The point of all this was to make room for a temple compound of an unprecedented scale. The work lasted less than a century (the Romans burned the Temple to the ground in 70 AD). The artificial plateau is almost the only remnant of the Temple on the Mount itself. Around the sides of the Mount, however, are a great many interesting ruins from this period.

The Mount was abandoned after the destruction of the Temple. Initially, under the Byzantines, this abandonment was deliberate as it demonstrated the victory of Christianity over Judaism and the fulfillment of prophecy. A new period of bustling development on the Mount began after 638 AD, when the Arab Muslims conquered Palestine and Jerusalem. The Umayyad dynasty established itself towards the end of the 7th century in Damascus as leader of the Muslim world. Umayyad caliphs initiated the development of Jerusalem as an Islamic holy center near their capital, as a counterweight to Mecca and Medina in Arabia and due to the sanctity of Jerusalem in Judaism and Christianity.

The association of Jerusalem with the tradition of Muhammad's night-time journey was also born during the Umayyad period. The Koran mentiones a voyage during which Muhammad reached 'the farthest mosque' (Arabic: *al-masjid al-aksa*). While this ancient tradition apparently had referred to a heavenly edifice, the Umayyads identified it with a real mosque on the Temple Mount in Jerusalem. Thus we find Al-Aksa Mosque on the Temple Mount today. In the Dome of the Rock there is the footprint Muhammad left the moment he ascended heavenward from this spot. A profusion of legends has sprouted around the night-time journey. Muhammad, they say, rode his wonder horse *Al-Buraq* (Lightning) from Mecca to Jerusalem. When he dismounted, he tied the horse near the Western Wall. There he met and prayed with all the previous prophets, after which he ascended to heaven with the Angel Gabriel, crossed all seven spheres of heaven and returned to Mecca. All this happened so quickly that Muhammad, upon his return, caught a goblet filled with wine which the horse had kicked over, when he set out on this journey, and set it down without losing a drop... Another Muslim tradition relates that the Mount's sanctity dates from the reign of Caliph Omar who had to look for the Temple Mount during his conquest of Jerusalem. Once he found it, he had the debris cleared away and erected a wooden mosque. The large Temple Mount structures, however, were actually built by the Umayyads — the Dome of the Rock by Caliph Abd al-Malek in 691, and Al-Aksa by his son, Al-Walid, in 705. Both have been extensively modified and renovated over the years; still the Dome of the Rock is the oldest existing Muslim structure in the world.

The sanctification of Jerusalem had its occasional opponents, especially in the Muslim religious establishment. However, once the Christian Crusaders seized Jerusalem, the city's sanctity became a matter of consensus and liberating the Temple Mount from the 'infidels' became a unifying goal in the Muslim world. In the meantime, the Muslim structures were 'baptized' by the Crusaders and served as churches. The Dome of the Rock became 'The Lord's Temple' (Lat. *Templum Domini*) and Al-Aksa was used first as a royal palace and then as 'Solomon's Temple' (*Templum Solomonis*). The accumulated Muslim rage found its release under the leadership of Saladin who put the

Crusader kingdom to an end on October 2, 1087, sending tremendous reverberations throughout all of Islam. Subsequent Muslim rulers (the Mameluke and the Ottoman) developed the Temple Mount extensively. Most of the hundred or so ancillary structures on the Mount date from these periods. The two major buildings underwent different modifications, such as the facing of ceramic tile added to the Dome of the Rock.

The Temple Mount walls have 10 gates opening onto the Old City (some are closed). We begin our tour at the **Gate of the Chain**. Enter the Old City at Jaffa Gate and follow David St.(the main market street), to a slight bend where it becomes Shalshelet (Chain) St. If the gate at the end of the street is closed or if you have come from Dung Gate, enter via the Mughrabi Gate at the edge of the Western Wall plaza (to reach it from the Gate of the Chain, walk back a little and turn left at Hagai St.).

The Gate of the Chain is an interesting example of Muslim architecture. The double dome gate structure incorporates various Crusader elements, such as the slightly worn capitals on its left side, with their carvings of animals and human figures. The name 'Gate of the Chain' is linked in legend with the court which convened beside the Jewish Temple. The court had a chain which, if held by one of the litigants, proved him innocent. When a certain litigant deceived the chain and grasped it despite his guilt, it vanished forever. The structure over the gate is a minaret, from which Muslims are called to prayer five times daily. To the right is the impressive entrance to an important Mameluke building: **Madrasat** (Academy) **Al-Tankiziyya**, built by Emir Tankiz in 1328-29. Though we deal at greater length with interesting 14th and 15th century Mameluke buildings when we leave the Temple Mount, several conspicuous features of Mameluke architecture should be noted here. The most ornamented part of the building is the entrance, inset almost to roof height. A conch on top of three-dimensional stylized 'stalactites' rests over the entrance aperture. The walls are inlaid with an interlacing pattern of stone in black and white, while decorative stone benches grace either side. The front facade bears a strip-like inscription across it. The round emblem with the goblet in its center denotes Tankiz's title as Chief Cupbearer. Notice the drinking fixture (*sabil*) opposite the Gate of the Chain. It recalls the reign of Ottoman Sultan Suleiman the Magnificent as its inscription (1537) indicates. The *sabil* incorporates ancient architectural elements, such as a Crusader rosette on top and the Roman sarcophagus functioning as its basin. The water supply for the *sabil* came from the aqueduct which ran from Solomon's Pools under the Street of the Chain. Finally, look for the contemporary unpretentious

THE TEMPLE MOUNT

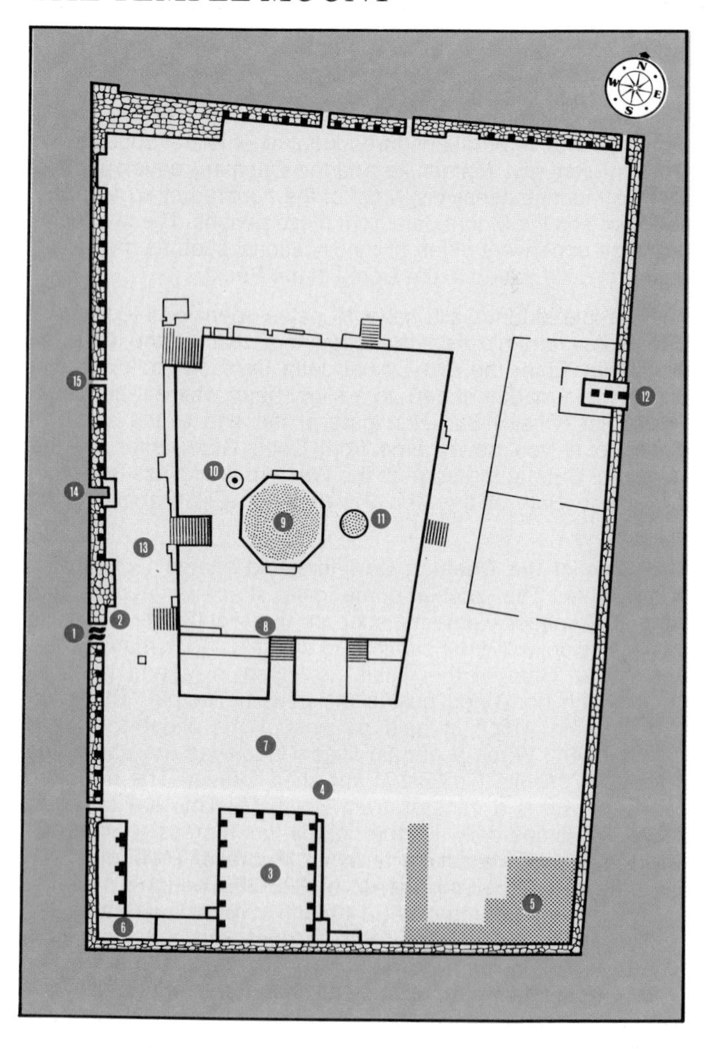

Index

1. Gate of the Chain
2. Madrasat Al-Ashrafiyya
3. Al-Aksa Mosque
4. Al-Aksa Al-Qadima
5. Solomon's Stables
6. Muslim Museum
7. Basin
8. "Summer Pulpit"
9. Dome of the Rock
10. Dome of the Ascension
11. Dome of the Chain
12. Golden Gate
13. Sultan Kait Bey's "Sabil"
14. Gate of the Cotton Market
15. Iron Gate

painting on the wall depicting holy places in Islam — Mecca and the Holy Black Stone, Medina, and the Dome of the Rock in Jerusalem. Though it may not be there when you arrive, you'll encounter many others like it in Muslim sections of the Old City.

We now enter the Temple Mount compound — an area of about 35 acres, some one-sixth of the Old City. As stated, some of this space is the artificial product of Herod's engineering. Minarets stand at its corners. The Dome of the Rock occupies a raised area in the middle of the mount; Al-Aksa is to our right, at the southern end of the compound. A total of about one hundred ancillary structures are situated here and there; underground are numerous water cisterns and chambers.

Just inside the Gate of the Chain and to the left, notice the **Madrasat Al-Ashrafiyya**, a Mameluke building completed in 1482. Study its facade and notice again the typical elements of Mameluke architecture. Look inside for an impression of a beautiful Mameluke ceiling.

To our right (south) is Al-Aksa Mosque. On the way, we notice two characteristic types of Temple Mount ancillary structures: the raised open surface reserved for prayer, with an open niche (*mahrab*) at its southern end facing Mecca; and ablution fixtures which pious Muslims visit before prayer to wash themselves. Before entering Al-Aksa, buy an admission ticket (good for all Temple Mount sites) at a small pavilion to the right of the mosque.

Al-Aksa Mosque, the Temple Mount's major prayer house and center of activity, was erected in permanent form by Umayyad Caliph Al-Walid in the early eighth century. The Umayyad mosque was destroyed in an earthquake in 747-748 and the few surviving remains include the southern wall which worshippers face in prayer. When the Umayyads' successors, the Abassids, set out to renovate the mosque, fundraising problems forced Caliph Al-Mansur to have the gold and silver plating of the mosque doors melted down to finance the reconstruction. Over the centuries Al-Aksa has been damaged and repaired many times, resulting in a melange which reflects various stages of building. The mosque is substantially narrower now than it was at first. The eighth century Abassid plan envisioned 15 aisles — seven on either side of a central passageway. In the 11th century, after yet another devastating earthquake (1033), the mosque was restored with only seven aisles as seen today. The Crusaders, taking Jerusalem in the 12th century, used the mosque first as a royal palace and, from 1118 onward, as center of the Order of Knights of the Temple. When Saladin recaptured Jerusalem in 1187, he reconsecrated the mosque, restored the *mahrab* (the niche in the wall facing Mecca) and donated an impressive pulpit. Further modifications were made under the Mamelukes in the 14th century. With the mosque on the verge of collapse in the 20th century, extensive renovation was undertaken (mainly from 1938-42); accounting for the modern columns and capitals.

Al-Aksa has subsequently been the scene of two dramatic events. On July 20, 1951 (when the area was under Jordanian rule) King Abdallah of Jordan was assassinated as he entered the mosque for Friday prayers. On August 31, 1969, after the Six-Day War, a crazed Australian set fire to the mosque and caused serious damage — especially around the dome. Renovation has progressed since then. Today certain parts of the mosque are closed off due to the political and religious sensitivity of the site.

The facade is punctuated by seven ornate entrances corresponding to the seven interior aisles. The central doorway is higher, deeper and more richly embellished than the others. It is graced with a number of arches which rest on older, 'recycled' pillars which are set inside one another in a manner which creates a sensation of depth and disperses the feeling of heaviness which the thickness of the wall would otherwise produce. The integration of Crusader elements in the ornamentation is especially interesting. One example, in the facade, is the central of the three ornamental mini-columns to the right of the main entrance; it bears a carved relief of griffins. We proceed from the facade to a portico (covered porch) and thence to the mosque itself. Take your shoes off; and leave your things outside.

The interior is basically a broad rectangle (250 x 175 ft); parted lengthwise by six rows of columns which create seven aisles. This is the first mosque to have arcades perpendicular to the southern wall rather than parallel to it, which the worshippers face. This presumably reflects Christian basilica influence which may have been introduced by Christian builders. Note the lack of uniformity and the different styles of columns and supports in various parts of the mosque — a phenomenon which stems from the many stages of building here. The white columns in the central and left-hand aisles are the most recent (20th century) while the two dark specimens with the gold-plated capitals, to the right and the left of the large arch in the central aisle, are among the oldest. The western wings (to the right) feature heavy supports bearing cross vaults, apparently from the 14th century.

Muslims, of course, face Mecca in prayer from wherever they may be. The direction (Arabic: *qibla*) — south in our case — is marked by an apse (Arabic: *mahrab*) in the southern wall. A Muslim can usually perform his five daily prayer services alone.

Only on Friday — the Muslim Sabbath — must he participate in a public service in a mosque such as this. Al-Aksa is devoid of any furnishings which might obstruct the masses of worshippers in their rows, who prostrate themselves and touch the carpeted floor with their foreheads during the service.

The *mahrab* wall has been under renovation and thus inaccessible since the 1969 fire. Accordingly, the ornamentation of the dome over the transverse hall in front of this wall is hard to see. In any case, the dome dates from the 11th century and its embellishments from the 14th century. The fire damaged an extremely important piece of furniture here — a 12th century wooden *minbar* (pulpit). Its remnants have been preserved, and may one day be restored. To the right of the transverse hall (northwest of the dome), we notice two columns which almost touch one another. In Muslim tradition, one's ability to pass between them is proof of success; inability means failure, both in the here-and-now and in the world to come... (today, one cannot approach the columns). The most handsome ornamentation which can be seen clearly today is the floral embellishment in a golden mosaic covering the arch which faces the central aisle, in front of the dome. To see it at its best, stand away a little. The 11th century ornamentation had long been covered with mortar and was rediscovered only in 1927. Another interesting detail comes into view if you face left from the front of the hall: a round, rosette style window with a crown of six leaves — a Crusader element lifted intact from a church dedicated to Zechariah.

To the right of the exit from Al-Aksa, a staircase descends to a locked iron door. Known as **Al-Aksa al-Qadima** — the 'ancient' Al-Aksa — it is actually an underground passageway which served as a main entrance to the Herodian Temple Mount from the south and has nothing to do with the Al-Aksa Mosque. It emerged at the Hulda Gates which may be seen in the Western Wall excavations. The passageway cuts through the filling by which Herod expanded the Temple Mount; a row of supports bolsters its central section; four stone domes rest on one central pillar at its southern (lowest) end. Their Second Temple dating evidently establishes them as belonging to the oldest of their type in the world. In the two southernmost domes we can still make out (with a powerful flashlight) a stone relief with gorgeous floral and geometrical designs; these, too, date from the Second Temple. Unfortunately, this important site is seldom open to visitors; admission requires a special permit from the *Wakf*.

Another interesting and impressive site which is usually closed to visitors (unless the Wakf decides otherwise) is **Solomon's**

Al-Aksa Mosque

Stables, at the southeastern corner of the Temple Mount compound. The entrance is through a small metal door against the eastern wall, not far from the corner of the mount. Solomon's Stables, under the artificial surface of the Mount, comprise a cavernous hall (300 x 150 ft) with parallel systems of vaults borne on scores of supports. Most of the structure is Medieval, though it also uses the Herodian architectural device of exploiting the area under the support vaults of the Temple Mount surface for storage. The name 'Solomon's Stables' stuck to the site during the Crusader period, when the name of Solomon was applied to several sites on the Temple Mount. The Crusaders themselves

Washing before prayer

may have kept their horses here. Solomon's Stables became a focus of discord in 1986 when several Israeli legislators challenged the *Wakf's* exclusive right to control access. The incident contributed to the tension surrounding the Temple Mount.

A small **Muslim Museum** is located at the South-western corner of the Temple Mount, between Al-Aksa Mosque and the Mughrabi Gate. Though not especially well-endowed, its display includes lamps and other mosque implements, weapons, and beautiful manuscripts (including ancient Korans and a monumental Mameluke Koran). An interior chamber houses cypress beams from the eighth century ceiling of Al-Aksa, together with the remains of the 12th century pulpit which was damaged in the 1969 fire.

The Dome of the Rock is our next stop. On our way to the stairs which lead to the raised area we pass a goblet-shaped basin six feet in diameter. Though it is essentially a 14th century fixture, it has additions from the 20th century. The stairs open onto an arcade, one of eight arcades which surround the Dome of the Rock (each at the head of a staircase which leads to it). The arcades are known in Arabic as 'scales'. According to tradition, the Scales of Justice will hang from an arcade like this in the End of Days. Some of the arcades are medieval; the one through which we passed was renovated in the late 1800s. Note the sundial at the southern side. On the raised area to the left of the stairs we just navigated is another small monument — the 'summer pulpit', a *minbar* used for summer sermons. Again, notice on it the Crusader pillar capitals and other architectural details.

The Dome of the Rock is the oldest Muslim monument in existence today. The structure was erected by Umayyad Caliph Abd al-Malek and was completed in 691/2 AD, as an interior inscription attests. Though the name of another caliph — Al-Mamun of the ninth century — appears in the inscription, one should not be fooled. Al-Mamun 'amended' Al-Malek's inscription in an attempt to attribute the famous building to himself; but he forgot to change the date. He may have been acting under political motivation, i.e., a desire to erase the memory of the seventh century Umayyad dynasty. Though the building has been modified and renovated throughout history (and even served as a Crusader church at one time), its seventh century design has basically been preserved — in contrast to Al-Aksa.

Size up the Dome of the Rock from a distance. Its interior will be described first, since its major importance lies indoors.

The interior: The name commonly used for the Dome of the Rock, 'the Mosque of Omar', is wrong on two counts; it is not a mosque but a shrine (built around the holy stone in its heart) and Caliph Omar was not the man who built it. Jewish tradition calls the holy stone 'the foundation stone', for here the world was founded. According to another Jewish tradition, Abraham sacrificed Isaac here. It may have been the site of the Holy of Holies (the innermost sanctuary) of both Temples; the Holy Ark stood in it during the First Temple years, while the chamber was left empty in the Second Temple. In Islam, the stone marks the spot from which Muhammad ascended to heaven in his night-time journey.

That the development of the Umayyad Dome of the Rock reflects significant Christian influence is beyond doubt. One of the Umayyads' important goals in erecting the building was the creation of a monument alongside the Christian churches, the Holy Sepulchre in particular. The existence of such an impressive edifice would place the Muslims on a par with the Christians. Abd al-Malek was also in competition with Mecca and Medina in Arabia, where Ibn al-Zaubayr declared himself rival Caliph until Abd al-Malek routed him in 693. One aspect of this rivalry was enacted in the principle of an *ambulatorium* based structure enveloping a holy stone; thus viewed, the Dome of the Rock is an imitation of the Kaaba in Mecca.

The Dome of the Rock is distinctive for its precise geometrical proportions. The structure is built concentrically around the stone in a ring of four supports and 12 pillars. The pillars were probably appropriated from Byzantine churches which were damaged in the Persian invasion of 614. The circle is enclosed in an octagonal structure — each side measures 65 feet. It functions as an *ambulatorium* — a circular concourse. Eight piers and 16 columns split the *ambulatorium* into two processions, the interior one wider than the exterior. Some believe this design is meant to symbolize the world — the Foundation Stone at the hub and the two rings representing land and water. The pillars of the inner circle are slightly irregular, enabling one to view all the building's pillars at once. The *ambulatorium* is sheltered by a flat sloping roof. Entrances are built into four sides of this octagon, each facing a different direction — today one enters by the western gate.

The Dome of the Rock was the first Muslim monument to use a dominant central dome. This design was chosen in response to the Byzantine Church of the Holy Sepulchre (with its rotunda dome over the sepulchre). The fact that the two domes are nearly identical in diameter lends credence to the presumption that this was deliberate. Both edifices, had ratios of four piers to 12 pillars. The dome in this case is in fact a double structure — an interior dome of wood and a slightly convex exterior structure coated with metal. Between them was a layer of hair and wool which insulated the interior against extremes of temperature and also permitted easy access whenever renovations became necessary. The dome rests on a drum with 16 windows. The original dome was destroyed in an earthquake in 1016 and the

Taking shoes off before entering the Mosque

present dome dates from later in the same century.

Apart from its physical distinction, the dome is also the most conspicuously ornamented part of the edifice, dating mainly from the 14th century. Surveying the dome from the bottom up, we start at the drum and its two bands of ornamentation — one under the windows and the other between them. The dominant motifs in these mosaics are amphoras (tall jars) from which colored scrolls curve outward. A gallery is situated over the drum; over the gallery, an inscription against a black background commemorates a 14th century renovation. The ornamentation of the dome itself comprises an array of spirals and Arabesque designs which diminish in size as they approach the center of the dome, making the dome look deeper and larger than it is. The technique used is relief in stucco which stands out for its golden color on a red background. Above the reliefs is another inscription with the central circle overhead.

The dome shelters the holy stone, secure behind a high wooden grille. The stone is pocked with man-made marks. Most have been associated over the years with various holy traditions: fingermarks left by the Angel Gabriel, a tongue which the stone stuck out at Muhammad... The most important artifact of all is a separate piece of stone enclosed in a cabinet with bars, a little to the right of the gate through which we entered (at the south-western corner of the grille which protects the holy stone itself). Identify it by the crowd of people who push one another to reach in and touch it. It bears the heelprint which Muhammad left in the stone as he ascended to heaven during his night-time journey (when the Christian Crusaders ruled Jerusalem, they claimed it was Jesus' heel). The cabinet over the stone holds a silver box with three hairs from Muhammad's beard, donated by Ottoman Sultan Ahmed I in 1609, which is on display only once a year.

From here we turn left and walk clockwise around the stone. Again, the area around the stone is divided by supports and columns into two concourses. The inner (and wider) of these is also embellished more impressively than the other. Pay special attention to the mosaics over the inner arches, on top of the middle row of columns which turn toward the center of the structure. Again, their motifs are primarily floral, but we also find amphoras, jewelry designs, gem motifs and more. The dominant colors are various shades of green, blue and gold, with delicate touches of other colors. Notice how the motifs are matched with the area they cover. The octagon ceiling is faced with 18th century artistically embellished wood; the exterior concourse ceiling, even more ornate, dates from the 14th century.

Proceeding around the stone clockwise, we first reach the northern (closed) gate of the Dome of the Rock, named the Garden of Eden Gate. The supports and walls are faced with marble cut into two or four slabs laid out like the pages of a book. The veins of the marble combine into a natural ornamentation in which various shapes may be perceived. For example, we can easily identify the face of a *kefiyya*-clad Arab at the exterior side of the support between the western and northern gates, at the bottom of the central panel.

In the support between the northern and eastern gates, at the side facing west, one may find another face of marble, a slightly frightening one, within a golden frame. Follow this face to the King David (eastern) Gate. Remains of the original Dome of the Rock mosaics are preserved in the ceiling of the outside entrance structure of this gate. If it is open, you can get a good look at them from here. We continue to the southern gate. This side of the shrine is the *qibla* — the direction facing Mecca. Notice the *mahrab*, the prayer alcove to the left of the gate.

From here we descend to a cave — a crypt of sorts — under

the holy stone. As we go down, we may perhaps understand the origin of the legend which describes the stone as 'floating in the air'. According to tradition, the stone tried to detach itself from the ground and ascend to the heavens together with Muhammad, only to be stopped by a touch of the Angel Gabriel's hand (who left his imprints). Once inside, notice the various niches. Each is named for one of the prophets who prayed with Muhammad. At the right-hand corner farthest from the entrance, is the spot dedicated to Elijah. The little niche next to the stairs at the left is Solomon's; it is distinctive for the way its arch and little pillars create a flat alcove rather than an inset one. This is an ancient and archaic form of the *mahrab* — one of the oldest in existence.

The Exterior: We leave the Dome of the Rock and walk around the building. Originally, the exterior tiles were applied either during 16th century renovations by Suleiman the Magnificent, or in the course of later repairs. Originally the exterior was faced with a magnificent mosaic. Only negligible bits of it have survived; one sample is visible in the ceiling of the eastern gate portico. The tile ornamentation, with its geometric and floral themes, is especially impressive from afar. Its many inscriptions are verses from the Koran.

While maneuvering clockwise around the Dome of the Rock, notice the great number of domes and other structures strewn across this part of the Temple Mount. Each has its own significance. To the left, 70 ft. northwest of the Dome of the Rock, is an octagon known as the **Dome of the Ascension.** The Crusader era structure was originally open in the middle; the Crusader capitals around it are decorated with reliefs. According to Muslim tradition, Muhammad prayed here before his ascent. There are many other structures which cannot be described in detail here. One especially important building near the eastern face of the Dome of the Rock is the **Dome of the Chain**. It's lines are similar to those of the Dome of the Rock, but there is no basis to the supposition that it was built as a model for the Dome of the Rock, and dated earlier. From here we notice the lovely view of the Mount of Olives. At the southern gate of the Dome, between the two pairs of columns to the right of the gate, inside a black square, is an interesting interplay of veins of marble: supposedly a pair of birds drinking from a goblet. According to tradition, the birds turned into stone while speaking insultingly about King Solomon (who understood the speech of all animals, of course).

Before coming down from the Temple Mount, we shall mention the **Golden Gate** at its eastern wall and its adjacent building (closed to visitors). We come down from the Dome of the Rock plaza via the western staircase (facing the main entrance to the Dome). While descending, notice the tall, narrow structure to the left: a handsome 15th century Mameluke drinking fixture, named for Mameluke Sultan Kait Bey. Its main splendor is its dome, with its floral relief embellishment and crescent crown. We turn right, following the Temple Mount wall. The first gate we pass (the gates are marked) is named the Gate of the Cotton Market. It leads to a covered market dating (in this form) from the 16th century, and from there to Hagai St., the main thoroughfare in this part of the Old City. However, to continue exploring interesting Muslim structures and additional sites, exit the Temple Mount via the Iron Gate, farther to the north.

Mameluke Quarter

The major Muslim buildings along this route are Mameluke and in fact, we are approaching a **'Mameluke Quarter'**. Among the many buildings of this type is one outside the Iron Gate to the left — a *madrasa* (academy) established in 1357-58. Again, notice a beautiful Mameluke facade, inset entrance, use of multicolor stone (*ablak*), and other patterns of interlocking stones over the windows and elsewhere. The inscription in the facade provides an example of a Mameluke heraldic symbol, a playing card diamond in this case.

We stray momentarily from our Muslim subject matter and turn right through a small passageway to the **Small Wall**, another section of the western wall of the Temple Mount ('the Wailing Wall') . It is used as a synagogue by extremist ultra-Orthodox Jews who reject the Western Wall plaza because of its crowds, and because the plaza in front of the wall has been created by the Zionists. The Small Wall is also used by members of a special Jewish group who devote themselves to mastering the ancient priestly rites, should the Temple ever be rebuilt.

After passing the Mameluke structures outside the Iron Gate, we go through an underpass and come out on Hagai St. (a major and easily identified thoroughfare). Turn right and proceed to a crossroads (Salah-ed-Din St. to the right, Aqabat et-Takiyeh St. to the left). Here, on the right, is another drinking fixture: a *sabil* installed by Sultan Suleiman the Magnificent in the 16th century (with the recently painted inscription in black and light green). Notice its stone flowers, each different from the others. Turn left onto Aqabat et-Takiyeh St. The third building to the left, where the street begins to rise, is a Mameluke structure identified immediately by its multicolor *ablak*. In one sense, this building may be quite unique: its layers of stone are held together not by mortar but by **lead**!

THE MAMELUKE QUARTER

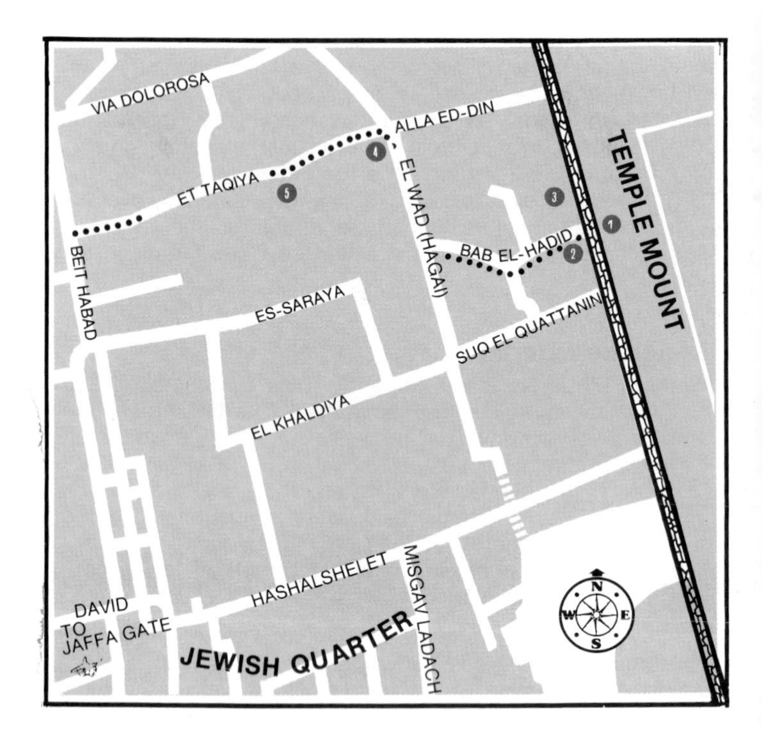

Index
1. Iron Gate
2. Madrasa
3. Small Wall
4. Mameluke Structures
5. The Palace

We walk uphill to the last pair of beautiful Mameluke buildings on our tour. To the left is a palace (note the four large entrances); to the right is a domed burial structure. They belonged to a matron named Tunshuq who lived here in the late 14th century. Tunshuq, began life as a slave of Turkish or Mongolian descent. She was bought by a wealthy man, and died a wealthy widow in

Jerusalem in 1398. The lovely structures display all the definitive features of Mameluke architecture (e.g. exceptionally beautiful friezes and inscriptions). A little farther on is Beit Habad St. If we turn right, we reach Damascus Gate; a left turn takes us to the Church of the Holy Sepulchre or the heart of the marketplace and thence to Jaffa Gate. A third option is to stay right here and enjoy some Old City delicacies.

The Armenian and Jewish Quarters

Today's Old City still maintains the Roman-Byzantine layout of four quarters demarcated by streets which are still used. Shalshelet and David Sts. run east-west, linking the Temple Mount with Jaffa Gate; Beit Habad, Ha-Yehudim and Habad Sts. run north-south, connecting Damascus and Zion Gates. (A third axis, Hagai St., links Damascus and Dung Gates.) Roughly speaking, these major streets set the boundaries of the Old City's contemporary four quarters — the Christian, the Muslim, the Jewish and the Armenian.

We now focus on the Old City's southern quarters, the Armenian and the Jewish. Apart from their own attractions, they include impressive remains of the Roman-Byzantine street system.

Jaffa Gate

We begin at Jaffa Gate (bus 19 or 20). The rampart seen today was built in 1537-41 by the greatest of the Ottoman Sultans, Suleiman the Magnificent, as part of his extensive development work in Jerusalem (see 'Walls and Ramparts — From Damascus Gate to the Citadel'). Jaffa Gate, in the western section of the wall, is the most important gate of the city since the road leads from it to the port city of Jaffa, which gave it its name. We actually stand before two different openings in the wall. One admits a wide paved street, the major vehicle entrance to the Old City. The other, to its left, is the original gate. It is equipped with a large iron door and is crowned with an inscription in Arabic which commemorates Suleiman the Magnificent and his endeavors. The passage forces one to follow a right angle — a relic of pre-artillery military strategy which forces invading charioteers or foot soldiers to slow down.

As Jerusalem began its push outside the walls during the 19th century, the ramparts became decreasingly functional and ultimately, an obstacle. In 1898, when it became necessary to prepare a modern wide passage into the Old City, the moat between the original Jaffa Gate and the Citadel was filled in to construct a paved road. The pretext for this project was the visit of Kaiser Wilhelm II of Germany who — so the story goes — announced in advance that he would not climb down from his white horse during his visit. According to convention at the time a sovereign's passing through the city gate on horseback was considered an act of conquest. Therefore, Wilhelm had to be directed through an opening which was not a 'gate' as defined. Thus, the new Jaffa Gate prevented an international crisis.

The **Jaffa Gate Plaza** has been modified often and extensively in recent times. The most sweeping change was a soaring clock tower built in 1909 and later torn down in the 1920s by order of Sir Ronald Storrs, Governor of Jerusalem under the British, who decided that it spoiled the aesthetics of the square.

After going through Jaffa Gate (the original one), notice a low picket fence affixed in the wall to the left, encasing a tree and two adjacent Muslim graves. According to Jerusalem tradition, the engineers who designed the wall for Suleiman were interred here after Suleiman the Magnificent had them beheaded. Tradition offers several possible reasons for Suleiman's act. One is that he was so ecstatic about the wall built for him that he wished to prevent its ever being duplicated. Another version says the opposite: Suleiman was angry at his engineers for having left Mt. Zion and David's Tomb outside. A third account attributes the affair to a defense problem: Suleiman was simply preventing the leakage of intelligence concerning the wall's weak spots by the men who knew them best. A fourth hypothesis — the cynics' favorite — is that it was far cheaper for Suleiman to pay an executioner for five minutes work than the engineers for four years...

Beyond Jaffa Gate we look down the major street of the **Oriental Market of the Old City** (which we shall enter at the end of the tour). Turn right before the market and follow the street around the Citadel. Opposite its rear gate (it leads to a staircase) is the **Old City Anglican Compound**. **The Christ Church** in its center is especially important to Protestants, since it was the first Protestant church in the Middle East. After years of Ottoman refusal, permission to build was given by Muhammad Ali of Egypt, ruler of Palestine during the 1830s. For Jerusalem, too, the building is especially important. It symbolized the new policy toward Europe which was first adopted under Muhammad Ali and which coincided with the first modern boom of development in Jerusalem. Christ Church, consecrated in January 1849, was the first sizable modern building in Jerusalem and the very first built of stone. Stonemasons were brought in from Malta and a special quarry was opened for the project. Subsequently, a "Protestant Quarter" of sorts — largely comprising missionaries, including many converted Jews — congregated around the Church, becoming an extremely active force in Jerusalem development.

The church was built in the neo-Gothic style of 19th century

THE ARMENIAN AND JEWISH QUARTERS

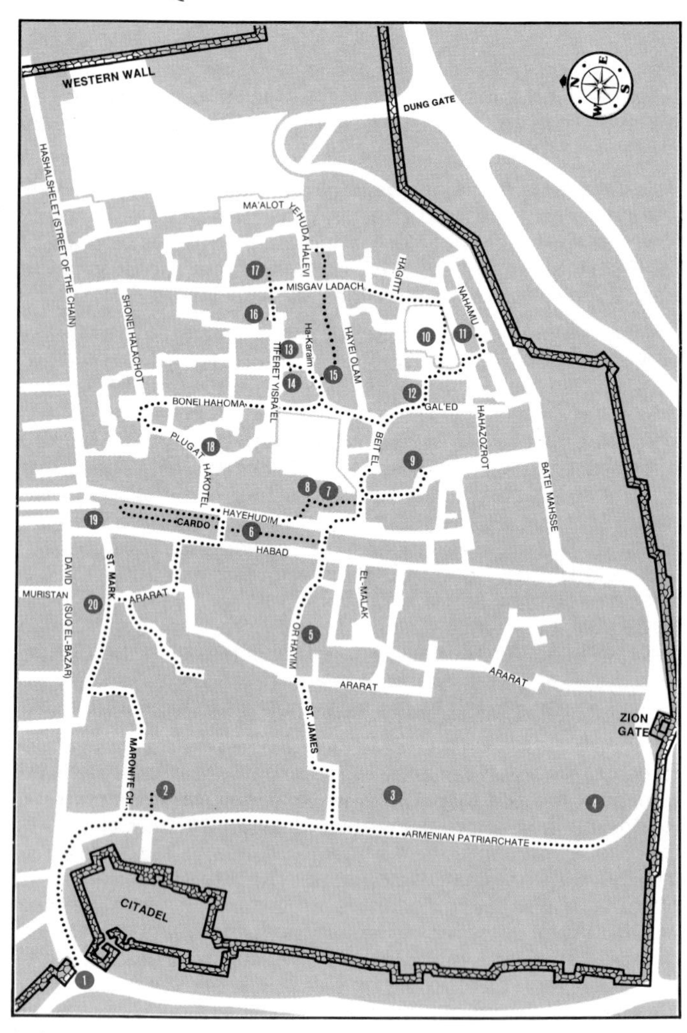

Index

1. Jaffa Gate
2. Christ (Anglican) Church
3. Church of St. James
4. Armenian Museum
5. Old Yishuv Court Museum
6. Cardo
7. Ramban Synagogue
8. "Hurva" Synagogue
9. Sephardi Synagogues
10. Batei Mahse Square
11. Nea Church
12. Monument to the Defenders of the Jewish Quarter
13. Tiferet Yisrael Synagogue
14. Karaite Synagogue
15. Wahl Museum of Archeology
16. "The Burnt House"
17. Church of Holy Mary of the German Knights
18. "The Broad Wall"
19. Markets' Rooftops
20. Watson House

Jaffa Gate

England. Its interior reflects simple, modest and pleasant good taste. One conspicuous singular characteristic is a proliferation of inscriptions in Hebrew — at the apse (which resembles the Ark of a synagogue), the windows and elsewhere. This use of Jewish and Hebrew elements was an outgrowth of the Protestants' missionary policy of doing whatever possible to approach Jerusalem's Jews. The cross too, was kept out of the church so as not to offend Jews. The cross we see today was introduced only in the 20th century. The Protestants' missionary frame of work led them to open Jerusalem's first modern hospital near the church. In the church courtyard some of the wings are named for the Protestant bishops during several decades when a 'United Jerusalem Bishopric' of Anglican and German-Lutheran Protestants existed. The first bishop under this arrangement was Solomon Alexander, a former Jew who assumed the post in 1841. His successor was Samuel Gobat, an active figure in Jerusalem, who held the position between 1846-1879. (The partnership fell apart in 1887). These and many other prominent Jerusalem Protestants are buried in the cemetery on Mt. Zion (see 'Old Traditions and New Beginnings'). The massive building which borders the court to the right of the Church was the home of the English consul in Jerusalem. The church, as defined in its building permit, was actually the consul's private chapel.

We exit the Anglican Church and turn left in the direction of the Armenian Quarter.

The Armenian Quarter

Among Jerusalem's Christian sects, the Armenians are perhaps the most surprising. They own an entire quarter in the Old City and claim important possessions in the Holy Places — especially in the Church of the Holy Sepulchre, where only the Catholics and the Greek Orthodox have more extensive rights. The surprise is that, unlike these denominations which have hundreds of millions of believers worldwide, there are but a few million Armenians. In Jerusalem, too, they are a tiny community of 1,000-2,000. Their success may perhaps be explained by the diplomatic skills they have displayed throughout history, and in the good relations they have maintained with Jerusalem's various conquerors. It appears that only the Armenians have never been expelled from Jerusalem and they can boast of an uninterrupted presence from the early Middle Ages until today.

The Armenians, originating in an area divided today between the Armenian Soviet Socialist Republic and Turkey, are proud of being the first people to have officially adopted Christianity. Their king converted in 309 (or 303), several years before Emperor Constantine the Great of Rome, under the influence of St. Gregory the Illuminator. They are 'monophysite' Christians, i.e., members of the group of churches which does not accept the orthodox doctrine concerning Jesus' two natures. Because the Armenian Church is a national one, one can enter it only by adopting Armenian nationality (i.e., through marriage). Evidence — including some of the loveliest mosaic floors ever discovered in the area — attest to the presence of Armenian monasteries in Jerusalem from the fifth century onward.

The Armenian "Quarter" is in fact a large monastery bordered by a high wall with a number of gates, a city within a city. Notice the impressive wall, bordering St. James street to the right (to the south). According to the Armenians, they were given title to this area by Muhammed himself. Until the 20th century, the Armenian presence in Jerusalem was essentially religious, comprising a community of monks who dwelled in the cloistered monastery built around the Church of St. James. The Armenian genocide during World War I, resulted in a stream of refugees, thousands of whom reached Jerusalem. A secular community burst into existence inside a monastery. Though the newcomers had no religious motivation for living here; they were dependent on the religious establishment for their most basic services. To this day, the atmosphere of the Quarter is that of a monastery and not an ordinary neighborhood. The gates are shut early in the evening. For us, the Armenian Quarter has two major attractions: the Church of St. James, and the Armenian Museum.

The Church of St. James is entered via the main Armenian

Quarter gate left of the main street. Open Mon.-Fri. 3-3.30pm, Sat.-Sun. 2:30-3:15pm. Two interesting details may be noted. Stylized stone crosses known as *katchkar*, an exclusively Armenian element, are affixed in the square stone panels in the walls. Another feature is the narrow wooden panels suspended to the right: monks would knock on them during a period (until the 19th century) when the Muslims forbade the sounding of church bells in Jerusalem.

The church is named for James 'the Great', the Martyr Apostle who, by tradition, was buried here. During the Middle Ages his sarcophagus miraculously appeared in Spain, where the Santiago de Compostela Church was built for it. Even so, his head remains here. Though most of the church was built during the Crusader era (mid-12th century), it incorporates some previous elements. The church interior is embellished with tiles imported from the Istanbul area in the 18th century by Armenian Patriarch Gregorius, known as 'the Chain Bearer' by virtue of having chained himself for four years to a pillar in the church in Istanbul, until money was raised for his co-religionists in Palestine, the funds he raised bought the 8,000 tiles. On the left side of the church, is a little chapel with shell-studded wooden doors where according to tradition, St. James' head is buried. Beside it is **St. Mennas' Chapel**, the oldest part of the church (the fifth century, or the Byzantine period). Another chapel to the church's right houses three stones originating from the Jordan River, Mt. Tabor and Mt. Sinai. Another interesting artifact in the church is a 17th century Patriarch's Throne, which is built on the chair of St. James the brother of Jesus (he too, a martyr), the first Bishop of Jerusalem. Today, the Patriarch mounts this throne only once a year.

The Armenian Museum (open 10am-4pm, closed Sun., tel. 282-331) can be reached from the main street or (if the locals permit) through the spacious and beautiful courtyards of the Armenian Quarter. In order to reach it by the main street, leave the Armenian quarter through the gate onto the street running parallel to the Old City wall. Turn left (south) and follow the street to a sign on the left which marks the entrance. The building was a seminary for Armenian priests until the seminary moved and it became a museum. The first floor has an exhibition of general Armenian national history including documentation of the Armenian genocide of 1915-18 and the Armenian in Jerusalem community. On the second floor is an exhibition of Armenian stone floors; archeological findings from the Armenian Quarter area, including Herodian-era frescoes with a bird motif — almost unheard of at a time when all depictions of man or animal were frowned upon; Armenian *objects d'art* and holy implements, including ceramic tiles and illustrated scrolls;

parts of the Armenian printing press; photographs taken by an Armenian Patriarch in the 1860s, among the oldest in Jerusalem; and an explanation of Armenian writing — a special medium which, according to tradition, was communicated in Divine revelation to an Armenian monk in the early fifth century. The museum exhibits only a small portion of the Armenian Patriarchate's treasure of culture and art. The Patriarchate Library is especially interesting for its collection of some 3,000 Armenian manuscripts, about half of them illustrated. The two oldest specimens (of the three in existence from this period) date from the ninth century; the latest is from the 18th.

Jewish Quarter

We proceed to the Jewish Quarter. Follow the road back to the corner of St. James street and turn right between the high walls on either side. The wall on the right is an extension of the Armenian Quarter wall. A striking change is apparent as one crosses Ararat St. into the Jewish Quarter, with its distinctively renovated buildings.

This Quarter has been populated by Jews for at least 700 years, when Jerusalem's Muslim rulers rescinded a previous Crusader-imposed ban on Jewish settlement here. Little is known about the location of the Jewish district in pre-Crusader times and firm conclusions cannot be drawn from the available material. The Jewish Quarter was never clearly demarcated; it expanded and contracted with fluctuations in the Jewish population. The major growth of the Jewish population and Quarter occurred in the 19th century and ultimately led to the move outside the walls. The Quarter gradually thinned out, ending with the Jordanian conquest of 1948. Much of it was leveled, concluding seven centuries of continuous Jewish presence. Change again swept the Quarter after the Six-Day War (1967). The Israel Government decided to rebuild it within pre-determined borders as a modern residential neighborhood, while preserving some of its traditional features.

Most of the houses today are modern, which makes it difficult to imagine the Quarter before the mid-19th century. At that time, it was the only place in Jerusalem where Jews lived. A traditional element preserved during the reconstruction is the narrow, winding, staggered streets (there is only one road into the heart of the Quarter, which is reserved for emergencies and supply). Local stone, has been used to reproduce and repair broken facades and arches. Regrettably, the traditional scarcity of greenery remains as well. Houses were renovated, even though rebuilding would have been cheaper and more convenient. All this posed political and legal problems because land had to be expropriated from Arab tenants and because the Old City's Arabs viewed the huge investment and modern spacious design with jealousy and frustration.

Though the traditional Jewish Quarter way of life has indeed yielded to the times, something of its past traditions may be seen in a special museum — the **Old Yishuv Court Museum** (open Sun.-Thurs. 9am-4pm). This is the first stop in the Quarter and may be reached by following the street we're on and keeping an eye on the right. The street has two names; its Jordanian name, El Arman Rd., at first, and its Israeli name, Or Ha-Hayim St., farther down. The term 'court' most aptly describes the traditional Jewish way of life in the Quarter, unlike the term 'quarter' which was imported to Jerusalem by European travelers. The court was a structure in which a number of dwelling units opened onto an inner open space (the 'court' itself). Very few windows and doors faced the street and most activity went on inside the structure — at its own pace and ambience. Court life was communal in many respects with several families sharing many services, such as cooking facilities, synagogue and water cistern (which, in later and well-built structures, was under the interior court). This way of life was well-suited to the socio-economic structure of the Jewish community of the 19th century. The Jews here received financial support from Diaspora communities. As they grew in number, they split into groups by countries of origin (Heb. *kollel*), each distributing the funds received from the 'old country' among its members. This fragmentation paralleled the physical division of the Quarter into courts. Jews in a given court may have felt more attached to a town in Hungary, say, than to tenants of a neighboring court who were of different origin.

The museum grounds incorporate two courts and two synagogues — a density of synagogues which is typical of the entire Jewish Quarter. One, named for the great rabbi and mystic Isaac Luria, known in acronym form as the **Ari**, is Sephardi (descendant of Spanish Jewry). According to tradition, the Ari himself was born here in the 16th century. Next door is the **Or Ha-Hayim Synagogue** which, though founded by a leading Moroccan rabbi who settled in Jerusalem in 1742, became Ashkenazi and henceforth maintained the rituals of Central European Jewry. The rest of the museum displays household wares, clothing and tools, which recreate the slow pace and special way of life of the period. Bear in mind that you are seeing an immeasurably greater quantity of such implements here than would have been found in any individual home since the standard of living here was rather low.

Notice too, the typical Sephardi and Ashkenazi hosting rooms and the characteristic differences between them. Ashkenazim sat in the middle of the room and Sephardim rested along the walls. In the bedrooms, notice the bride's dress, the delivery bed which went from mother to daughter and the oil lamps over the crib (taken from the synagogue as lucky charms for the infant; rabbis would recite mystical verses for the newborn by their light). There is also a kitchen, a laundry corner, a workshop and business room, where we see universal tools of the pre-modern world and other implements specific to the Jews (such as those for producing Torah scrolls, etc.).

We now follow the lane into the heart of the Quarter. After we cross Habad Rd., we reach one of Jerusalem's most conspicuous Roman-Byzantine sites — the main street or the **Cardo**. After looking into its open-air section to the right, descend to its floor level through the arched passageway to the left. The Cardo is a remnant of Aelia Capitolina, the Roman city built atop the ruins of Jerusalem following the Jewish rebellions of 70 and 135 AD. Like others of its genre, it invoked a grid street-system based on two broad thoroughfares intersecting at right angles. The north-south axis was **Cardo Maximus**; perpendicular to it, running east-west, was the **Decumanus**. Byzantine Jerusalem stuck to this layout. A sketch of the elaborate Byzantine Cardo, whose remains we see today, appears in the sixth-century Jerusalem map discovered in a mosaic floor, in Madaba, Jordan and a replica is on display here. After the Six-Day War, when the Jewish Quarter reconstruction got underway, about 500 feet of the grand Byzantine street was uncovered in intervals. The street, 70 ft. wide, was bordered on the west by massive walls and on the east by an arcade. Covered passageways sheltered both sides. The rows of monolithic columns — which show up well in the Madaba map — carried the weight of the beams of the roofing which protected passersby from sun and rain. The column bases, capitals and other details are not uniform, indicative of the typical Byzantine nonchalance about detail (a marked departure from the rigid norms of the Roman Period). The Cardo was so wide that later Old City developers ran a row of buildings down its middle, thus leaving two narrow streets on either side — Habad and Ha-Yehudim Sts. One section of the Cardo has been restored in its entirety, including the roofing, and a certain stretch has been restored in the form of a small shopping center. There, among the shops, are segments of other archeological discoveries — such as part of a city wall dating from the end of the First Temple Period (see 'the Broad Wall', below).

We follow the Cardo back to its open, unroofed area, and climb the steps at the leftmost end. We turn left and right around the minaret and we reach the structure adjacent to the mosque

— **the Ramban (Nahmanides) Synagogue**. Usually open only for prayers. In many ways, this is the heart and soul of the Jewish Quarter in geographic, historical and Jewish national terms. The Ramban — acronym of Rabbi Moses ben Nahman, or Nahmanides — reached Jerusalem from Spain in 1267 at the age of 70 and is considered the father of the reborn and permanent post-Crusader Jewish settlement in Jerusalem (even though several Jewish families preceded him). Upon arrival, he described the city in a well known letter to his son: *'I'll tell you this about the Land: it is terribly rundown and desolate... The holier something is, the more decrepit its state... Jerusalem is the most ruined of all... We found a hovel made of four marble columns and a beautiful dome, and we took it for a synagogue; the city is open for the taking, and anyone who wants a ruin simply claims it...'*

A tradition advanced by 19th century scholars identifies the structure near where we are standing as that house which was transformed by Nahmanides into a synagogue. Even if it really began to function as a synagogue only a hundred years after Nahmanides' arrival, as most of today's Jerusalem scholars believe, it (together with the Karaite synagogue) is the oldest synagogue in Jerusalem. Its interior — not always open to visitors — comprises a double chamber partitioned by a row of handsome marble pillars originally found in the Roman Cardo. The synagogue was closed in the 16th century following a dispute within the Jewish community which led a Jewish family to convert to Islam. Ostracized from the community, the heads of this family dedicated a plot they owned next door to the Muslims. When a quarrel broke out over the right to use the synagogue, the Muslims closed it down and built the adjacent mosque.

Observe the slender arch soaring over the Ramban synagogue. It marks the location of the most famous and important of all Jewish public institutions in the Old City: the *Hurva* (Ruin) of Rabbi Judah Hehasid, or simply, **The Hurva.** To enter it, walk around the minaret, into Ha-Yehudim St., turn right, and find the gateway on the right hand side. The opulent structure was called a 'ruin' not because of its ruination in the War of Independence of 1948 but for a different earlier destruction. In 1700, one of the largest contingents of Jewish immigrants in Jerusalem's pre-Zionist history reached the city from Poland, led by Rabbi Judah He-Hasid ('the Pious'). They bought a plot of land and began building a synagogue. The rabbi died but his disciples went on — financing the project by taking loans from Jerusalem Moslems. When they found themselves unable to repay, the creditors burned the synagogue to the ground, and the Ashkenazi Jews left town. It has been 'the ruin' ever

The Hurva and the Ramban Synagogue

The Cardo

since, even after it was rebuilt in the mid-19th century. This new Hurva revolutionized the status of the Jewish community in Jerusalem; a towering, grand structure (75 ft. to the tip of the dome). The Hurva became the center of Jerusalem life even after other large houses of prayer were built. The community's important institutions were also centered around it. During the War of Independence, its roof was a key position in the struggle for control of the Jewish Quarter and as such, was destroyed by the Jordan Legion after its was taken. This episode provoked the following telegram sent from the Quarter: *'The Ruin — ruined.'* Various reconstruction proposals were considered after 1967 but in the end it was left virtually untouched (aside from repair of the court) in remembrance of the Quarter's devastation between 1948 and 1967. The courtyard provides sketches and descriptions of the synagogue's history.

Worth a visit is the **complex of Sephardi synagogues** which serve the vibrant Sephardi community. Open Sun.-Thurs. 9am-4pm; Fri. 9am-1pm. Turn left at the Hurva doorway and follow the street south (it's a little tricky; use the attached map). After a bend in the road, the Sephardi synagogues appear to our left. A staircase leads from street level to the first floor — which, until the 19th century, was the only floor. The use of a sunken cellar as a synagogue is indicative of the situation of the Jews of Jerusalem under Islamic rule. Synagogue construction was a particularly sensitive matter which entailed complications and, at times, subterfuge.

The complex includes four adjoining synagogues. The site was apparently first used for prayer in the early 16th century when Jews ousted from Spain in the great expulsion of 1492 reached Jerusalem. During the 1830s, when Palestine was under Egyptian rule, the Jewish community was allowed an unprecedented freedom of action. The Sephardi synagogues were thoroughly renovated, taking on their present form. The building, once the hub of Jerusalem's Sephardi community, was destroyed in 1948, and the furniture disappeared. The revitalization, which got underway just after 1967, included reconstruction of the furniture and the import of Arks (in which the Torah scrolls are kept) from synagogues in Italy.

The main entrance opens onto the largest and most famous of the four synagogues, named for **Rabbi Yohanan ben Zakkai** (a sage of the Second Temple period). Its double elongated design, with its central row of pillars and two frontal Holy Arks, may have been based on the layout of the older Ramban Synagogue. As in any Sephardi synagogue, the prayer leader's platform is in the center (as opposed to the usual Ashkenazi practice of setting it in the front). Look up at the window above the entrance. The *shofar* (ram's horn) and flask of oil, tradition claims, will be used by the Messiah upon his arrival. Notice that the vaults of the synagogues' ceilings are never allowed to meet in the shape of a Christian cross.

A passageway to the left leads to the **Elijah Synagogue**, the oldest of the four. According to tradition, nine Jews gathered here one Sabbath eve for prayer; one too few for a *minyan*, the mandatory public prayer quorum of ten adult Jewish males. Then a tenth Jew appeared — a man with a white beard who, after praying with them, immediately vanished. According to tradition, it was Elijah the prophet. The synagogue is built around a centralized design and appears more suitable for study than for prayer. The bench standing alone beside the Ark is the only original bench found after 1967 and returned to this site (the others are reconstructions). To the right and at the back is a room called a *geniza*, where holy writings no longer fit for use — which are never thrown out — are kept until a proper burial is arranged for them in a cemetery. A special chair for Elijah was also once kept in the synagogue.

Two other synagogues are worth seeing. One is the **Middle Synagogue**, a small structure named for its position in the complex. It was probably the newest of the four, put into service due to the needs of a growing congregation. The other is the **Istanbuli Synagogue**, used originally by Jews of Turkish descent.

Our next stop is the **Batei Mahse Square**, in the southern part of the Jewish Quarter. To reach the square, follow the street from the Sephardi synagogues, turn left onto a narrow alleyway (Ha-Hazozrot Rd.) to its end. Take another left onto Gal'ed Rd. and immediately go right through the gate opening onto the square. The full name of this mini-neighborhood is **Batei Mahse la-Ani'im** — Almshouses for the Poor. It was the first residential neighborhood built in Jerusalem by Jews on land purchased by themselves. Construction, commencing in 1858, initiated by Jews from Germany and Holland, was a preparatory step for the development of neighborhoods outside the Old City walls. Though the handsome, bustling square is now ringed with many new houses, several of the original ones remain. The most conspicuous is the **Rothschild House**, a two-story structure with an arched facade bordering the square (note the Rothschild coat of arms in the center of the facade). The buildings around the square (known as *Deutscher Platz*) were of above average quality in many respects. Building innovations were incorporated which were previously unknown in Jerusalem, including chimneys. The stairs at the coffee house at the eastern edge of the square lead to an excellent view of the Temple

Mount and the Western Wall.

Interesting archeological findings surfaced during the reconstruction of Batei Mahse. One of them, on display in the square, is the impressive pillar from the Second Temple period which certainly belonged to some large public building. Its present reconstruction is much shorter than the original and is therefore misleading. Perhaps the most interesting and impressive archeological find in this area is wholly unrelated to the Jewish Quarter and is hardly visible: the Byzantine **Nea Church**, one of the largest churches ever built in Jerusalem. *Nea*, Greek for 'new', is used here as an abbreviation of 'The New Church of Holy Mary, Mother of God'. Built by Emperor Justinian in the sixth century, the church is described at length and with great praise by the contemporary historian Procopius. The church had vanished and until 1967 was known only in literature. The archeological digs of the 1970s produced several highly impressive relics, in particular a side apse, now kept in a special room (open 9am-5pm). To find it, follow the stairs from the right (south) side of the Batei Mahse square to a lower level; turn left and look for an iron door with a grating. The great thickness of the apse's walls attests to the strength of the building to which it belonged.

Another great find associated with the Nea Church, however, will leave anyone agape. In 1973, during a routine excavation in the open area alongside the wall south of the Batei Mahse Square, the earth split open, revealing an underground space much too deep to be an ordinary water cistern. Further investigations revealed a system of vault-roofed halls, separated by arches and embellished with plaster. The chambers had been the foundation for the floor of the Nea — a necessary solution because Justinian's church was too large for the area's natural ground. This manner of engineering was conventional in Jerusalem, where the mountainous terrain made building difficult. Procopius, in fact, described the project in detail. The paramount find in the Nea Church was an inscription, unique in Palestine, now kept in the Israel Museum. It commemorates the impressive enterprise and its builders — Justinian Caesar and Constantine, Father of the monastery, which is part of the church complex. Closed to the public today, the underground chambers are expected to open in the near future (make inquiries).

We return to the Batei Mahse Square, which we leave by the narrow lane which borders the Rothschild House on its right. The monument on the way marks the mass grave of the last defenders of the Jewish Quarter in 1948 who were hastily buried here before the Quarter's surrender to Jordan. The unmarked tomb was rediscovered only after 1967. The remains were reinterred in the Jewish cemetery on the Mount of Olives, and this spot was marked with a memorial stone. Turn right. While following the lane back to the open plaza in the middle of the Quarter, notice the door to the left embellished with stone reliefs. It is one of the original entrances to the Sephardi synagogues. Cross the spacious plaza and exit on its eastern end (opposite the Hurva) at Tiferet Yisrael St. (look for the bank).

Here we make a detour, Climb the stairs to the right on Tiferet Yisrael St. Facing you is the ornate facade of a ruined building — the **Tiferet Yisrael Synagogue** which, until the Jordanians demolished it in 1948, was one of the largest and most dominant buildings on the Jewish Quarter skyline. The story goes that when it was built, the funds for its construction ran out before the completion of the dome. When the Crown Prince of Austria visited Jerusalem in 1869, his Jewish guide brought him here. 'Why does this building have no dome?' the Prince asked. 'Your Highness,' the Jew answered, 'the synagogue has taken off its hat in your honor!' The prince got the message and donated the necessary funds...

Across the way from Tiferet Yisrael is a unique site, the **Karaite Synagogue**. The Karaite sect, which broke away from rabbinical Judaism in the eighth century AD, acknowledges only the literal precepts of Old Testament and disavows the Jewish oral tradition and later teachings. In certain periods, Karaites outnumbered other Jews in Jerusalem. Today however, the Karaite community in Israel has dwindled and Jerusalem has a mere handful. Their synagogue is in a partially underground rectangular structure partitioned by a central pillar. Worshippers pray on rugs in the unfurnished hall. It may be viewed from an interior balcony which opens onto it. Call the caretaker who lives in the adjacent court (at the doorway opposite Tiferet Yisrael); he will be glad to help.

From Karaim St. we enter the **Wahl Museum for Archaeology** (open Sun.-Thur. 9am-5pm, Fri. 9am-1pm), better known as 'the Herodian Quarter'. This is the principal archeological site of the Jewish Quarter, excavated during the rebuilding of the quarter after the Six Day War.

The site consists of six Herodian buildings, i.e., dated to the first century AD. We are also sure as to the last date of the use of these houses, the eighth of the Jewish month of Elul, 70 AD.

The buildings testify to the riches of some of the Jerusalem families of the time; the nobility and the priestly families who built their houses in the Upper City. The remains include mosaic floors, Fresco and stucco covered walls and everyday artifacts.

The Western House is the first on our tour. Here we can see

the ground floor. A barrel vaulted *mikve* (riutal bath) is in the underground level. Next to it there's a small bathroom with a mosaic floor. Take note that the mosaics and frescos depict no man or animal form. The Jews of the time were very strict in observing the prohibition on picture or likeness, thus most of the decorations are with geometrical or floral motifs.

In this house like the ones that will follow, archeologists have discovered a great number of mikves, although most of them do not conform to the specifications of the Jewish Law.

The mikves were used for purification only, thus we find bathtubs next to them, supposedly for cleaning purposes.

Along the corridor there are enlarged photographs of the site before, during and after the excavations. Further on there is a small archeological exhibition, with amphora handles carrying stamp inscriptions such as '*Lamelech*' (of the King). These date from the first Temple era. The multitude of stone artifacts is explained by the Jewish law stating that a stone cannot become impure, contrary to other materials such as ceramics, wood etc.

Also in the exhibition a *menora* (candelabra) engraved on plaster, is found in one of the houses. This is the earliest depiction of a *menora* by someone who probably saw it often inside the Temple. (This is a copy, the original is in the Israel Museum).

North to the central building there are some architectural parts. One of which is a beautifully carved Corinthian capital.

The main building is **The Mansion**, the most spacious and most fabulous of all the houses discovered. It has some 1,700 square feet of rooms and courts.

Note the large hall with the white plaster covered walls, designed as wide stone slabs. The red fresco walls of a room that has been badly burnt, the number of storage rooms and underground mikves.

We leave the site, and climb back by the Yehuda Halevi staircase. To our right are remnants of the Crusader era — the **Church of Holy Mary of the German Knights**, part of a complex (hospice, hospital and banquet hall) erected in the 12th century by the German knights. The church and the hospital have been revitalized as an archeological garden. The hospice is used as a residence.

Cross Misgav Ladach St. and continue to **'The Burnt House'**, perhaps the most exciting archeological find in the Jewish Quarter. It has tremendous historical, symbolic and emotional significance for archeologists. Open Sun.-Thurs. 9am-5pm, Fri.

9am-11:30pm; 12 minute audio-visual show in English every two hours from 9:30am, in German and Spanish by advance arrangement. This ancient private residence was destroyed in a great fire which consumed the wooden beams and toppled the walls and ceiling, burying everything inside. The archeologists, setting to work in 1970, discovered a thick layer of soot and ash and underneath, at floor level, various artifacts. Coins found on the site were dated up from 69 AD. This factor, among others, led scholars to conclude that the conflagration had been none other than the outcome of the Great Rebellion of 70 AD. The Burnt House then, is testimony to one of most traumatic events in Jewish history. The indications that objects had been gathered there as loot, also verify Josephus' account of the entry of the Roman Legionnaires.

Among the discoveries found here, the most exciting were the arm bone of a young woman with fingers clinging to a step at sharply distorted angles and an iron spear resting against a wall — as if waiting for use. The interesting contents on display *in situ* include pitchers, utensils and one-legged tables, all of stone. The abundance of stone utensils — despite their considerable expense compared with utensils of baked clay — reflects the fact that they made the Jews' ritual purity laws easier to cope with. The owners of this house belonged to the priestly caste, who had to be meticulous in their observation of such laws.

Another exceptional find was part of a stone coin die. This device, the great number of kilns in the rooms and other evidence, led researchers to hypothesize that a workshop of some kind had operated here. One of the stone weights bears the inscription 'Bar Katros' revealing the identity of the landlord. The Katros family was a large priestly clan which is mentioned in quite derogatory terms in Talmudic literature. Such a family might be found in the rich quarter of the Upper City. Here is a complete chapter of history, corroborated by the archeology as accurately as possible. A good idea of the family and its fate can be formed from the findings, which tally with literary accounts and events; the devastation of 70 AD, the looting of the houses, the destruction by fire with the occupants inside. Other residential houses, including additional 'burnt houses', have been unearthed in the Jewish Quarter; some were truly opulent. These, however, are still closed to visitors.

Return to the central Jewish Quarter plaza next to the Hurva and turn right on Tiferet Yisrael St., noting that it changes into Plugot Hakotel St. On the way, notice a large archeological find underground below the street level; the Jerusalem wall from the late First Temple period, known as '**the Broad Wall**'. The name originates in the Book of Nehemiah which mentions a wall in northwest Jerusalem that was abandoned when the First Temple fell. The account, by all appearances, refers to the wall observed here. The discovery ended years of controversy as to the dimensions of First Temple Jerusalem. The question was whether, as the 'minimalists' argued, the city was confined to the City of David area or, as the 'maximalists' contended, it had already climbed into the Upper City. The discovery of the Broad Wall gave the maximalists a resounding victory — though an argument over the precise course of the wall persists.

Plugot Hakotel St. winds around the wall left and right. At its very end, steps lead to the marketplace. Stop before them; turn right onto Bonei Hahoma St. On your right is another site which is worth a visit. **The Model of Jerusalem in the First Temple Era** (open Sun.-Thurs, 9am-5pm; Fri. 9am-1pm). This is a topographical model of the terrain of Jerusalem. The only buildings that have been included, are the ones that have been verified beyond doubt as belonging to the era. The building to your left covers the site of **The Israelite Tower** (ticket obtained with the above), a remain of the First Temple City wall.

This tour of the Jewish Quarter ends with an extraordinary experience — a **climb onto the Old City rooftops** and those in the market area in particular. Follow the street downhill, turn left at the covered passageway underneath the house, take another left and head up the stairs leading to the roof. It may take a moment of trial and error but you'll suddenly find yourself on the rooftop of the Old City. (One can also get here by iron steps leading from Habad St.) This spot affords an unusual bird's-eye view of the market — including the main street from Jaffa Gate to the Temple Mount (David St.) and the three parallel markets running north-south: the goldsmiths, the spices and the butchers' streets, all essentially of Crusader origin. This roof lies approximately at the intersection of the Cardo and Decumanus, the Roman-Byzantine streets noted above and the major axes of the Old City to this day. Observe to the East the Mount of Olives and its three spires, the Temple Mount which looks so close from here, the Church of the Holy Sepulchre and the Lutheran Church of the Redeemer (with its white pyramidal bell-tower). Notice the conspicuous difference in rooftop design in the reconstructed Jewish Quarter and the rest of town. Closer by, there is lovely rooftop garden, on one of the adjoining rooftops. It's the **Watson House**, a center of Jerusalem's Protestant community in the 19th century, and a Lutheran hostel today.

On the way down to where we pass a site which, like many in Jerusalem, combines history and politics. Its entrance is marked by a patch of prickly pear which thrives on the rooftops

A view from the Church of The Redeemer

as if they were a field in Arizona. The prickly pear, *sabar* in Hebrew, is a nickname for native Israelis; prickly outside, but sweet inside.

To the right of the cacti notice a gate and go through it and you will find a row of buildings inhabited by Jews, above the market, in a wholly Arab area. We see this by the Hebrew inscriptions and the *mezuzut* affixed on the right side of the doorways. The largest building, with the sloping roof, is a synagogue. This cluster, the **Galician Settlement**, was established in the latter half of the 19th century by Jews from Galicia (Poland). At that time, the high population density in the Jewish Quarter was forcing people out. Some began to settle outside the walls; others built mini-neighborhoods within the Muslim Quarter and elsewhere in the Old City. This neighborhood, of course, had a synagogue — the same one in use today. During the 1920s and 1930s, amid mounting tension between Jews and Arabs, the Jews abandoned their neighborhoods in the Muslim Quarter, this one included, and returned to Jewish areas. Since the Six-Day War, a group of Israelis from rightist, religious and generally extremist circles have begun to organize in an effort to restore Jewish control of once-Jewish properties in the Muslim Quarter. It is a controversial ambition. Many Israelis, including Jerusalem Mayor Teddy Kollek, fear that Jewish-Arab relations in Jerusalem will take a radical turn for the worse, if Jews penetrate the heart of the Muslim Quarter. The small Jewish presence includes several families who maintain a sort of

Strolling through the Old City

The colorful market

community life around the renovated and reopened synagogue.

The staircase at the end of the passageway in the Galician settlement descends to a spot near the marketplace. To reach the main market thoroughfare, Shalshalet St. (which is an extension of David St.), walk straight and take the first right. The market is yours to explore without any further commentary. Nevertheless, one final recommendation is in order: about 150 ft. into the market, on the left, is a shop which presses sesame oil and grinds sesame paste — *tahina* — in a large stone press. This 'technology', long dead in most places, is a rarity, on the verge of disappearance, even in the Old City of Jerusalem.

Past and Present — The Western Wall

The only surviving relic of the magnificent Temple built by Herod is the Western Wall. It is a site of paramount importance in Judaism and to the Jewish people, symbolic of the glory of ancient times and the anguish of the destruction, the yearning of the Diaspora Jew and the survival of the People of Israel. Over time, the Western Wall has come to be the holiest site in the Jewish world. It may be reached by buses 1, 38 and 99.

Due to its sanctity and character, it should be visited in proper attire. If you visit on the Sabbath eve (Friday night), the Sabbath or on Jewish holidays — an interesting experience in its own right — do not take pictures, write, or arrive by car. Such acts, on these days, offend religious Jews anywhere, let alone here.

The Western Wall was not part of the Second Temple proper. When Herod set out to rebuild the Temple with an expansive peripheral plaza which could accommodate the multitude of pilgrims, he decided to expand the top of the relatively small natural hill on which the Temple had stood. He built massive retaining walls on all four sides, filled the spaces between them and the hill with earth and with hollowed out vaults and laid a new Temple Mount pavement on the resulting artificial surface termed *podium*. The Western Wall is a section of the longest wall (1,500 ft.) which supported (and still supports) the Temple Mount podium from that direction. Originally, this was not a holy site. What's more, it was not considered especially important. The worshippers originally entered the Temple Mount from the south (as we'll see in the Temple Mount excavations). The area in front of the Western Wall, by contrast, was taken up by a street and a shopping center.

When Roman forces under Titus destroyed the Temple in 70 AD, the western wall of the Temple (according to Jewish tradition) survived. But we must not confuse this interior wall of the Temple itself which has since vanished, with the Western Wall which we see today. Parts of the other Temple Mount retaining walls remained intact as well. For centuries, Jews who came to lament the destruction of their Temple made a point of doing so at the eastern wall, the direction seen from the Mount of Olives or at the southern wall, formerly the front approach to the Temple Mount.

The Western Wall

The Western Wall evidently earned its special importance only in the post-Crusader period, probably bacause it was inside the city and adjacent to the Jewish Quarter. Given its new status, many have indeed confused it with the western wall of the Temple itself. At the beginning of the Ottoman period (16th century), the new rulers looked kindly on the Jews of Jerusalem and helped them renovate the Wall area, even recognizing it officially as a Jewish holy site. As the Wall developed into the premier attraction for Jewish pilgrims, the traditions concerning its sanctity multiplied. The Jewish national rebirth which began in the 19th century created an ambivalence concerning the Wall: many considered it a symbol of exile, and of values which the proud national movement insisted on shedding. At approximately the same time, a Muslim tradition developed, which told of Muhammad tying his wonder horse *Al-Burak* before ascending to heaven.

The Wall became a constant friction-point between Jews and Arabs. Over the years, Jews made several futile attempts to buy the site. In 1948, during the War of Independence, the Wall fell to the Jordanian Legion. Though the Israel-Jordan armistice acknowledged visitation rights for Jews, the agreement was never honored. During the Six Day War (1967), the Wall area became an Israeli domain, as did the entire Old City.

Extensive development of the area began after the war. A poor Muslim residential quarter alongside the Wall was evacuated, giving way to a broad plaza. Previously this quarter had come within 10 ft. of the Wall, leaving only a narrow alley for prayer. Some say the Wall actually looked more impressive that way. After 1967, another two layers of stone were excavated, exposing in all seven strata of huge stones belonging to the original Herodian wall. The four or five layers above them are also built of large stones, but these are chiseled differently. They were part of repairs performed by the Umayyad caliphs in preparing the Temple Mount for construction of Al-Aksa Mosque and the Dome of the Rock. The layers above these, consisting of smaller stones, are even more recent. Today's Western Wall plaza is defined as temporary, and current development plans, if carried out, will transform the entire area.

The Western Wall is a bustling religious shrine. The right-hand side is reserved for women, as in an Orthodox synagogue. The Wall does function in the main as a synagogue today, attracting throngs on Jewish holidays. The Wall is a favorite site for *bar-mitzva* ceremonies (roughly parallel to confirmation). The best days for witnessing these rites are either the Sabbath and the Holy Days or Monday and Thursday, when the Torah is read during morning services. If you hear the vociferous wailing of women, do not be concerned; it is the way some Oriental Jews express joy. You may even come upon one of the occasional military ceremonies held at the Wall. Not everyone is pleased with these new customs. The Wall never served either as a synagogue or a venue for festivities prior to 1967. Some consider its use for 'parties' a perversion of the traditional significance of the Wall as a place where the destroyed Temple is lamented and bewailed. Others stress the new national significance of the Wall related to its liberation, and to the reunification of Jerusalem in the Six Day War.

One entrenched Western Wall custom is the writing of requests to God on bits of paper which are pushed into the cracks between the stones. In the past, some would use nails for this purpose. Others, by contrast, are careful never to stick so much as a finger between the Wall's stones as to do so would amount to entering the Temple Mount, forbidden under Jewish religious law, since the destruction of the Temple.

Several important archeological relics are visible north of the Wall (to the left of the prayer area). Among the most significant of these is **Wilson's Arch**, named for the British scholar who discovered it in 1867. The arch — presently part of the roofing over the plaza edge — dates from the early Muslim period, when it replaced a Herodian arch. Wilson's Arch, like Robinson's Arch, carried traffic to the Temple Mount over the paved street which ran along the base of the wall. It can be reached either from the prayer area or via a series of medieval vaults beginning in an entrance at the north (left) side of to the Western Wall plaza. The *Western Wall Tunnel* is open Sun., Tues. and Wed. 8:30am-3pm; Mon. and Thurs. 12:30-3pm; Fri. 8:30am-noon. Women use this entrance only. North of here, a tunnel running almost the full length of the Western Wall has been excavated almost as far as the Wall's northwestern corner. A part of this excavation has been opened to the public in 1987.

The entrance to the site is situated in the northern part of the plaza (next to the public lavatories). A few feet after the entrance we reach a long and narrow vaulted corridor. Along the corridor we will notice a group of arches to our left. This area was originally discovered by the scholars of the Palestine Exploration Fund survey in the 19th century. The function of these arches is unclear. Most scholars presume that it dates to the Early Muslim period, and that the Street of the Chain, that leads to the Temple Mount was built above it. Ideas differ as to their original function. Maybe they were originally built to bridge the gap between the Temple Mount and the Western Hill, and that these are a reconstruciton of an early second Temple bridge. However, due to similarity in building plans from

Egypt, the building could have been an Early Muslim barracks for soldiers.

As we continue along, we pass over the so called **"Hasmohean Hall"**, at which we can peep through the slits in the floor. This is one of the most beautiful vaulted rooms that have been preserved in Jerusalem from ancient times, and could have belonged to an important second Temple building.

After crossing the large hall, the tunnel will lead us next to the Wall. Observing the size of the stones, and the lack of chiseled frame design that characterize the Herodian buildings, we can assume that this part of the Wall was rebuilt during the Muslim Era. On the left side of the wall in front of us, a large arch stands out, alluding to an entrance into the Temple Mount. This is **Warren's Gate**, named after it's British discoverer, Sir Charles Warren. The originally Second Temple gate, appears today in its Early Muslem reconstruction. Due to its proximity to the Temple itself, scholars presume that it was used for functional activities such as bringing firewood and sacrifical animals to the Temple.

The stairs will lead us to the tunnel that runs along the wall. Here we can appreciate the quality of the workmanship. Take note of the dressed stones, and the attractive chiseled frame of the huge stones. One of the stones is 40 ft. long, 10 ft. high, 2.5 ft. wide and weighs 200 tons!

If we continue along the tunnel we will reach a cut rock that protrudes from the wall. This was probably the edge of the Second Temple citadel of Jerusalem, named 'The Antonia'. A few feet further on, we will reach a narrow tunnel that was rediscovered in 1987, and dates to the second century B.C. The tunnel ends at a vaulted underground pool, that had been partitioned off from the Strotion Pool (see the Via Dolorosa tour). A staircase will lead you out to the Via Dolorosa. When you reach Ha-Gai St. turn left and return to the Western Wall, for the second part of our tour.

The Temple Mount excavations

The major Temple Mount excavation site is to the south past the grassy bank leading to the Temple Mount. Enter the excavation area through a gate on the left side of the road leading from the Western Wall to the Dung Gate (open Sun.-Fri. 7am-7pm).

Note: If you are especially interested in Second Temple Jerusalem, it is a good idea to first visit the model of Jerusalem of that period at the Holyland Hotel (see 'Ancient Jerusalem at its Peak — A Model'). Visiting procedures and opening hours at this site may vary and it may be closed altogether for several months. Verify the situation in advance; you may not be able to

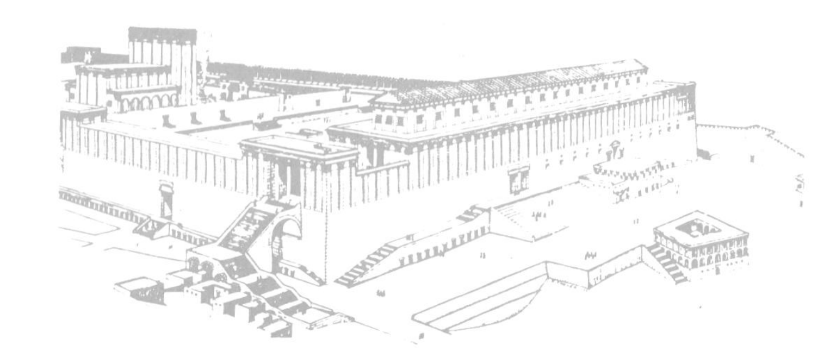

Reconstruction of the Temple Mount: the Hulda Gates on the right leading towards the temple, and the gate above "Robinson's Arch" leading towards the Basilica

follow every detail of the tour described here. Daily guided tours of the site are usually available in English.

Southwest of the Temple Mount, the excavations comprise some of the most important archeological sites in Jerusalem and some of the greatest in the world. The work here uncovered one of Jerusalem's key areas in all its periods and, in so doing, unearthed a wealth of fascinating discoveries.

To gauge the volume of the excavation, look back at the earthen ramp which carries the foot path to the Temple Mount (the Mughrabi Gate). Before work commenced in 1968, ground level of the dig area was just as high! Since then, 45 feet of debris have been hauled out to expose 25 layers of settlement. This profusion makes the findings difficult to display. Since the archeologists can leave only one layer visible at any given point, they are faced with destroying the village in order to save it. Since a representative sample of the various periods must be left, the picture of each is fragmentary. As you proceed, bear in mind that a step down or up means a different period. Of course, we won't explore all 25 layers in depth. We shall concentrate on three — the Second Temple (King Herod's works, destroyed in the rebellion of 70 AD), the Christian-Byzantine period and the Umayyad early Muslim period.

We begin at the southwestern corner of the Temple Mount. To reach it, follow the path into the site and turn left towards the western wall of the Temple Mount. To the right of the path is a massive wall which belongs to a complex of **Umayyad** (early

Muslim) **palaces**. The discovery of a cluster of giant structures from this period abutting the Temple Mount to the south and the west was one of the great surprises of the dig. Until then, scholars had never imagined their existence. The Umayyad structures are post-Temple, as can be inferred from their use of many large stones which belonged to the Temple. Some are laid as Herod intended, face forward, while others rest sideways, with the less beautifully chiseled side exposed. Reaching the corner of the Temple Mount, we see the wall of another Muslim palace to our left which demarcates a path running along the side of the Mount.

The corner of the Temple Mount: The walls of the Temple Mount are the most impressive element in the excavations and in the remains surviving from the ancient Temple Mount. Bear in mind that you're seeing only the base on which the Temple was built; no trace is left of the Temple itself.

At the corner where we stand, many layers of stone from the original wall remain, attesting to the quality and strength of the work. Originally the walls were 16 ft. thick and 66 ft. high, with another 40 ft. of free-standing wall (i.e., not supporting the Temple Mount floor) atop this. The total height was about 25 ft. higher than seen today. For the sake of stability, the walls were always anchored in bedrock, even if this required 65 ft. of foundation.

The most stunning fact about the walls' stones is their size: the smallest weighs several tons but many are larger. Observe some of these tremendous stones at the corner where we're standing. In the corner itself, they lay alternately lengthwise south and west. They reach 30-40 ft. in length, 6-8 ft. in width, and 3 ft. in height, and weigh 40-50 tons! The most massive specimens of all, uncovered at the Western Wall, are exceptional in the entire ancient world. One weighs about 200 tons! The tremendous bulk of these stones, of course, guaranteed the walls' stability, though they were rather difficult to quarry, transport and hoist into position. For the latter, a moderately sloping bank of earth was erected and, after the operation, taken down. To make sure the stone would not come down too hard and break at the corners, small balls of lead were laid under the corners which would be crushed slowly when the stone was put in its place and left in position. Traces of these lead balls can still be found at the site. Notice that the walls are all built 'dry', without mortar or any other adhesive substance. Some explain the use of these giant stones as an energy saving device. How so? Small stones would have required the use of cement which consumes great quantities of limestone in its preparation. Burning limestone was a procedure which required vast quantities of firewood in the ancient world — always an expensive and scarce commodity in Palestine. Another measure of ensuring the walls' stability was the reduction of pressure on them from inside. To this end the Temple Mount surface was laid not on a filling of earth alone (which would have placed great stress on the retaining walls) but on a system of hollowed out vaults. This tactic also created vast underground chambers for storage and other Temple needs. The stones of the walls are superbly chiseled in a frame design. The choice may have been aesthetic, enabling individual stones to stand out from one another when viewed from a distance.

An especially dramatic find was made at the base of this corner of the Temple Mount. Josephus tells of the presence of a tower at this corner, where a priest would herald the beginning and the end of the Sabbath with blasts of a trumpet. During the Western Wall digs, the cornerstone of this tower was found right here, identified as such by having careful chiseling on three sides. It bears a Hebrew inscription — *'For the trumpeting house to announce...'* — which, by all appearances, was installed in the tower we mentioned. A momentous discovery, since findings from the Temple, in general, let alone written findings, are extremely rare. The inscription itself is on display in the Israel Museum.

We continue between the western wall of the Temple Mount on our right and the Muslim wall to our left. Looking up, notice a disruption in the smooth surface of the wall — protruding square dentils, and above them, a huge sloping stone curving out of the wall. This is the beginning of an arch which extended from the Temple Mount. First discovered in 1838 by American scholar Edward Robinson, it bears his name. **Robinson's Arch** was once assumed to have combined with other arches in bearing a bridge from the Upper City (on the hill across the way where today's Jewish Quarter stands) to the large structure which stood at the southern section of the Temple Mount in the Second Temple period — the **Royal Stoa**, or basilica. Recent excavations however, prove that it was a solitary arch which functioned as an interchange above the street alongside the Temple Mount wall — the first flyover in history, if you will. The main entrance to the Royal Stoa was above the arch and from it, steps descended to the street. The 1,000 ton arch, which carried a street about 50 ft. wide (like a four lane highway!) was the world's largest at the time. Walk to the edge of the Muslim wall to your left and look down and behind to the lower story of the pier on which Robinson's Arch descended. Recognize it by its four openings above whose lintels are semi-circular stones. The coins, weights and storage vessels found in these openings attest to the presence of shops here, part of the Jerusalem bazaar of the time. Stairs from this support descended southward on vaults to street level. A few of these vaults and stairs have survived. The stairs to the right of the four openings belonged to a cross street from the Upper City. The purpose of all this complicated, unprecedented project was to facilitate the movement of the 'heavy traffic' which converged at once on the street parallel to the Temple Mount and the ascent to the Royal Stoa at the south of the Temple Mount. It was especially necessary during the bustling pilgrimage seasons.

To your right, a glass plate covering a small section of the Temple Mount wall will catch your eye. It protects a shallowly engraved Hebrew inscription, a slightly variant version of Isaiah 66:14: "*...And their (instead of 'your') bones shall flourish like young grass...*" Its height dates it at the fourth century AD or slightly later. The message — consolation, a vision of the End of Days and the resurrection of the dead — is intriguing. How had Jews engraved such topics into a wall of their shattered Temple, which they were commanded to lament forever? A tempting hypothesis, which seems reasonable if unproven, ventures that the inscription was engraved during a short-lived episode in the early 360s. When Julian the Apostate, assumed the throne of Byzantium in 360, he decided to return his empire to Hellenistic philosophy and to abandon Christianity in the process. Considering the Jews his allies, he actually permitted them to rebuild the Temple. Three years into his reign he was assassinated and the Third Temple still hadn't been built. The optimistic inscription may have been engraved just then, when Jews were returning in anticipation of restoring their Temple — a fleeting episode which left no other trace.

We continue along the western wall of the Temple Mount (access procedures may change here). We pass a small Byzantine pool whose grooved walls indicate that a marble facing had been installed here, as a few surviving traces indeed prove. To the left we come upon a gaping pit, its bottom beautifully paved and ending in a lip. The pavement belongs to the street which ran alongside the Temple Mount from today's Damascus Gate to the Siloam Pool, a distance of about a mile, during the Second Temple days. A few of its flagstones appear to be cracked. Observe the amount of debris piled up on the street and you'll see why. Giant stones of the wall and the mount crashed into the street from tremendous height; tangible evidence of the fall of Jerusalem in 70 AD.

Before retracing our steps, approach carefully, (if access is permitted at all) to the farthest point in the site along the wall. Notice a deep pit, a shaft in fact, which originally reached bedrock. Like several others, it was sunk by a British expedition in 1867 led by Charles Warren. Although the Turkish

Government hindered the British, their findings were virtually the only information available to scholars until 1967. Another detail worth our attention is a pair of post-Herodian canal-like slots in the Temple Mount wall. Dating from the Byzantine and Muslim periods, they were used as conduits for pipes.

We now return to our point of departure, passing the corner of the Temple Mount and the Muslim palace once again. A left turn brings us to a position inside the Muslim palace, facing the southern wall of the Temple Mount (notice the dome of Al-Aksa Mosque in its center). Seen on the left side of the Temple Mount wall, at great height, is a blocked-up gateway crowned with an arch, which had originally led to a passageway from this Muslim palace to Al-Aksa. Part of today's Turkish wall, much more recent than anything described here (only about 450 years old) was built on the walls of the Umayyad Muslim palace.

We can climb now to an **observation point** at a tower alongside the wall and mount a foot path on the wall, originally intended for the guards. Turn left from the path leading to the gates in the wall to a metal staircase; follow the signs to the stairs which climb the medieval-Crusader tower. From its top, look in the direction of the **Valley of Kidron**. To our left is the **Mount of Olives**; the towering spire belongs to the Russian **Church of the Ascension**, while the arcaded modern structure is part of the **Seven Arches Hotel**. **Siloam Village** (Silwan or Shiloah) rests on the slopes of the mountain. **The Hill of Evil Council** lies opposite us. Atop it is the former British High Commissioner's residence, now UN headquarters. To the right, inside the walls, is the **Jewish Quarter** and its yeshivas. Outside the walls we see the **Church of the Dormition** on **Mt. Zion** (notice its black pointed roof and its belfry) and another church — St. Peter in Gallicantu. Immediately below, is the Temple Mount excavation site. The excavated buildings inside the wall, seen from here and from the walkway, are Byzantine. Outside the walls are other excavation areas. Worth noting among their findings are the stairs leading to the Temple Mount, towards which we shall proceed.

After descending from the tower, there are two routes which may be explored. One is to stroll through the openings in the wall to the stairs on the other side which, together with their vicinity, add up to the most important area yet to be seen

The southwest corner of the walls — a daunting climb for any would be invader

in the site. The other route illustrates the complexity of this site. A slightly athletic option, it takes one through the various structures discovered during the digs, under the wall and out on the other side.

For this tour, turn left at the metal spiral staircase just in front of the gates in the wall. Here is a cluster of **Byzantine houses**, part of an entire Byzantine residential neighborhood (the remains of 18 residences have been exposed here). Recall that the Byzantines left the Temple Mount itself in ruins as proof of the Church's victory over the Jewish Temple. The area around it was not used, as in other periods, for public buildings.

Turn right, go through the little tunnel and explore the rooms of the Byzantine houses, some reconstructed. Impressions of the houses as they were — rooms, wooden ceilings and a few Byzantine embellishments may be seen. The mosaic floor is most conspicuous, as almost every Byzantine house discovered here seems to have had one. Most are ornate; some have inscriptions in Greek. Though the rooms are empty today, the archeologists found them filled with objects. Some 25,000 coins were found at this site. The largest collection dates from the late Byzantine period when soaring inflation developed and the value of the coins constantly diminished, explaining why they were left behind by the thousands... Another spiral staircase leads us into a water cistern hewn into the rock. We exit at the rear via its own stone steps — a slightly complicated maneuver — and find ourselves alongside the Turkish wall, but on the other side. Looking back and up at the wall, notice a 'recycled' section of lintel installed there.

If you enjoy clambering through excavations, you can go down to the right into other cisterns and sections of reconstructed buildings. Otherwise, take the short staircase toward the small gates in the wall. On the way, notice the Jewish ritual pools (*mikve*). The steps which lead down into them are sometimes partitioned in the middle. The partitions separated the 'impure' on their way to immersion from the 'pure' on their way out. Reaching the openings in the wall, notice to their right another handsome section of 'recycled' lintel. Its design integrates a cross, some flowers and the blurred, upside-down letters A and W. This magnificent lintel may be a relic from the great Byzantine Nea Church, located in today's Jewish Quarter.

Climbing a little more, we reach the broad staircase leading to the southern wall — the facade of the Temple Mount for worshippers (as opposed to 'business' visitors to the Royal Stoa, who ascended on Robinson's Arch). We may also appreciate why this direction was chosen: it affords the clearest sensation of ascent to the holy place, as befitting an acropolis, an abode of

God. The Temple Mount had two gates — the **Triple Gate** (three-aperture) as its entrance, and the **Double Gate** (two-aperture) as its exit. The broad staircase on which we stand led to the plaza of the latter. Though most of the steps are reconstructed, the original ones are unmistakable. An interesting feature of the steps is their variable widths. The idea was to keep people from racing on the stairs, especially when leaving the sacred place, but without resorting to drastic measures such as those used in the Acropolis in Athens — where each step is up to 1.5 ft. high.

Climb to the southern wall and note another *mikve* to the right, with a partition on its steps. Only one exterior layer of Herodian stone in the wall has survived here; the others are obviously more recent. The gate in the Temple Mount wall, partially obscured by the later Turkish wall, is on the left. Identify it by the window which attests to the space behind it and by the relatively small stones which obstruct it. Note the massive monolithic lintel overhead; though it appears to be the original lintel, it is not in the original position. Above it is an arch, and above the arch is a dentil embellishment. These are superceded by later (Muslim) ornaments attached to the outer face of the wall. Inside the wall, the gate opens onto a two tunnel underground passageway which originally led under the Royal Stoa to the Temple and which exits on the other side of Al-Aksa Mosque today. The passageway, presently closed to visitors, incorporates two original stone domes from the Second Temple period.

We head east along the southern Temple Mount wall to the Triple Gate. The gate may be identified by the relatively small stones which obstruct it. Note the original side stile on the left-hand side of the gate which bears a Hebrew inscription. Such inscriptions were engraved by Jewish pilgrims during the Middle Ages after a successful trip. We have covered the most important sites. Look to the south, just to see that many more unexplored sites and relics abound including a collection of Byzantine pillars, which you may explore on your own.

Walls and Ramparts — From Damascus Gate to Dung Gate

Damascus Gate is the most beautiful in the Ottoman Old City Wall. Legend relates that Sultan Suleiman the Magnificent resolved to build the wall after dreaming about lions pursuing him. The religious sages whom he consulted for an interpretation told him that he was really being chased by Jerusalem which his father had conquered but had left "naked" — without a wall. Immediately he set to work on a wall for the Holy City, embellishing it with stone lions in memory of his dream. (These lions can be seen at the Lion's Gate.) The wall (length: 3 miles, average height 40 ft; thickness 9 ft.) was built between 1537-1541. It incorporates various defense features: a serrated top rim, towers and narrow firing slits. Most of these were largely decorative from the outset since firearms had already made such traditional defense features obsolete. Furthermore, the wall was too weak to withstand a truly massive attack. The real purpose of the wall was the defense it provided the population of Jerusalem from nomads, bandits and creatures of the wilderness. Atop the wall, concealed behind the sawtooth design, is a path for guards and soldiers. We recommend following the path from here to Jaffa Gate.

Damascus Gate is named for the main highway which heads north to Damascus via Nablus (its Hebrew name is Shechem Gate, Shechem being the Biblical name for Nablus). From this point, the meaning of Jeremiah 1:14 can be understood, '*From the north shall disaster break loose.*' Jerusalem is protected from the east and west by steep valleys. To the north of the wall, however, the terrain is flat or moderately hilly, and thus relatively easy to attack. Hence Damascus Gate is the best-fortified opening in the Old City wall. Compare its double right-angle turn designed to impede a charging enemy, with the single hairpin turn of the other gates. This is the most magnificent and ornate of the gates. Note the pointed arch over the entrance, the ornamented window over it, the little turrets beside and over the windows, and the towers framing the gate structure. The inscription of course, is dedicated to Suleiman the Magnificent. The plaza in front of the gate is modern, and a replica of an ancient Muslim *sabil* (drinking fixture) stands in the middle.

From the Damascus Gate — and the constant commotion in and around it — walk down the path to the right of the plaza. Follow it under the overpass and progress a little way downhill to remnants of the most ancient walls and gates built at this site (Suleiman's wall incorporates such ruins throughout). Opposite is a gate installed in the wall; note the round arch and the bases of columns on either side. Gate and wall are open daily 9am-5pm; there is an admission fee. To the left is the rugged base of the wall. The gate (one of three in a row) is Roman. It belonged to Aelia Capitolina, the Roman city built on the ruins of ancient Jewish Jerusalem. Underneath it is supposedly a city gate from Herod's time. The entrance area is known in Arabic as *Bab al-'Amud*, meaning 'Gate of the Column'. The name recalls the Roman period when a towering pedestal bearing a likeness of Hadrian Caesar soared over the broad plaza in front of the gate. The column was used to measure distances (which were marked with Roman milestones) for the extensive Roman highway system in Palestine. The pillar and plaza appear in the Madaba Map, a sixth-century mosaic depiction of Jerusalem discovered in Madaba, Jordan. Turn left inside the gate, to a passageway which leads to recently discovered sections of the Roman street and plaza (the famous pillar has not yet been unearthed). The slots in the floor were meant to keep horses from slipping. Today a little museum houses several archeological findings, an explanation of the history of Damascus Gate, a hologram of the plaza and the pillar, and a model of the Madaba Map including a general presentation (on the wall) and a magnified view of Jerusalem.

Back at the entrance we turn right (or left from the outside) to the large, well-built Roman gate rooms. Observe the stones. Those which are chiseled in a way which emphasizes their edges are typical of the Herodian period. This room houses a reconstruction of an ancient olive press of stone, and a model of the *ballistra*, the ancient 'cannon'. From here we climb the impressive Roman stairs, which wind around a pillar hewn out of the rock, to the top of the 'new' Ottoman gate.

We proceed along the northern section of the Jerusalem wall, from Damascus Gate in a westerly direction to Jaffa Gate. One may also head east; the rampart promenade is open as far as Lions' Gate, about half a mile from here. One ticket permits entry to the ramparts four times during two days, so you do not have to take the entire two mile concourse on one morning.

Looking out from Damascus Gate you again see several of Jerusalem's prominent landmarks. For a better view, climb to the top of the gate. Within the Old City, the **Temple Mount** and the **Dome of the Rock** to the left are the most conspicuous. The tower with the white pyramidal roof belongs to the **Lutheran Church of the Redeemer**. The two grey domes to the right of the tower mark the **Church of the Holy Sepulchre**. Our observation point is one of the few places which afford a clear look at almost all of ancient Jerusalem, especially the **Tyropoean Valley** which crosses the Old City from Damascus Gate south to Dung Gate. This watercourse, one of the most dominant elements in Jerusalem's structure and landscape, originally demarcated and defended the City of David and subsequently separated the Lower City (to the left from this angle) and the Upper City (to the right). Three millennia of recurrent pillage has filled the valley with accumulated rubble and from most angles its existence can hardly be discerned. Two streets leading from Damascus Gate follow the Roman layout: to the left, within this valley, is **Hagai St**., known in Hebrew and Arabic as **Street of the Valley**, i.e., the Tyropoean Valley; the right-hand street, Khan ez-Zeit heads toward Zion Gate.

Turn around and look over the wall. Down below (if you're at the top of the gate) is a fine view of the new Damascus Gate plaza. To the left, the road heads uphill along the wall. To the right is a giant structure which dominates the landscape; **Notre Dame de France Hospice**. Known universally as Notre Dame, it is the largest and most impressive French undertaking in the Holy Land. The late 19th century building was built as a hostel for Catholic pilgrims, perhaps to counterbalance the Russian Compound hospices. (See 'A Nostalgic Walk — Nevi'im Street and Beyond'). Notice the large rooftop statue of the Madonna. Notre Dame was the first Jerusalem building to have electric lighting — the machinery was imported from France. War damage was repaired during recent renovations and the building today serves as a hotel.

Closer to us, across the Damascus Gate plaza, stands a large, conspicuous white building with little stone domes on the roofs. It is the **Hospice of St. Paul**, a German-Catholic establishment founded at the turn of the century as their center in Jerusalem. Perhaps it was established by the German-Catholics in response to the establishment of hospices of competing denominations. It is an excellent example of the way various European powers competed for influence and footholds in Jerusalem from the mid-19th century. During World War I, St. Paul's Hospice was used to accommodate General Kris von Krassenstein's German division. After the war, it became a British administration office building and Royal Air Force staff headquarters. Today it houses a school for girls.

As we proceed along the walls, another building attracts our attention with its high square tower. Built as an **Italian**

hospital just before World War I, it houses Israel's Ministry of Education and Culture today. An excellent example of interpower rivalry, it was designed as a replica of medieval Italian buildings, and will be familar to anyone who has visited Florence or Siena. Before climbing down from the Damascus Gate, peer through the slits in the wall. Through them, Jerusalem's defenders could pour boiling oil on to her attackers.

We continue west on the wall. The distance from here to Jaffa Gate is well protected with railings. The major structure within the walls is the great Franciscan monastery, **San Salvador**, conspicuous for miles around by its towering spire. To the right Notre Dame is still visible. Behind it is the **St. Louis Hospital** with its impressive, elaborate facade.

As the promenade heads uphill, the Mount of Olives appears on the horizon to the east. The three towers on the ridge, from right to left, belong to the Russian **Church of the Ascension** in Et-Tur, the German **Augusta Victoria Hospital**, and the new **Hebrew University** campus on Mt. Scopus.

Pay attention to an interesting phenomenon evident along the way: the short clay pipes which create triangular openings in the roof balustrades of many Old City houses. This roof design is a Jerusalem tradition either for ventilation or a means by which women might sit on the rooftop balcony and look about without being seen.

Once opposite Notre Dame, pass over the **New Gate**. One can climb down here, but cannot return the same way. The gate was pushed through in the late 1880s, mainly to enable convenient access for residents of the 'French Quarter' outside the walls. The gate is also known as the **Abdul Hamid Gate,** after the Sultan who permitted its construction. The project attests to the potency of French influence, and for the trend of developing Jerusalem beyond the city walls. As you stand over the gate, turn around. There, abutting the wall on the inside, is the entrance gate to the Franciscan compound. Its inscription, Terra Sancta, is an abbreviation for *Custodia di Terra Sancta*, or 'Guardians of the Holy Land'. The Franciscans were awarded this distinction after the period of Catholic-Crusader rule in Palestine.

The wall now takes a left turn, on to a new vantage point to the west. Here another French building stands out across the street near the wall: the **Convent of St. Vincent de Paul**. Note that most of Jerusalem's conspicuous edifices which are more than 20 years old are Christian public buildings. Only the Christians had both the means and the motivation to erect such grand structures. Behind St. Vincent de Paul, we see one of the monuments of this period — the **Plaza Hotel**. The wall now takes two turns to circumvent a garden outside. Here,

DAMASCUS GATE TO DUNG GATE

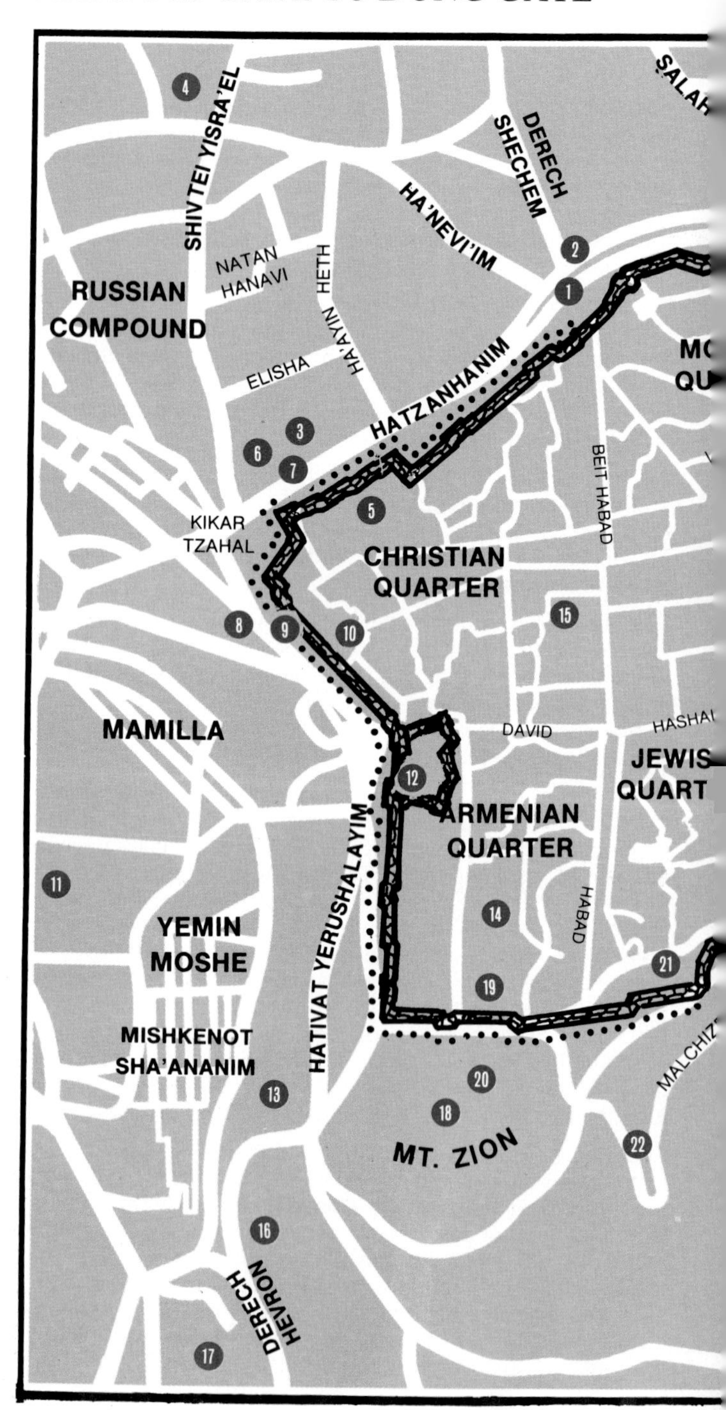

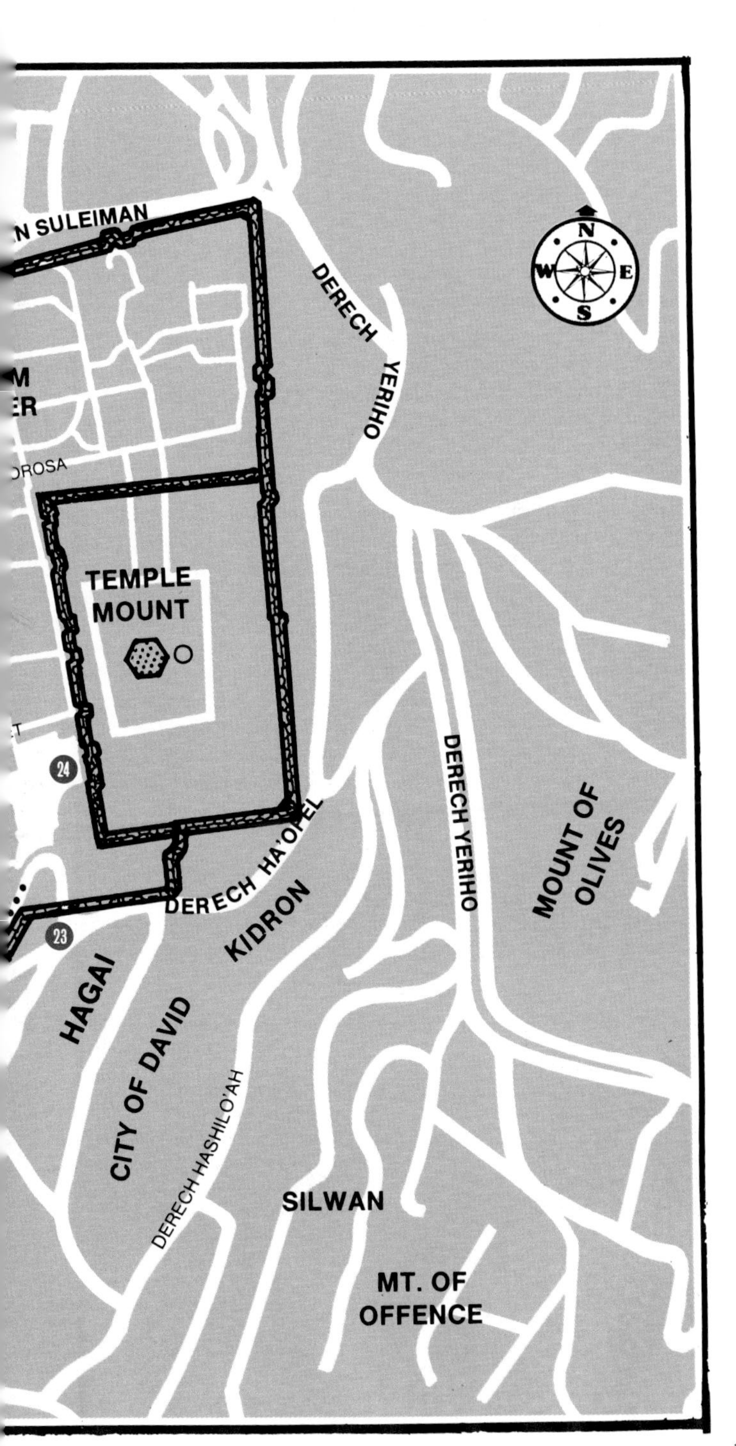
N SULEIMAN
M
ER
DEROSA
TEMPLE
MOUNT
DERECH
YERIHO
N
W
E
S
24
23
DERECH HA'OFEL
KIDRON
DERECH YERIHO
MOUNT OF
OLIVES
HAGAI
CITY OF DAVID
DERECH HASHILO'AH
SILWAN
MT. OF
OFFENCE

alongside the wall, we observe ruins of a Crusader fortification which ran under the Ottoman rampart. The complex, a tower with a protective trench, was known as **Tancred's Tower** after the Crusader commander who camped in this area during the conquest of Jerusalem (also known as **Goliath's Tower**). At this section, too, the wall passes a large French building on the outside: the **College de Freres**.

Observe the beautiful view of the entire western stretch of the rampart, as far as Mt. Zion, from the northwest corner of the wall. Identify Mt. Zion by the **Church of the Dormition**, with its pointed black roof and adjacent tower. The round **Tower of David** appears to its left next to Jaffa Gate. Here we end our tour of this part of the wall.

Across the street, parallel to the wall, are half demolished buildings which still display something of their original grandeur. These belong to the **Mamilla neighborhood**, now the subject of one of the most ambitious and controversial plans Jerusalem has ever known. (During the partition years, 1948-1967, the Israel-Jordan border ran through the area). An earlier and truly grandiose plan to renovate the area was abandoned owing to budgetary and other reasons, and the area was left as a scar of partial destruction, and a dead zone between Arab and Jewish Jerusalem. The present program calls for the demolition of most of the structures in favor of a large modern commercial center which will unify the city's Arab and Jewish sectors. Work on the present program began in 1986.

During the partition years, the wall was manned by Jordanian Legion troops, and sniping at Israeli pedestrians was a frequent occurrence. Israel met the danger by erecting protective concrete walls across the entrances to the streets leading from

---

Index

1. Damascus Gate
2. Hospice of St. Paul
3. Notre Dame de France Hospice
4. Italian Hospital
5. San Salvador
6. St. Louis Hospital
7. New Gate
8. Convent of St. Vincent de Paul
9. College de Freres
10. Latin Patriarchate
11. King David Hotel
12. The Citadel and Jaffa Gate
13. Sultan's Pool
14. Armenian Church
15. Church of the Holy Sepulchre
16. Cinemateque
17. Scottish Church
18. Church of the Dormition
19. Zion Gate
20. House of Caiphas
21. Remnants of the Nea Church
22. Church of St Peter in Gallicantu
23. Dung Gate
24. Western Wall

---

the wall. These were torn down after the Six Day War. The marker we pass along the way commemorates a Jordanian position on the wall.

Continuing south, notice inside the walls on the left a large building with a triangular facade and towers on each of the four sides. It is the **Latin Patriarchate of Jerusalem**. Outside the walls, across the Vale of Hinnom (below) parts of the New City can be seen: the famous **King David Hotel**, a massive building of pinkish stone with green windows and the handsome tower next to it, the **YMCA**. As we approach Jaffa Gate, we notice the string of red shingled roofs on the right-hand slope of the valley. It is the **Yemin Moshe** quarter; note **Montefiore's Windmill** in its midst. Opposite are the towers of the Citadel, part of Jerusalem's fortifications and our next destination. We now reach Jaffa Gate; and return to earth and the bustling street.

Turn left and walk along the inner city wall of the citadel. The building facing the corner of the wall is a Franciscan information center. Information is available here on Christian activities in Jerusalem and hours of church visitation, services, etc. Open daily 8:30am-12:30pm, 3-6pm; winter till 5:30pm, tel. 287-647.

The Citadel

We enter the citadel via its eastern entrance which used to be the only entrance into the compound (today there is an entrance just outside Jaffa Gate). It is open Sun.-Thurs. 8:30am-7pm, Fri. and Sat. 8:30am-4pm.

The monumental gate itself was built by Ottoman Sultan Suleiman the Magnificent, builder of the walls. Here, on the steps of the plaza in front of the gate, General Allenby of England officially accepted Jerusalem's surrender on December 9, 1917, ending 400 years of Ottoman rule. Note the Herodian tower which can now be viewed from outside, together with the trench system, the slope, and the reconstructed wooden bridge which defended the Citadel.

By virtue of its location on the highest point in the Old City, the Citadel enjoys obvious strategic advantages. For this reason, it was an important center of government and a fortified bastion as far back as the second century BC. The first construction here was a wall with towers, erected by the Jewish Hasmonean kings. Herod built a palace nearby, reinforcing the complex with three towers — **Hippicus, Phasael and Miriamne** — of previously unheard of dimensions and grandeur. **Phasael's Tower**, the largest of the three, is an imitation of the lighthouse in Alexandria which was one of the Seven Wonders of the Ancient World. In 70 AD, during the Roman siege of the rebellious city, the Citadel

remained in Jewish hands about one month after the Temple had been captured and burned. After the rebellion had been crushed, Titus left the three towers standing; the base of one has survived (as we shall see). In subsequent periods the Citadel was a Roman army base, the seat of Byzantine monks, an Umayyad Muslim fortification, a Crusader fortress, a Mamluk bastion and an Ottoman citadel. In other words, everyone settled and fortified this spot. Only the British sought to turn it into a museum — and failed. In 1948 it served as a military installation for the Jordanian Legion facing Israeli western Jerusalem. After 1967, the Citadel was renovated for visitors. The appellation 'David's Tower' first stuck to the Citadel in the Roman-Byzantine period when this area was apparently misidentified as the City of David. 'David's Tower' was associated chiefly with the large Herodian tower and, since the Ottoman period, with the round minaret we see today. This minaret has become a symbol of the Citadel and, to a certain extent, of the entire Old City.

Today the citadel houses the **Museum for the History of Jerusalem**. There is also an audiovisual presentation on summer evenings in English, French and German (check the days in the tourist bureau).

The museum is divided into halls, according to the different periods in the history of the city. In all of them there is an emphasis on the importance of the city to all three religions — Judaism, Christianity and Islam. There is a special emphasis on its important role in the life of the Jewish people.

As you enter the citadel through the eastern gate, you pass into the hexagonal hall, and from here you start the tour in the museum.

Before you tour the museum, climb to the top of the **Hexagon Hall** with its distinctive and interesting cupola. From here we continue upstairs to the top of the highest tower. A beautiful view of the Old and New Cities — perhaps the most impressive sight from the Citadel — awaits you. On your way, pause at an exhibit of dolls which, demonstrate the great ethnic and religious variety of Jerusalem.

The view: First look again into the Citadel complex and study its walls. To the west, toward the New City, is **Yemin Moshe**, a lovely

Damascus Gate

neighborhood of red roofed houses beyond the Vale of Hinnom. **Montefiore's Windmill** is next to it, though it does not stand out from this angle. Conspicuous among the newer buildings are two hotels — the **King David** (made of pinkish stone with green windows) and the **Plaza**. Looking south from the stone staircase to the right, we cannot miss the **Church of the Dormition** on Mt. Zion, with its pyramidal black roof. Behind it, half concealed in a grove of pines on a bluff in the background are the **UN Headquarters**, originally the British High Commissioner's Residence (Hebrew: *Armon Hanatziv*). Closer, inside the walls, is the **Armenian Church** with its flat dome; and closer still is the **Church of the Messiah** (Anglican). Looking east from the stone staircase to the left, you will see on the horizon the **Mount of Olives** with its three spires; (right to left) the **Church of the Ascension** (Russian), the **Augusta Victoria Hospital** (German) and the **Hebrew University** tower on Mt. Scopus. Inside the walls, we see the **Temple Mount** and its mosques, the **Church of the Redeemer** (Lutheran) with its soaring white turret, the **Church of the Holy Sepulchre** (two domes of different sizes), and, to the left (north), a tower belonging to the **San Salvador Monastery** (Franciscan). From this view one may also glimpse **Hezekiah's Pool** or 'the Pool of the Towers'. It stands between the buildings and appears (from this angle) in front of the Church of the Holy Sepulchre. The reservoir was part of Jerusalem's water system during the Second Temple period. As such, it is not actually associated with Hezekiah, and amounts to another example of erroneous Jerusalem folklore. Though the pool basin survives among the Old City rooftops, its feeder pipes have disappeared. It gathers a bit of water in the winter but none of it is usable.

The Eastern Tower exhibits the history of Jerusalem in the First and Second Temple eras. The south-eastern tower houses the Roman-Byzantine era exhibition. The mosque displays the Muslim and Crusader periods and the western tower the Ottoman period. Before you start there is a screening of a short movie about the history of the city.

We entered the Citadel by its northwestern tower (from outside Jaffa Gate). Note the iron grating over the entrance, and the beauty of the well-preserved Crusader and Ottoman fortifications. We pass through the second doorway to the left and climb the tower. Here several exhibit halls display pottery, oil lamps, catapult stones and arrowheads, and sketches describing Citadel history. A separate room houses a unique exhibit — an enormous model (13 ft. x 15 ft; on a 1:500 scale) of Jerusalem as it appeared in the late 1860s. A Hungarian named Stefan Illes built the model for an international exposition in Vienna in 1873. It was displayed in Europe but later forgotten.

The model was recently rediscovered by several Hebrew University students and brought to Israel for display. The period depicted marks the first pioneering stages of development outside the walls. Note, for example, the Jewish neighborhood of **Mishkenot Sha'anannim** and the **Russian Compound** west of the Old City. One touching detail is the telegraph line — a wire drawn from western Jerusalem into the Old City. This innovation indeed reached Jerusalem during the 1860s.

From here we climb to the top of the Citadel's second tallest tower. A gloomy, narrow corridor (part of the medieval-era fortification system) opens from the roof plaza. From the apertures, known as *mashikuli*, defenders would pour boiling liquids on besieging enemies (from the outside they look like protrusions with curl-shaped supports). This tower dominates Jaffa Gate, though the gate itself is hard to see through the slits. Look into the Citadel from the tower to see the archeological and structural maze which this site exhibits.

To the left (north) we see the Citadel's massive main tower. Its base, built of large, well-chiseled stones with indented edges, is the survivor of Herod's fortifications; it is either the **Tower of Phasael** or **Hippicus**. We climb down and cross the courtyard to the south (right), approaching the round minaret built by the Turks in 1635 and misnamed 'David's Tower'. Examine the base of the Herodian tower and marvel at its impressive construction. Throughout the courtyard, there are remains of walls and towers and also what appears to be a Mameluke arch attached to nothing.

A glance into the valley beyond the wall will explain the origin of one of Jerusalem's legends. In the watercourse (the Vale of Hinnom), in front of the road which crosses the valley, is a broad lawn; the site of the **Sultan's Pool**, known in Jerusalem folklore as **Bathsheva's Pool**. Although this would be a convenient spot to watch Bathsheva bathing in the pool as we recall, David observed Bathsheva as she bathed on her rooftop; but who are we to argue with folklore?

If you want to proceed the tour of the wall — go out of Jaffa Gate to the foot of the Citadel until you are just below the Tower of David. We will enter the ditch surrounding the citadel, there you will see the remains of an old quarry and a *mikve* from the second temple period. Spiral stairs lead us to the top of the wall. Below is the Vale of Hinnom and across it, facing us, is the flag of the French consulate. From here we can see the Mamilla neighborhood from a new angle. It is now being rebuilt. Inside the wall we see the *Kishleh* which was a prison and a camp of the Ottoman army in Jerusalem and today is a police station.

The Citadel

From the east-southern corner of the wall we can see Sultan's pool below and the road to Bethlehem, built on the dam that created the pool. At the foot of the wall there are remains of fortifications from different periods.

To the left of Yemin Moshe neighborhood there is a long building. This is Mishkenot Sha'ananim, built by Montefiore, one of the first built outside the walls. To its left is the Jerusalem **cinemateque** with the red tiled roof, standing where the former Jewish Sham'a neighborhood used to be. On the top of the hill, above the cinemateque there is the **Scottish Church** with the white dome and the blue and white Scottish flag on its top. Far away, on the mountain on the horizon we can see the Gilo neighborhood.

The wall turns east, look to the south in the direction of **Mount**

Along the walls of the Old City

Zion. To our feet is the Franciscan cemetery and behind it is the Greek-Orthodox cemetery. The outstanding building with the dark cone-shaped dome and the oriental-like bell-tower is the **Church of the Dormition**. Proceeding, we will walk over (above) **Zion Gate**, built, like most of Jerusalem gates, in an L shape. From our position we can see only the inner side of the gate. The building close to the gate belongs to the Armenian patriarchate. Here, according to Armenian tradition, stood the **House of Caiphas**, the High Priest in front of whom

Jesus was tried and imprisoned. At the side of the building is the Caiphas Armenian church and next to the church are the tombs of the Armenian Patriarches. The low dome of a mosque, a bit higher than the houses of Mt. Zion, marks the traditional tomb of David. The buildings to our left, inside the walls, are the houses of the Armenian Quarter. Proceed for an impressive view of Mount Scopus and Mount of Olives. Mount of Offense, facing us, is crowned by trees and on its slope are the houses of the picturesque village of Silwan. To the right is the Judea desert, crossed by the Kidron Valley.

To the left of the new buildings of the Jewish quarter there are remnants of buildings which used to belong to the **Nea Church**, the biggest of Jerusalem churches in the Byzantine period. The horizon is hidden by a hilltop of trees, where you can see Armon Hanatziv which was the residence of the British High Commissioner in Palestine from 1931 to 1948.

After we pass the iron gate we will observe the Kidron. From this point we will see a shallow valley below us. This is the Biblical 'Hagai', which marked Jerusalem's western border in the days of Hezekiah. The City of David sat on the hill between this valley and the Kidron Valley, and therefore is not seen from this point. The church to the right, on the slope of Mt. Zion, is the St. Peter in Gallicantu.

According to Christian tradition here is where the house of Caiphas the High Priest used to be. The church was completed in 1931 and named after Peter, one of Jesus' disciples. The word *Gallicantu* means the voice of the cockerel; according to the New Testament, Jesus sat here with his disciples in the evening before he was imprisoned, and when Jesus doubted their faith and Peter declared his, Jesus said: 'Tonight, before the cockerel crows twice, you will deny me three times'. That night Jesus was caught by the Romans and Peter had denied him three times before he heard the cockerel crow twice.

Proceed along the wall in the direction of Dung Gate. In the garden at the foot of the wall are remains of fortifications, cisterns and houses from different periods, especially from the Byzantine and Muslim epochs. There is a section of a paving of the continuation of Hagai street (El-Wad), one of Jerusalem's main streets in the Byzantine time, probably proceeding till 'Hagai' (The Valley). Remember that in Byzantine times the walls surrounded all of Mt. Zion and also the City of David. Further on we will see the domes of the mosques on Temple Mount and the Western Wall.

We finish this tour at the Dung Gate.

Old Traditions and New Beginnings — From Mount Zion to Mishkenot Sha'anannim

This tour will trace Jerusalem's first steps out of its traditional confines, heralding the establishment of the New City. We start at **Mount Zion** with its array of holy sites and splendid observation points and end at the first Jewish neighborhood outside the walls — **Mishkenot Sha'anannim**, and the adjacent windmill built by Sir Moses Montefiore. The neighborhood and the mill mark an important chapter in Jewish history in general and Jerusalem history in particular. Between here and there, we cross the **Vale of Hinnom** (Hebrew: *Gai ben-Hinnom*), a patch of lush greenery, one of Jerusalem's loveliest and least-known jewels, where surprises are in store.

Mount Zion

The point of departure is **Zion Gate**, southwest of the seven Old City gates, most conveniently reached from Jaffa Gate. Zion Gate is used when entering or exiting the Jewish and Armenian Quarters. The portal was also known as the 'Jewish Quarter Gate' because Jews held its keys during the late Medieval period. Like the other original apertures in the Old City wall, the interior of Zion Gate is a right angle — a traditional strategic element meant to break an invader's momentum. As for the outer facade, one can hardly fail to notice the large number of marks left by bullets and shells, most dating from Israel's War of Independence (1948). An Israeli attempt to break into the Jewish Quarter while it was under siege via Zion Gate took place on May 19, 1948. After almost six months' combat, during most of which the Quarter was cut off, 22 fighters broke through Zion Gate and joined up with the Quarter's defenders. Efforts to hold the gate failed and the Jordanian Legion retook it the next morning, forcing the Jewish Quarter to surrender shortly thereafter. Undeterred, Israeli forces mounted another attempt to re-enter the Old City on July 18, 1948, this time by blowing up the wall, but the quantity of explosives was hardly enough to scratch the rampart. The little indentation about 230 ft. west of Zion Gate, in a section of tower protruding from the wall beside the path, marks this last Israeli attempt to wrest the Old City from Jordanian control until the Six Day War of 1967. The indentation has been filled recently with mortar but is still distinguishable.

FROM MOUNT ZION TO MISHKENOT SHA'ANANNIM

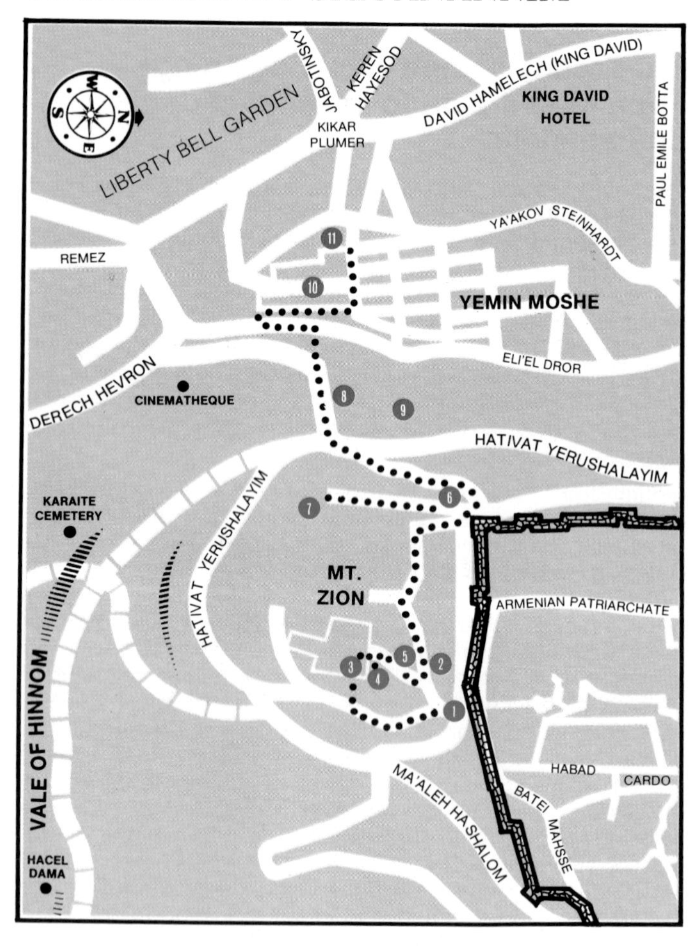

Index
1. Zion Gate
2. House of Caiphas
3. King David's Tomb
4. Cenaculum
5. Church of Dormition
6. View Point
7. Eretz ha-Tzvi School
8. Sabil
9. Sultan's Pool
10. Mishkenot Sha'anannim
11. The Windmill

The new church under construction opposite Zion Gate belongs to the Armenians and occupies the spot where, according to Armenian tradition, Caiphas the High Priest lived, and where Jesus was imprisoned before his trial. The Armenian Patriarchs are buried in the courtyard. The path branching to the right from Zion Gate heads for the Vale of Hinnom and Mishkenot Sha'anannim. Now however, we choose the longer way which takes us to the major attractions of Mt. Zion. The name *Zion* originally referred to the low hill on which Jerusalem (the City of David) was built, and was applied to this location only after the city's destruction. As early as the Byzantine period in 390 AD, a massive Church named 'The Holy Zion Church' was consecrated here although its remains have not yet been found. The most conspicuous building on Mt. Zion today, the Church of the Dormition, occupies its site. Another church on the southern slope of the mountain is the **St. Peter in Galicantu**, built on the site where according to tradition St. Petra denied Jesus (Mathew: 26).

Our exploration of Mt. Zion begins at **King David's Tomb** and **Cenaculum** (the Hall of the Last Supper). To get there, proceed straight from the Zion Gate, turn right at the second alleyway and follow it to the gate of the site. Open 8am-sundown, Fri. 8am-1pm, closed Sat. The association of this site with David's Tomb dates from the Middle Ages. Though David was actually buried within the Jerusalem of his day (the City of David on the hill to the east), it just may be that the last Kings of Judah, who ruled during a period when Jerusalem had expanded this far, were indeed buried in this vicinity. The earliest Jewish source which mentions rediscovery of David's tomb is the famous traveler Benjamin of Tudela, who stopped here in the mid-12th century although he does not mention the site. A wall, he notes, had collapsed 15 years before his arrival, and the Patriarchs of Jerusalem had it repaired. During the work, when nearly all the laborers were taking a lunch break, two men who remained at the site discovered the mouth of a cave. Benjamin relates: *'The one said to the other: let us go in and see if there is any money in it. So they proceeded through the cave until they reached a great palace built on columns of marble coated with silver and gold, with a table of gold, a sceptre and a crown in front of it. It was the Tomb of King David... The two men wished to enter the palace, when a sudden gust of wind came from the mouth of the cave and struck them. They fell to the ground as if they were dead, and lay there until evening.'* Leaving the cave, they reported that God did not want them to show this site to anyone. With this in mind, the Patriarch had the cave entrance sealed and concealed from view... as it remains to this day. Mere legend? An Italian archeologist claimed to have found an opulent burial crypt in this area in 1859 — but no one since has succeeded in corroborating the discovery...

In any event, the present structure known as **King David's Tomb** and its interior cenotaph (gravestone) were built in greater part during the Crusader period, though a late Roman building lies underfoot. Controlled today by Israel's Ministry of Religions, the site serves as a prayer hall and attracts throngs of pilgrims. The interior itself is not spectacular. The arcaded court leading to the tomb itself was once the cloister of a 14th century Franciscan monastery. When Jews and Christians waged a pitched battle for control of the site during the 14th and 15th centuries, the Muslims finally stepped in and turned it into a mosque. Its *mahrab* (apse) is visible to this day.

From the courtyard, climb to the roof next to the minaret. Though today it is no longer the most impressive view available, between 1948 and 1967, it certainly was for the Jews of Jerusalem. With the Old City and the Mount of Olives in Jordanian hands, this spot offered the best view of holy places. A rooftop room was occupied at times by Izhak Ben-Zvi, the second President of Israel.

Adjacent to the tomb there is the **King David's Museum** that exhibits articles relating to the site and to King David (open Sun.-Thurs. 10am-5pm, Fri. till 2pm).

The upper story of David's Tomb is the **Cenaculum**, the Hall of the Last Supper. To reach its separate entrance, leave David's Tomb as you entered, turn left, and left again at a narrow passageway. Upon reaching a courtyard of a Jewish Yeshiva, follow the stairs to the Cenaculum (open 8:30am-sundown). According to Christian tradition, this is the site of Jesus' Last Supper — a Passover *seder*. It was on this occasion that Jesus gave his disciples bread saying: "*This is my body*", and wine, saying: "*This is my blood.*" Tradition also associates this site with the miracle of Pentecost, the *glossolalia*, when the Holy Spirit induced the apostles to speak in many tongues.

The hall is a Crusader structure which once belonged to the Church of Our Lady of Mount Zion. A lovely vintage Crusader marble column commemorates the Last Supper. Its capital supports the arch over the staircase at the southwest corner of the hall opposite the entrance. The capital is embellished with two carved pelicans pecking at the chest of a third. The scene depicts a legend of the pelican which feeds its offspring from its own body. Over time, this story has come to symbolize Jesus' sacrifice as well as the bread and wine of the Eucharist which represent his flesh and blood. Additional Crusader relics may be seen beside the entrance to the right. A pair of faded color frescoes of Crusader coat-of-arms, includes one which depicts the city of Regensburg. The *mahrab*, (niche) is in the southern wall. Note the inscription by Suleiman the Magnificent, the Ottoman Sultan, which describes how the ancient Church (like King David's Tomb) became a mosque.

Go down the stairs, exit through the gate facing you, turn right and then turn left. You arrive at the **Church of the Dormition**, a structure recognizable from far off for its black conical roof and its belfry. Jerusalemites call the belfry 'guardian of the walls' because its top resembles the head of a helmeted soldier, especially at night. Open 7am-12:30pm, 2-7:10pm. This institution is a Catholic church erected by Germans between 1906 and 1910. It occupies the site where, according to tradition, Mary, mother of Jesus, went to her eternal rest (hence *dormition*). Note the spacious interior and the apse, adorned with figures of Jesus and Mary above the prophets. The three rings in the mosaic floor symbolize the Holy Trinity. Around them are the prophets, the four mystical 'beasts of the chariot', the 12 apostles and the Zodiac. A lower story crypt contains a statue of Mary made of cherry wood and ivory.

Turning left at the church exit, we reach the western flank of Mt. Zion and its splendid view of the Vale of Hinnom. Across the valley, the **Yemin Moshe** quarter stands out for its ranks of one and two story houses with red shingled roofs. To its left is an elongated structure with a sawtooth roof gable, **Mishkenot Sha'anannim.** Montefiore's **Windmill**, a famous landmark, rises above. To the left of the windmill is the **St. Andrew's Scottish Church**, a building of yellowish stone with a single white dome and another half-dome at a lower level. It was built after the British conquest in World War I in commemoration of Scottish soldiers. Of all structures in modern Jerusalem, this church is considered by some to be the most well-proportioned, and best suited to local landscapes.

Above Yemin Moshe rises a monumental rectangular structure of pinkish stone with ranks of green windows — the **King David Hotel**. Constructed in 1931, it was considered the most important and opulent hotel in British Mandate Palestine. The hotel made the history books with the blowing up and utter destruction of its southern wing by the Jewish anti-British underground, the Stern gang, in July 1946. The British failed to heed warnings and refused to evacuate the building. As a result, a great many Jews and Arabs, as well as British officials, were killed in the explosion. The restored hotel has maintained an old-world ambience and hosted the Israeli Government's most important guests; Richard Nixon, Henry Kissinger and Anwar Sadat were but a few. To the hotel's right is the French Consulate, distinctive for the tricolor

The Church of the Dormition

Yemin Moshe

flag on its sawtooth roof. The Jaffa Gate area is visible at the extreme right. Before starting the descent into the Vale of Hinnom, look down at the large grassy basin to the right of the road. This is the **Sultan's Pool** originally a real pool, but now used as an arena for outdoor performances.

We follow the path into the Vale of Hinnom and the road crossing it. If you get permission, you can visit the *Eretz ha-Tzvi School*, located to the left of the road descending Mt. Zion toward the valley. There is a lovely courtyard, and also a Protestant cemetery on the premises. The building, one of the first structures built outside the Old City walls in the mid-19th century, housed a school founded by Protestant Bishop Samuel Gobat. The cemetery contains the graves of many Protestant personalities who left their mark on Palestine and Jerusalem over the past 150 years. Buried here are Sir Flinders Petrie, the founder of Palestine archeology and an Egyptologist, Conrad Schick, perhaps the most important architect in 19th century Jerusalem, Johann Ludwig Schneller, who lent his name to a massive and impressive Jerusalem building, and Bishop Gobat himself.

The Vale of Hinnom

We have reached the Vale of Hinnom. Its association with *Gehenna* (hell) evidently originated in descriptions by the Prophets and various legends of a religious rite once practiced here which featured human sacrifice among other things. As you reach the road, look up and notice the cable which stretches over the valley from the Gobat School to Mt. Zion, attached at its other end to a building which once housed a British institution, St. John's Opthalmic Hospital. A little green cablecar with two yellow stripes dangles from the cable to the right. These are the remains of an ingenious engineering solution to a sticky problem which arose during the 1948 War of Independence. Though Israel controlled both sides of the valley, the crossover was exposed to Jordanian snipers positioned on the Old City wall. Thus a cablecar was stretched across the valley. It operated at night only, and after use the cable itself was lowered by a special mechanism so as to protect the secret. The cablecar conveyed supplies, hauled equipment and — some say — evacuated the wounded. Just below St. John's Hospital which today houses the Mt. Zion Hotel, is another building that houses the **Jerusalem Cinemateque**, it is one of the few buildings that remained from the Jewish neighborhood of Shamah.

From this point, on the road crossing the Vale of Hinnom, you can leave the path to tour the watercourse itself. This is Jerusalem's only 'canyon', and it offers a variety of surprises. Spend an hour or half a day — as long as you desire. Follow the watercourse on the right bank (not on the road to the left). The olive trees lead to a Karaite cemetery, property of a special sect which broke away from Judaism during the Middle Ages and interpreted Scripture in its own way. Then note the many burial caves (free to explore — an uncommon phenomenon!), some ornamented and others with inscriptions in Greek. Explore the ruins of a large Crusader burial structure at the site known as **Haceldama**, where corpses were interred by being dropped from the ceiling through holes which are still visible. *Halcedama* (Aramaic: the field of blood) was the area bought by Judas Iscariot with the money he received for betraying Jesus. Visit the Greek Orthodox **Monastery of St. Onuphrius**, the long-bearded hermit. One of the elderly nuns may agree to show you a fingerbone of his which is kept here. Past this are more burial caverns (larger and even more interesting). When you get tired, return to the road which runs parallel to the watercourse along its left bank and ascend back to the bridge.

Cross the valley via the bridge (watch out for traffic). It is in fact a large dam which allows water to gather in the **Sultan's Pool**. The pool takes its name from 16th century Ottoman Sultan, Suleiman the Magnificent, who constructed the dam. The reservoir is far more ancient, appearing in Crusader sources, and may even be the 'Pool of Snakes' mentioned in accounts of the Second Temple period. On the bridge, alongside the road, is an installation which Suleiman built alongside the pool — a *sabil*, a water trough for the convenience of passersby. It bears an inscription noting its location, the name of its builder, and the Muslim date of construction — June 1536. Popular tradition has another name for the Sultan's Pool — 'the pool of Bathsheva', where King David supposedly saw Bathsheva bathing from the roof of the nearby David's tower...

Cross the bridge, take the stairs at its end and turn left to an observation point. Approach the green rail and look down on a section of the aqueduct which brought water to the Temple area in Roman times. Farther along the path is an open wooden gate in a high stone wall, leading to Mishkenot Sha'anannim, the first Jewish residential area outside the Old City walls.

Mishkenot Sha'anannim: the Montefiore cottages

Jewish history lends this quarter, with its two houses and its windmill, more importance than it really deserves. Just the same, their construction was significant. The Jews of Jerusalem began to overcome their fear of life outside the walls and this marked the beginning of Jewish urban development — the 'new city' of Jerusalem. Until then, the Jewish presence had been confined to the Old City and its Jewish Quarter. By the first half of the 19th century, that neighborhood had become a suffocating example of extreme urban density, miserable sanitary conditions and rampant disease. The desolation outside the walls however, was frightening. The city walls, whose gates were locked at sunset every evening, protected Jerusalemites from the bandits, wolves and evil spirits (real or imaginary) which roamed the wilderness. The fears proved to exceed the actual peril by quite a margin. Given the conditions inside the walls, a move into the country would have been a marked improvement. Jerusalem's Christian communities were the first to acknowledge this. The Protestants built several early structures outside the walls, including the Gobat School on Mt. Zion; the Russians erected a vast enclosure known today as the Russian Compound (see 'A Nostalgic Walk Nevi'im Street and Beyond'). It was in 1860 however, only four or five generations ago, that the first Jewish breakthrough occurred, resulting in new Jewish Jerusalem — a move catalyzed by Sir Moses Montefiore.

Montefiore was an English Jew of Italian extraction and a dignitary in the upper echelons of English society. A businessman until the age of 40, he decided in mid-life to devote his remaining years to philanthropic activity. Quite a few years remained — Montefiore was alive and busy past the age of 100. He worked towards bettering the situation of Jewish communities throughout the world. His efforts took him to the courts of the Czar of Russia, the King of Morocco and the Shah of Iran — to mention but a few of his quasi-diplomatic contacts. He visited Palestine seven times, laboring to improve the circumstances of the Jewish community in various ways — some successful, others less so. Among them we should mention a modern Jewish-owned printing press, a citrus plantation in Jaffa, the first Jewish-owned pharmacy, a weaving plant in Jerusalem, and a census of the Jews in Palestine. This neighborhood is an example of one of his best received and most successful initiatives — the first Jewish quarter outside the walls.

Visiting Jerusalem in 1855, backed with funds inherited from the Jewish-American philanthropist Judah Touro of New Orleans, Montefiore bought a large plot of land opposite the walls on the other side of the valley. His first thought was to establish a hospital there, but he quickly realized that the Jews had no urgent need for one and that the distant site was unsuitable for such an institution in any case. The new decision was to found a neighborhood which would alleviate the housing shortage within the walls. An English architect was invited to handle the project. The first structure in the neighborhood was the long building (1860), as the star-shaped inscription in its facade explains. Progress was difficult in the early stages as it was difficult to persuade fearful Jerusalemites to move to the new neighborhood. The name chosen — Mishkenot Sha'anannim, Hebrew for 'tranquil residences' — wasn't enough. Neither were the neighborhood's circumferential wall, solid gates and sawtooth roof rail, meant — perhaps — to give the impression of a mighty rampart... On the other hand, relatively high standards were painstakingly maintained in the new neighborhood to make sure the miserable conditions of the old Jewish Quarter would not be reproduced there. The number of tenants was limited to prevent overcrowding, and cleanliness and sanitation were excellent (by the standards of that period). The results became apparent in 1866 when a vicious cholera epidemic struck Jerusalem — but not a soul in Mishkenot Sha'ananim. The Jews of Jerusalem then understood that life 'out of town' represented not a menace but quite the opposite; a guarantee of life. Development outside the walls gained momentum. In Mishkenot Sha'annanim, another building — the upper, shorter one — was erected that very year.

During the partition years (1948-1967), Mishkenot Sha'anannim lay on the border and began to crumble. Revitalization work ensued after 1967, as seen in adjacent Yemin Moshe. The original Mishkenot Sha'anannim building was renovated into a Municipality-owned guest house set aside for visiting artists and dignitaries. The guest list includes authors Saul Bellow and Milan Kundera, musicians Arthur Rubinstein, Pablo Casals and Isaac Stern. Visitors are not welcome, as might be expected, and one must be content with a tour of the fringes.

The gate leads us to the middle of the long facade. We turn right and follow the central section of the building where the original dwelling units, more than 20 in number, are laid out in a row. Each apartment had a front door and window, two rooms and a kitchen. Today, every other door is sealed; every two apartments have since been merged and expanded. The 19th century standards of spacious, high quality living would not suit today's guests in Mishkenot Sha'anannim.

Reaching the steps at the edge of the long house, we climb a little for a glimpse of the so-called 'short house'. Note the iron pergola on the front porch: The original sign of the manufacturer in Ramsgate, Kent, England is on some of its columns (the third or the seventh to the right). Montefiore, who had an affinity for artisans in his native Ramsgate, actually had everything metal imported from England.

Continuing up the steps, we reach the neighborhood's most famous landmark — the **Windmill**. The mill, a tall, tapering cone with four wings attached to the top (a modern reconstruction) is a conspicuous fixture in the Jerusalem skyline. Montefiore built it as a source of livelihood for tenants of his neighborhood. Despite tremendous efforts and large-scale investment, the mill was of little practical use. The milling equipment (all

The Windmill

sent from England) proved unsuitable for the wheat in Palestine, but more importantly, steam-powered flour mills were brought to Jerusalem shortly thereafter, consigning Montefiore's technology to obsolescence. This special attempt to provide employment for a population used to receiving aid from Jewish communities abroad nevertheless became a symbol of Jewish enterprise.

The mill structure houses the **Sir Moses Montefiore Museum** and is worth a short visit. Open Sun.-Thurs. 9am-

4pm, Fri. 9am-1pm. The museum depicts Montefiore's life, his contacts with various world leaders and his activities on behalf of Jews worldwide, especially those in Palestine. The exhibit also includes photographs from the mid-19th century which portray actual physical conditions in Jerusalem at the time, in particular, the desolation which reigned outside the walls. Notice the first photo to the right — Mishkenot Sha'anannim in its infancy — and a photograph of Jaffa 'Road' in 1866, Jerusalem's main road today. Montefiore's coach was kept behind the mill, but arsonists set fire to it in December 1986.

We conclude our tour of this area and continue by meandering through the streets of Yemin Moshe, a neighborhood adjacent to Mishkenot Sha'anannim. Yemin Moshe begins just beyond the stairs by which we reached this point. This Quarter was built in the 1890s on the adjacent ground purchased by Montefiore 40 years previously. The *Moshe* in its name refers to the illustrious Montefiore. Situated on the Israel-Jordan armistice line between 1948 and 1967, this neighborhood, like Mishkenot Sha'anannim, suffered serious damage. After the unification of Jerusalem, an innovative experiment in urban renewal was enacted here which proved to be very expensive. Many of the poorer residents at the time were forced to move out and, in exchange, were compensated. The houses were sold to painters, artists, and affluent individuals. The project, harshly criticized, became the subject of pointed public controversy, and was never repeated. In order to preserve the neighborhood's character, construction which violates its original character is not permitted. The streets are paved with flagstone, and closed to motor vehicles, and all utility lines are underground. Imagine returning from the supermarket and having to lug heavy baskets up the steep stairs of this neighborhood and you'll appreciate that the preservation of a distinctive quality of life also has its price...

In a nearby garden there is a burial chamber that is traditionally indentified as **Herod's House Tomb**. Discovered in 1892, its size and good workmanship, led explorers to believe that this is the site of the tomb of members of Herod's family. Herod himself is supposedly buried in Herodion outside Jerusalem.

A Nostalgic Walk — Ha-Nevi'im Street and Beyond

The area in this tour is not one of highlights, exceptional historic sites or 'musts', but rather an attempt to recapture the character of 19th century Jerusalem. Here we'll explore pleasant streets, visit institutions and examine residences in once prestigious areas which have since been swallowed up 'downtown'.

We begin in the heart of downtown, on the north side of Jaffa Rd. Most city bus lines will take you there. From 32 Jaffa Rd., walk up Heshin St. to our first stop, the Russian Compound (drivers should note that there is a large parking lot beside the Russian Orthodox Church). In mid-19th century Jerusalem, when the Old City walls were breached, two concurrent processes made their mark on the city (see '3,000 Years of History'). The Jews built new residential neighborhoods in response to the overcrowding and substandard living conditions inside the walls, whereas the Christians (i.e., the Churches and the European powers) built massive, grand public buildings as footholds in competition for influence in Jerusalem.

The **Russian Compound** is an example of the latter: a vast plot of land with buildings which dominated the Jerusalem skyline in the 1800s. It served mainly to accommodate pilgrims from Russia who were the most prominent element in Jerusalem at the time. The Church, with its distinctive green domes, was one of several structures which served the pilgrims as hostels. The entire compound was surrounded by a wall with gates. One gate and a remaining section of wall may still be seen on the side facing the Old City. While the few pilgrims from Western Europe were mostly affluent and demanded appropriate services, Russia produced an endless stream of simple village folk — mostly women. They set out on their trek almost penniless, crossed the Mediterranean in crowded vessels and, once in Palestine, set out for Jerusalem and other holy places on foot. A British traveler who joined such a group described it thus: *'Most of them reserved enough money to pay for their return voyage to Russia, apart from those who were convinced they would die en route...'* Their impact on the Jerusalem scene was noticeable. Construction of the Russian Compound which was intended for them, began in 1858. One of the first structures outside the wall, it could accommodate 1,500 people. Its scale and power was like that of an army barracks, and indeed the Turks, rulers of Jerusalem at the time, mistook it for a military base

HA-NEVI'IM STREET AND BEYOND

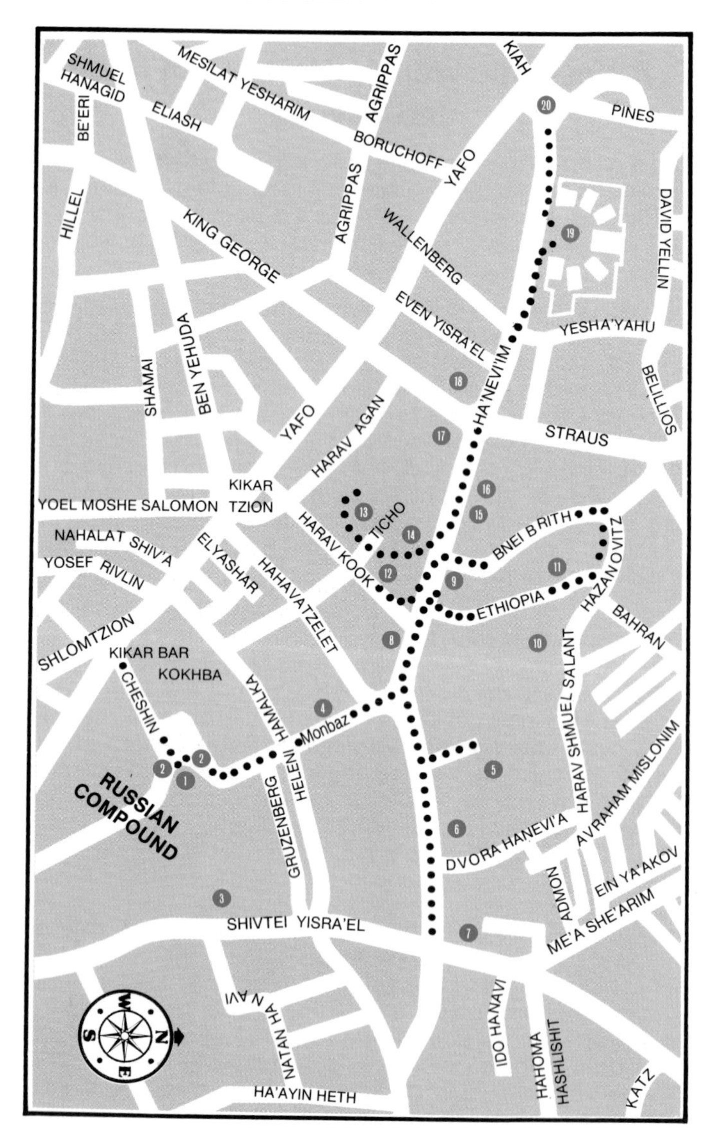

Church of the Holy Trinity — Russian Byzantine style

from which the Russians intended to set out to conquer the Holy Land... The Russian Compound was a 'Little Russia' of sorts — an enclave of Russian language, goods, cuisine and thought.

Part of the compound will be incorporated into the new Jerusalem municipality buildings that will border its eastern edge.

Located in the center of the compound is the **Church of the Holy Trinity**, capped with greenish domes, representative of Russian-Byzantine style. Built by order of Czar Alexander II, it

Index

1. Church of the Holy Trinity
2. Police Station and Supreme Court Complex
3. Shrine of Heroism
4. Sergei Building
5. German Probst Building
6. Ethiopian Buildings
7. Italian Hospital
8. Rothschild Hospital
9. Thabor House
10. Ethiopian Church
11. Residence of Eliezer Ben Yehuda
12. Beit David and Museum of Rabbi Kook
13. Ticho House Museum
14. Chaba Museum of Jewish Micrographics
15. Residence of William Holman Hunt
16. St. Joseph French Catholic School
17. German Hospital
18. Bikkur Holim Hospital
19. Anglican School
20. Davidka Square

was dedicated in 1872 in the presence of Prince (later Czar) Nicholas. Today it is usually open for Sunday mass only. Facing away from the church entrance, you can see two large buildings on the left and right, where male pilgrims were housed in conditions similar to those of today's rudimentary youth hostels. The building on the right is now a **police station** and the one on the left is the **Supreme Court** complex (we'll have more to say on these as we proceed). The building with a triangular gable to the left of the Supreme Court used to be the Russian Hospital.

Across from the church, next to the police station, you'll notice a grille which encases a stone column lying horizontally, half carved out of the rock. Discovered while the Russian Compound was under construction, it is believed to have been quarried for use as a monolithic column in the Second Temple, but was abandoned here after having been cracked during the chiseling (as may be seen). According to local folklore, on the other hand, it's the small finger of Og, the giant King of Bashan.

The large building behind the church to the right was originally a women's hostel. Its major claim to fame, though, belongs to the post-World War I British period, when the Mandatory rule requisitioned the massive structure for government service. This made the Compound a target for attacks by the Jewish resistance movements of the 1940s. The British used the women's hostel as a prison. Today it houses a small museum devoted to the Jewish underground movements and especially to those who were imprisoned here. The **Shrine of Heroism** is open Sun.-Thurs. 9am-3pm, Fri. 10am-1pm. In a cell, adjacent to the gallows, two members of the Jewish underground took their own lives just before their scheduled execution, and in another cell — the first to the right as you enter — prisoners left etchings in the stone floor. The exhibit includes photos, press clippings and posters related to the Jewish struggle against British rule and the subsequent arrests and executions.

There's nothing Russian about most of today's Russian Compound. The Russians retain only the great church, a smaller chapel and a residential wing inside the Supreme Court building. Today, there are two sects in the Russian Church. The 'White Church' is the ancient Russian Orthodox Church, which was expelled from the Soviet Union following the Bolshevik Revolution, and which relocated its center in New York. The 'Red Church' is a new denomination established by the Communist authorities. The properties in Israel originally belonged to the 'Whites'. However, during the brief post-1948 honeymoon in Israel-USSR relations, the two states reached an agreement in which Russian Church holdings in Israeli territory at the time were expropriated from the 'Whites' and handed to the

'Reds'. The church in the Russian Compound and other Russian properties in pre-1967 Israel are therefore 'Communist' Church holdings. Czarist 'White' Church properties may be found in the Old City and on the Mount of Olives — where the agreement did not apply because at the time these areas were Jordanian. In the talks between Israel and the USSR, these holdings were among the subjects discussed. Only in a country with a history as complex as Israel's could a Communist Russian Church and Israel's Supreme Court share a single building.

Cross the Compound and exit to the west (the left, facing the church) to the castle-like building at the edge. It is known as the **Sergei Building** after the great Prince Sergei Romanoff, son of Czar Alexander II, who headed the Pravoslav-Russian Imperial Pro-Palestine Society. The building, also a hostel, belonged to the Russian Compound even though it was built outside the compound wall. The single gate tower once had a partner, but it was removed to allow cars through. Studying the tower at the corner of the building, note the oval Russian emblem encircled by a Russian translation of Isaiah 62:1 *"For Zion's sake will I not hold my peace, And for Jerusalem's sake I will not rest..."*

The **Israel Nature Preservation Society** (an important address for visitors interested in unusual outings in Israel) shares the building's courtyard with a somewhat rundown **exhibit of ancient farm implements**, some reconstructed. Enter from Heleni Hamalka St.

Pass the **Sergei Building** to the right and follow Monbaz St. to Hanevi'im St. (Hebrew : Street of the Prophets). This street and its vicinity may well be the most interesting part of New Jerusalem but are far too complex for in-depth coverage. If time permits, turn right and follow the street downhill. On the left, is the former **German Probst Building**, today the ORT school (recognizable by its German inscriptions). Also worth seeing are some **Ethiopian buildings** identifiable by the blue and gold lion mosaic and inscriptions in Amharic, and the former **Italian Hospital** (used today by the Ministry of Education and Culture) unmistakable for its soaring tower: this is a highly accurate replica of a style typical of medieval Florence or Siena.

Now retrace your steps or, if you're still on Monbaz St., turn left on to Hanevi'im St. A few shops across the way sell fast-food, but only one serves the renowned Yemenite falafel — well worth tasting.

While walking down Hanevi'im St., note an old building at No. 37, set off a little from the road. Its facade and gate bear the inscription **Rothschild Hospital** in French, Hebrew and Arabic. This was Jerusalem's first Jewish hospital and the first built outside the walls by any community. No. 58, our destination, is a private residence which now houses the **Swedish Theological Institute of Jerusalem**. Private though it is, they usually answer the doorbell and welcome visitors into the courtyard. The building's extraordinary facade is worth a pause. The name of the house, *Thabor*, and its year of construction, 1882, are engraved over the gate. Once in the courtyard, walk into the interior garden. While enjoying the trees, well-tended bushes, flowers and grapevines, you can observe the unique architectural beauty of this house and its excellent upkeep.

Thabor House once belonged to Conrad Schick, a German who was one of the most prominent figures in Jerusalem in the late 1800s. After reaching the city as a Protestant missionary, Schick abandoned his calling and as an architect left a deep imprint on subsequent generations. He not only built some of Jerusalem's loveliest buildings (this is one example) but introduced new techniques of construction and design and developed urban and neighborhood planning. The original layout of Me'a She'arim, today's ultra-Orthodox Jewish center, was the work of this German ex-missionary. As an archeologist, he was a leading Holy Land scholar, publishing scores of articles on various discoveries especially the Temple Mount and its surroundings. Today's archeologists find it hard to compete with him for thoroughness. His home abounds with replicas of his findings.

While sitting in the Schick courtyard and enjoying its special atmosphere, it is hard to imagine that the noisy main street is right over the fence. On your way out, notice the little gate house with stairs on either side and the heavy wooden latch by which it was once locked up. To your right is a small church belonging to the Theological Institute.

From the Schick house, turn left, and left again at Ethiopia St. This special lane has been preserved in almost its original form since Turkish times and is not very suitable for modern transportation. The stone houses on either side, behind high fences and lush gardens, are truly lovely. Several were built by the Nashashibis, one of Jerusalem's most important Muslim families. The street takes its name from the **Ethiopian (Abyssinian) Church** located on it. It is the largest and grandest building belonging to this sect in the Holy Land. The church courtyard is worth visiting and an Ethiopian monk is usually happy to admit visitors into the church itself. There you'll find a round chapel with an altar in its center (note the tom-tom drums). The round design, it is said, denies Satan corners in which to hide.

Opposite the entrance to the Ethiopian Church, at No. 11, was

The Ethiopian Church

the **residence of Eliezer Ben Yehuda**, a Zionist movement leader in pre-Israel Palestine. Ben Yehuda is often credited with having 'invented' modern Hebrew. Obsessed with this goal, he tirelessly urged the people of Israel, returning to their land, to speak the tongue of Israel once again. His efforts were a major factor in adapting Hebrew from an archaic language, which for centuries had been used exclusively for prayer and study, into a modern language suitable for everyday use. This was his house from approximately 1905 until after World War I, when he moved to then distant Talpiot.

We follow Ethiopia St. to its end and turn left into Bnei Brith St. Jerusalem's ultra-Orthodox Jewish area begins to our right, down the hill, not far at all from its Christian neighbors. Looking to our left from Bene Berit St., is a handsome red stone building which housed the main Zionist library in Palestine (est. 1892). The institution subsequently evolved into Israel's National Library.

Follow Bnei Brith St. back to Ha-Nevi'im St. and cross over to the parking lot opposite the Schick house. Walk several yards down Harav Kook St. and turn right at the broad stone staircase for a look at two interesting houses. One of these, to the right of the path, has a rather narrow, uninviting iron gate. This house is actually an entire neighborhood in fact, the fourth neighborhood built by Jews outside the Old City walls. It was erected with a donation by philanthropist David Reiz and is therefore called **Beit David** (David's House). The building displays some of the features typical of Jerusalem homes of more than a century ago. For one, it was designed as a fortress with walls about three feet thick, which show nothing to the outside world but grille-faced windows and one little gate. Beit David's original surroundings were nothing but unpopulated exposed hills with two or three small settlements such as Nahalat Shiv'as. Danger was prevalent, or was at least perceived to be and residents tended not to leave their neighborhood after dark. The flagstones of Beit David's central court conceal a water cistern — a vital institution in every Jerusalem neighborhood until recent years. Though plugged, they still exist, as does the pump. This closed courtyard clearly illustrates the living conditions in the 19th century Old City as well. David Reiz's original contribution covered the construction of a one story structure only, designated for Jerusalem's poor Ashkenazi Jews. When the second story was built, it housed Rabbi Abraham Isaac Hacohen Kook, one of the greatest rabbis in Jewish Palestine of this century and the most important leader of Religious Zionism. There is a dedication inscription in Hebrew of the neighborhood, embedded in the wall opposite the entrance.

Follow the path from the gate of Beit David to another building known today as the **Ticho House Museum**. Open Sun-Thurs. 10am-5pm, Tues. also 5-10pm, Fri. 10am-2pm. Cafeteria open till midnight including Fri. nights. The building takes its name from the Ticho couple who lived there for many years. Abraham Ticho, the father of opthalmics in Jewish Jerusalem, opened an eye clinic in his home. His wife, Anna, who had studied painting in Vienna, devoted herself from the 1930s onward to Jerusalem art — landscapes and portraits. Her watercolors are on display in many important museums. After her death in 1980, the house became a public institution by her request. The museum exhibits the Tichos' home and personal effects on the upper story and a selection of Anna Ticho's paintings below. There is a pleasant cafeteria in the lovely garden — a charming nook in the heart of the bustling city.

This house has a curious place in the history of modern Jerusalem. Built by a wealthy Muslim, the house was purchased by Wilhelm Moses Shapira, a Christian ex-Jew who was one of the most colorful characters in Jerusalem's history. Shapira was a dealer in antiquities who earned notoriety for his involvement in two forgeries. One was a collection of 'Moabite' statuettes from the Biblical era which, after they were sold to Germany, proved to have been fashioned in his workshop. The other was a set of narrow strips of parchment. These, Shapira claimed had been given to him by Bedouins in the Judean Desert and contained the oldest existing version of Deuteronomy. The British Museum was about to pay Shapira one million pounds sterling for the cowhide 'artifacts', when a French archeologist denounced them as counterfeit. This spared the British Museum considerable public embarrassment and prompted Shapira, protesting his innocence to the last moment, to commit suicide. A minority of scholars, by the way, now believe that Shapira's scrolls were in fact genuine — the first of the important scrolls discovered in the Judean Desert in the mid-20th century. His daughter, French authoress Myriam Harry recorded the affair in her writings.

Tired? The Ticho cafeteria is at hand and other refreshment opportunities are nearby on Jaffa Rd. Left of the Ticho House gate is a unique museum of special Jewish art — the **Chaba Museum of Jewish Micrographics**, the art of miniature writing. Open Sun.-Thurs. 9am-noon. Here one may see a version of the Book of Ovadia, a mere half centimeter in length, which is thought to be the smallest Scriptural writing in the world. The Magna Carta and the United States Declaration of Independence are reproduced on eggshells; the 15 Jewish morning benedictions on grains of wheat, and the portraits of celebrities are produced by lines of print.

Return to Ha-Nevi'im St., turn left, and explore the homes and courtyards to your satisfaction (visitors are rarely allowed past the courtyards). Several of these are worthy of particular attention.

At No. 64 Ha-Nevi'im St. is a house with a lush garden and a conspicuous cross atop an iron gate. It was the Jerusalem **residence of English painter William Holman Hunt** (1827-1910), a major artist in the brotherhood of pre-Raphaelite painters. Hunt visited Palestine several times to acquire first-hand familiarity with Holy Land landscapes, painting some of

The massive walls of Beit David

his most famous works here. To produce one of these, *The Scapegoat*, he took the great risk of traveling to Sodom for the proper desert scenery. It was during his third visit to Palestine, in the 1870s, that he purchased this house. A private residence today, its courtyard alone is worth a visit. Note the water cisterns used for the storage of oil during Israel's War of Independence.

The **St. Joseph French Catholic School and Orphanage** at 66 Ha-Nevi'im St. was erected by the St. Joseph Order of Nuns in the 1880s during a vigorous French drive to establish a presence in Jerusalem. A large chapel was subsequently added on to the western side of the building. The truly impressive element here however, is the building's facade. Notice the anchor and cross emblem of the St. Joseph Order over the entrance and the cornerstone in the wall to the left of the steps. It bears the date March 19, 1887, evidently commemorating the beginning of construction.

The corner of Ha-Nevi'im and Nathan Strauss Sts. is flanked on either side to the south by impressive buildings belonging to **Bikkur Holim Hospital.** One of these, which originally functioned as Jerusalem's **German Hospital**, is notable for the metal turret on its roof. Its gate (on the Strauss St. side) bears inscriptions in German and Arabic, as well as the hospital's founding date and a relief of a dove (the symbol of the German Protestant Diakonishes Order which ran the institution). The building across the street is the original Bikkur Holim Hospital, a Jewish institution built in the early 1900s.

Continuing down Ha-Nevi'im St., to No. 82 we come to what was once the **English Hospital**, built in the 1890s by 'The London Society for Promoting Christianity Among the Jews'. It was designed by English architect A.B. Pite, who studied 20 hospitals in various countries before selecting the detached-pavilion design seen here. The layout, a horseshoe formation of detached structures linked by corridors, permitted the isolation of individual wings during epidemics. In the middle of the semicircle, various inscriptions are engraved into the facade: the name of the founding society, the date when the hospital was originally established in the Old City together with the dedication date and verses from the Scriptures. Other inscriptions on the various small buildings denote the benefactors by whose generosity they were erected. Some English names are familiar: Norfolk, Norwich, Cadbury, etc. No longer a hospital, the complex presently houses an **Anglican School** mostly for children of foreign residents — diplomats, scholars and others. The building is surrounded by an attractive lawn and garden.

We have reached the end of Ha-Nevi'im St., **Davidka Square**, named for the weapon set in a memorial at its center. The davidka, a home-made mortar which produced more noise than damage, was the most famous and terrifying weapon available to the Israelis in the 1948 War of Independence.

For a different though still nostalgic kind of Jerusalem cityscape, cross Jaffa Rd., walk up Kiah St. and cross Agrippas St. to the gate facing you. The portal opens onto **Mazkeret Moshe** — one of several Jerusalem neighborhoods named for Sir Moses Montefiore. Suddenly you find yourself in another world. Mazkeret Moshe, a Jewish residential area built in the last century, is composed of low stone houses with red shingled roofs arrayed in rows or rectangles, with broad public courtyards with an occasional synagogue in between. The tranquility of yesteryear still reigns and one is surely able to sense the spirit of a Jerusalem that was. You may wander into neighborhoods nearby, some of which are strictly Orthodox; so be sure you're dressed properly.

A Unique Ethnic Experience — Me'a She'arim

Me'a She'arim

On this tour we meet a unique Jewish community, one whose patterns of life, dress, organization and institutions appear to come from another century. These are the ultra-Orthodox Jews (Heb. *haredim*), a group who are intolerant of those who do not share their beliefs. Although we begin this chapter with a word of caution, it should not deter you from visiting this area. Anyone interested not only in sites but also in people and ways of life will find this a unique and memorable experience.

When visiting ultra-Orthodox neighborhoods, dress and behave accordingly. Women should wear dresses or skirts which cover the knees and modest blouses with long or three-quarter-length sleeves. Men should not wear shorts or other scanty attire, and are best advised to keep their heads covered. By adhering to these guidelines, you will avoid offending the community's sensitivities. The more modest your attire, the more receptive they will be towards you. Recall too, that this neighborhood is hostile to general Western norms. Demonstrative and raucous behavior is inadvisable. Don't even think of taking close-up photos of anyone or of carrying a radio or anything resembling one. It's recommended to visit in small groups so as not to arouse attention as tourists. If you have questions or require directions, it's advisable to approach someone of your own sex. The segregation of the sexes is very strict here and should be adhered to by visitors to the area. The best advice is to be inconspicuous. Any violation may be met with antagonism accompanied with shouting. If this occurs, leave quickly — for the next stage might be violent.

Special care needs to be taken on the Sabbath (from sundown on Friday until about two hours after sundown on Saturday). It is forbidden to drive in Me'a She'arim on the Sabbath and no cameras, radios, etc. should be carried. Though Sabbath activity here is especially interesting, it is not necessarily the most suitable day to visit.

Who lives in the Me'a She'arim area and what makes them special? The ultra-Orthodox faction in Jewry is distinguished for the uncompromising way in which it views Jewish faith and precepts. The result is an extremism in norms of life and in its stance vis-a-vis the 'other' Orthodoxy, a more moderate brand which has integrated itself into secular Jewish society in Israel.

Although the ultra-Orthodox are in fact a cluster of diverse groups, divided by fundamental differences, they do share certain features. Because Judaism is essentially a detailed code of behavior which includes every facet of life, the ultra-Orthodox creed is all-embracing and dictates a state of segregation from less observant Jews. This radically Jewish way of life is highly demanding. They resist all innovation and modern influence. The ultra-Orthodox dress and behave according to traditions practiced in Eastern European communities several centuries ago. It is easy to identify the ultra-Orthodox by the way the men dress. In all seasons, they wear heavy, multi-layered black suits with matching dress hats. It should be noted that not all Orthodox Jews in black consider themselves part of this particular community and each ultra-Orthodox sect dresses differently. In every Orthodox group, all women are required to dress modestly, and married women cover their hair. In some of the more extreme sects, married women crop their hair and wear scarves.

Like other ethnic minorities, the ultra-Orthodox have chosen to live in their own separate neighborhoods. This isolation permits cultural dominance and the freedom to enforce their essential values and norms undisturbed. Their vernacular is Yiddish, a German-Jewish dialect. Hebrew is used only for study and writing. Ultra-Orthodox schooling, strict and totalitarian, is at the core of implanting their values from one generation to the next. The children spend most of their time in schools, devoted primarily (sometimes exclusively) to a practical form of Judaism with virtually no contact with modern or secular disciplines of study. Here again, the aim is to minimize the impact of the outside world. The ultra-Othodox upbringing is so narrow that many children have never seen Jaffa Road or any non-religious neighborhood. Television has no place here, though radio has earned a position of some respect. The ultra-Orthodox are also known for community cohesion and a highly developed system of welfare and mutual assistance. Such a system is essential since many ultra-Orthodox families are large (they view all birth control as contrary to Jewish law and ethics).

The ultra-Orthodox are divided regarding the State of Israel. The 'moderates' have made their peace with it and are represented in the Knesset by Agudat Israel, Shas (Shomrei Masoret) and Degel Torah political parties which have, sat in Government coalitions in recent years. The more radical sects recognize neither Israel nor its legislature. They refuse to pay Government

ME'A SHE'ARIM AND THE BUKHARAN QUARTER

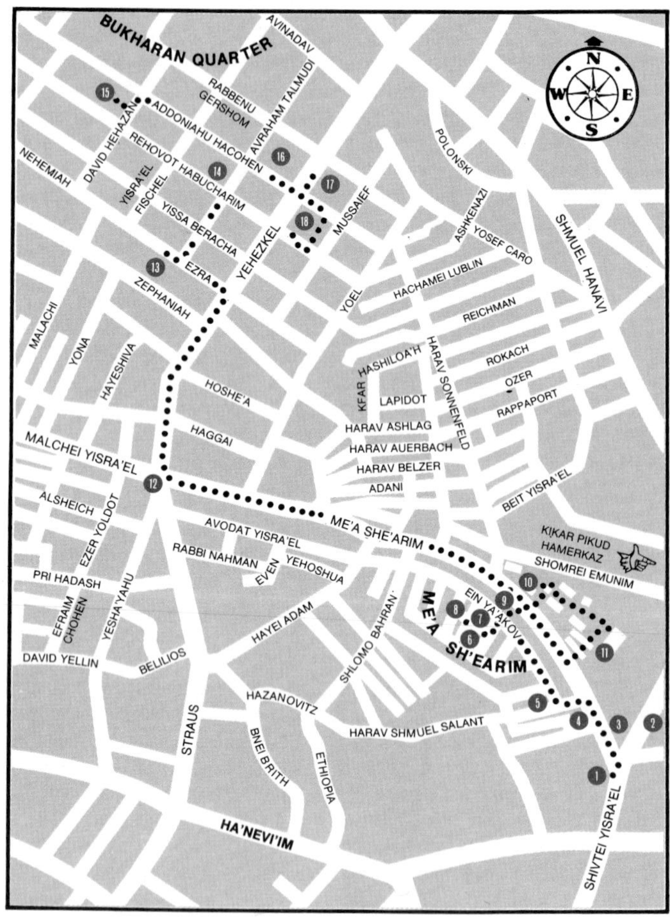

Index

1. Ministry of Education
2. Romanian Church
3. Toldot Aharon Yeshiva
4. Chasidei Breslav Yeshiva
5. Jerusalem Gate
6. Beit Avraham
7. "Shtieblach"
8. "Mikve"
9. "Muhammad's Gate"
10. Batei Ungarin
11. Batei Neitin
12. Sabbath Square
13. "The Palace"
14. Davidoff House
15. Mosheioff House
16. Adoniahu Hacohen Synagogue
17. Hamam
18. Baba Tama Synagogue

Walls and faces in Me'a She'arim

taxes, turn down payments from State-run welfare agencies and view the imposition of Jewish sovereignty in the Holy Land as a grievous sin until such time as the Messiah and the End of Days. Most of the ultra-Orthodox, including the "moderate", do not serve in Israel's army.

A state of constant tension exists between the ultra-Orthodox and the non-religious. One cause is the high birth rate and minimal generation gap which has increased the pressure to find new housing solutions for the ultra-Orthodox communities. The preferred locations, of course, are the fringes of today's ultra-Orthodox bastions. As a result, most of the area north of Ha-Nevi'im St. has become an unbroken ultra-Orthodox enclave. The post-1967 land reserves appeared to offer a solution. For various planning reasons (which in retrospect, seem to have been mistaken), new non-religious neighborhoods were built around the ultra-Orthodox community which has, once again, found itself fenced in and immobilized. This has created a new basis for friction. The ultra-Orthodox bloc is no longer at the edge of town but rather at its center, thereby forcing the non-religious to cross through it.

Tension often reaches a peak on the Sabbath. Public desecration of the Sabbath, by activities prohibited on that day in Jewish law, such as travel, cinema, business, football, is perceived by the ultra-Orthodox as a *casus belli.* In recent years the struggle has spread to new fields, such as archeological excavations at sites which are thought to have served as Jewish burial grounds (which cover practically every square foot of this history-laden city).

All this has led to rising tension and occasional outbreaks of violence between the secular and ultra-Orthodox communities. It is also aggravated by struggles within the ultra-Orthodox community itself. Fighting the secularists has become a calling card for ultra-Orthodox leaders who solicit support and contributions, especially in ultra-Orthodox communities abroad.

Tour of Me'a She'arim

With this in mind, let's begin our tour of Mea She'arim. The point of departure is the corner of Ha-Nevi'im and Shivtei Yisra'el Sts. This area is not part of Me'a She'arim; the **Ministry of Education and Culture**, and the **Romanian Church** are located here. The Education Ministry occupies the former Italian Hospital, a structure with a style of its own. Its turret is a replica of medieval buildings in Italy such as the Palazzo Vecchio in Florence. We head north on Shivte Yisra'el St. toward the little red building which houses the Rumanian Church. The atmosphere of the ultra-Orthodox area contrasts sharply with that of this adjacent street.

We turn left onto Me'a She'arim St., a major artery. Although it runs through the heart of the ultra-Orthodox area, it simultaneously serves as a main axis for Jerusalem traffic in general. Buses displaying immodest advertising might find themselves in trouble traveling this road.

The various ultra-Orthodox neighborhoods and courtyards may be reached from Me'a She'arim St. The first of these, branching off to the right, is demarcated by the **Toldot Aharon Yeshiva**, a modern white building at the edge of a plaza which reaches the street. A *yeshiva* is a college where boys and men pursue religious studies and is the most common institution in this area. Toldot Aharon is the epicenter of the most painstakingly observant and radical ultra-Orthodox faction — the Hasidim of Reb Aharon, who are 'popularly' known by the Yiddish nickname Reb Arelah. They are distinguished by their distinctive dress: striped robes (not black) and large white skullcaps which protrude from their hats. It is recommended to skirt this particular *yeshiva*, moving closer to the residences.

We now turn off the main street into the historic core of the ultra-Orthodox bloc and, in fact, of all of north Jerusalem: Me'a She'arim. Turn left onto Salant (R. Shemuel Salant) St. at the massive **Chasidei Breslav Yeshiva** (its ample representation of English speakers can answer questions). We shall pass through the gate on the right, noting the embedded iron bar — a remnant of the original Me'a She'arim gate.

Me'a She'arim was one of the first neighborhoods built outside the Old City walls and, at the time (1874) was the largest and most distant from the city and the road to Jaffa. By that time, settlement outside the walls was no longer the enterprise of eccentric individuals. Mea She'arim was the organized effort of several dozen householders who pooled resources toward a shared goal. Their hopes were articulated in the name they chose for their neighborhood taken from Genesis 26:12 — *'And Isaac sowed in that land, and found in the same a hundredfold...'* (Heb. *me'a she'arim*). The neighborhood was originally designed by a European Christian architect and ex-missionary, Conrad Schick. He designed a large rectangle of apartments with iron-grilled windows and six gates facing out. The central court (long since filled in) was set aside for open space and for public buildings. This design served two purposes. It created a fortress of sorts whose gates were opened in the morning and closed in the evening, against attacks of villagers or bandits. The second purpose involved the social imperatives of life in an isolated, autonomous community which in a sense, 'competed' with the Old City.

We entered Me'a She'arim through **Jerusalem Gate**. Turn right and follow the street to the row of houses at the northern side of the Me'a She'arim rectangle, to the marketplace. This nearly autonomous neighborhood is equipped with all its daily needs to avoid contact with the outside world. Notice the low rise houses, originally one story in height. Now we pass under a large multilingual sign which warns against dressing immodestly while in the neighborhood. After passing the vegetable stands, we turn left into the heart of historic Me'a She'arim. One of the most fascinating features of this area is the array of graffiti and posters. Though most of these are in Hebrew, an occasional specimen in your own language will give you a proper initiation.

We now stand in the heart of the quarter, facing an extraordinary two story building. This edifice, known as **Beit Avraham** (Abraham's House) originally housed several institutions: the **Great Yeshiva** of Me'a She'arim (the high academy of Jewish studies, meant to compete with similar schools in the Old City), a **Talmud Torah** (religious school for young boys) and a **free kitchen** for the destitute. Evidence of the advanced social thinking in these circles is a Me'a She'arim bylaw requiring even the well-to-do to take in an occasional meal at the free kitchen, sparing the truly needy from shame. The spacious synagogue, the neighborhood's largest house of prayer, occupies the front end of the upper story marked by a uniform row of windows. It is decorated with interesting ceiling frescoes depicting the Zodiac and the twelve tribes of Israel. Male tourists are occasionally permitted to enter — but don't insist. Today the building houses a school for young children. One can go around the building in order to reach the southern gate in the Me'a She'arim wall.

The group of buildings opposite the Great Yeshiva are *shtieblach* — little synagogues. They proliferate in Me'a She'arim and are constantly in use (in contrast to the Great Synagogue which is used mostly as a study hall) and tend to be more intimate and pleasant. There is an interesting clock which can be seen through the right-hand window. It displays traditional *Eretz Israel* time, calculated on a basis different than Western time. In 'Jewish' timekeeping 12:00 denotes sunset or sunrise and the other hours are calculated in accordance. Though most of the ultra-Orthodox have adjusted to standard Western timekeeping, this clock in the synagogue and certain announcements, still use the traditional reckoning.

Without entering or going offensively near, try to peer through the door to the left, to which the steps descend. There is a

A courtyard in Batei Ungarin

grey wall with a small, rectangular gap which is just one of several entrances to a sealed room known as a *geniza*. Pious Jews would never throw away a worn Torah scroll or other holy book. Instead, they set aside special rooms where the artifacts are stored until which they are ultimately taken out for burial. Especially painstaking Jews here treat any paper with Hebrew writing in this fashion, lest the name of God or some other holy word appear on it. Thus the residents of Me'a She'arim deposit all disposable written material (letters, newspapers etc.) in *genizas* such as this, until it receives proper burial in a Jewish cemetery.

Two other important institutions are situated near this entrance to the synagogue. To the left, across the alleyway, stands **Hachnasat Orhim**, (House of Hospitality) whose name reflects the religious command concerning hospitality. This is a special hostel for Jewish wayfarers which provides free or nominal fee accommodations for up to one month; another example of the unique tradition of mutual assistance. To the right is the *mikve*, conspicuously labeled in Hebrew. A *mikve* is a ritual bath in which married women undergo an essential ritual purification by immersing themselves after menstruation, childbirth and other circumstances. Especially observant men also frequent the *mikve* at regular intervals.

A right turn takes us back to the market street and the commercial center of Me'a She'arim. (For an alternative way back, turn left, walk to the end, turn right, follow the alleyway to the end and turn right again.) This section of the market street offers a little more open space with its broad flagstone pavement. We are standing over a giant subterranean water cistern which though plugged up, still protrudes above ground. One of Jerusalem's largest cisterns, it served the city magnificently during the siege in the 1948 War of Independence. We now turn right, back through the market and exit via the passage to Me'a She'arim St. This northern gate was once known as **Muhammad's Gate** for the Arab watchman who lived in a room beside it.

In the market, opposite the passageway to Muhammad's Gate, (20 Ein Ya'aqov St.) is a shop with a selection of copperware featuring distinctive Jewish religious themes.

Before proceeding to more conservative areas you can stop at the bakery to the left of the Me'a She'arim entrance. Note the pair of Hebrew signs overhead which indicate separate lines for men and women.

We turn left from the Me'a She'arim gate and turn right and downhill at the staircase leading to a triangular courtyard to the left. We have reached **Batei Ungarin** (The Hungarian Houses), one of Jerusalem's most beautiful and interesting quarters. Here one feels truly divorced from the 20th century. Two sides of the triangular court are demarcated by long apartment buildings (approximately 250 ft. long). The northern side features an arcade which has been partially built up in order to alleviate overcrowded housing conditions. The base of the triangle on the third side is a synagogue and study hall. The courtyard is paved with flagstones; here, again, the plugged-up underground cisterns are visible. You will see laundry hanging over the entire courtyard; laundry which by now you would recognize as typical of the ultra-Ortodox. This court is undoubtedly one of Jerusalem's unique corners.

The **Batei Ungarin Quarter** was erected during the 1880s and 1890s by an organization within the Hungarian Jewish community known as a *kollel*. Each Jewish national or ethnic community had such an organization and some still exist in the ultra-Orthodox world. *Kollelim* are responsible for distributing funds among certain community members and, at times, engage in public activity on behalf of the entire membership. The Batei Ungarin houses, built by the *kollel*, still remain under its ownership and are rented at nominal rates. Although this arrangement is financially beneficial for the tenants, it can also be a means of exerting pressure and enforcing those behavioral norms which the *kollel* leaders deem appropriate. This is reinforced by the courts' physical layout: everyone's front door opens onto the same open space, so no one can hide their activities from the eyes of their neighbors. Generally, the tenants of Batei Ungarin tend to be more painstaking in religious observance and more frequently opposed to the Jewish state than those of Me'a She'arim. Many affiliates of *Neturei Karta*, arguably the most famous of the extremist ultra-Orthodox factions, live here.

We go around the synagogue from its left and then turn right into another open courtyard, this one rectangular and narrow. Its two long sides are apartment houses with a synagogue in between. A metal fence on the upper floor of the building on the left marks the **Talmud Torah**, a school for young boys. On the building is a sign whose Latin characters spell out the institution's Hebrew name: *Lechem Lare'evim*, (Bread for the Hungry), another free kitchen. Note the tiny half-cylinder affixed to the wall alongside the right-hand side of every entrance door. This is a *mezuza*; the container holds a piece of parchment bearing Biblical verses. Jewish religious law commands Jews to affix a *mezuza* to each doorway in this manner. When passing through the door, the pious touch the *mezuza* with a hand, raise the hand to their lips and kiss it.

We continue through the narrow passageway to the right of the synagogue at the edge of the rectangular plaza, following the full length of another elongated building until breaking into open space. Orientation in Batei Ungarin is problematic because the streets have no names (apartment door lintels are numbered in Hebrew characters). To our right are three long parallel buildings which we face at their narrow side. These are the homes of Reb Arele's Hasidim, the extremist faction whose yeshiva we passed as we began this tour. Our goal now is to return to Me'a She'arim St. We turn right, and right again, now facing the direction from which we came. Then we take a left, another left and then a right — into a passage through the center of the building facing us. Tricky? Even if you get lost, you'll find other courtyards. If you have indeed followed these directions, you will have reached the mini-neighborhood of **Batei Neitin:** four rows of apartments connected by an unusual covered passageway by which we exit on to Me'a She'arim St.

You may terminate the tour here: turn left and take a few short steps back into the secular world. Since you are nearby and appropriately dressed, this might be a good opportunity for a visit to another lovely neighborhood on the fringe of the ultra-Orthodox residential area — the Bukharan Quarter. Its buildings radiate interesting character and extraordinary form, testimony to the Quarter's unique history. Turn right, go up Me'a She'arim St. between the ultra-Orthodox quarters. To the left, after the corner of Baharan St., you will see a sign in Hebrew and English: 'Shatnez Laboratory'. *Shatnez* is an interweaving of different kinds of fiber in a single garment, which is a violation of Jewish law. One may bring ones clothing here for laboratory testing. Under the sign appears a drawing, with Yiddish commentary, of a naive looking ultra-Orthodox man who, while rejecting non-kosher food in disgust, is willing to wear non-kosher clothing...

Note the narrow, handsome street branching off to the left and climbing the hill. Its name, *Hayei Adam* St., literally means 'life of man' and people here explain that it does indeed reflect the life of man. If you begin at the top, at the non-Orthodox neighborhoods, it's one long descent; while if you begin with the Orthodox quarters, you just rise and rise... A few hundred yards later we reach a bustling intersection (Me'a She'arim, Yehezqel, Yesha'yahu and Strauss Sts.) — known as **Sabbath Square** (Heb. *Kikkar Hashabbat*). The name was born in riots which were orchestrated here by the ultra-Orthodox until the authorities were forced to close the area to traffic on the Sabbath. To reach the Bukharan Quarter, turn right onto Yehezqel St. and continue to the top of the rise.

The Bukharan Quarter

The Bukharan Quarter (est. 1894), an outstanding neighborhood in Jerusalem's history, was built by wealthy members of the Jewish community of Bukhara (Central Asia, now in the USSR). These were among the richest Jews in the world at the turn of the century. They chose an area far out of town to the northwest to build their prestigious neighborhood. Its overall planning and houses radiated power, grandeur and affluence on a scale unknown in Palestine at the time. Most of these families continued to run their businesses (mainly large-scale textile plants) in Central Asia, sending representatives to their enormous patriarchal houses in Palestine. These — often retired adults, or children sent to Jerusalem for schooling — were supported from Bukhara. The homeowners themselves would visit every couple of years for two or three months. Though this may not sound impressive, those were days when such a trip required great effort, and took months. A few did relocate their businesses and homes to Palestine; such as the Musayoff family, today owners of a large jewelry empire. These however, were a minority. The neighborhood was at a physical distance from Jerusalem during its heyday and, due to its nature, was divorced from the city's social and economic

The Bukharan Quarter — at the market

life as well. Ethnically too, the Bukharans stood apart from other Jerusalemites who would come to gape at their exotic, colorful clothing and unusual customs.

World War I and the Russian Revolution sealed the fate of the Bukharan Quarter. The Bukharans were enemy (Russian) subjects, and the Turks blocked their financial support from Bukhara. Many of them fled the country. Hopes that the end of the War would mark a return to normalcy proved false. After the Russian Revolution all their assets were expropriated by the new Soviet regime. Overnight, the Bukharan Jews who had built this neighborhood, turned from lavishly wealthy tycoons into utter paupers. In many cases, they were left with nothing but their Jerusalem homes and the clothes on their backs. The houses were put up for rent.

The Quarter enjoyed a brief postwar renaissance as a center of Zionist activity, as many Zionist settlers who reached Jerusalem found above-standard housing in the stone mansions. However, they soon moved to more centrally located neighborhoods, and the Bukharan Quarter began a slow sad decline. Some of the homes have literally crumbled into ruins and hardly a trace of the neighborhood's original grandeur survives. In recent years, the ultra-Orthodox have begun to penetrate the area. Though the locals sometimes object, these efforts might halt the deterioration.

Tour of the Bukharan Quarter

Let us tour the Quarter, pointing out some of the more prominent homes in which the original character is still preserved. First we turn left on to Ezra St., easily identifying the two story house at No. 19 known as **The Palace**. The Quarter's largest mansion, it was apparently the largest in all of Palestine up to World War I. The dominating, ornate facade is its distinguishing characteristic. The original main entrance stood at the double spiral staircase which leads to the upper story from the east (from which we have come). Step back a little and notice the glass pyramid on the roof. Resting on rails, it is removable and served as a unique solution to a religious problem: how to convert a standard room into an open *succa* (tabernacle) during the early autumn festival of Succot. The house (c. 1905), built by the Yehudayoff and Hefetz families, is known in Jerusalem folklore as 'the Messiah's palace', where the Messiah would be greeted upon arrival... One important reception has already been held here: Jewish Jerusalem's welcome of General Allenby and the victorious British army after their conquest of Palestine during the first World War. Today, the house's two floors have been separated and each accommodates a religious school. If permitted, climb to the second floor (enter at the right-hand side of the building). You can see traces of the magnificent interior, such as wall frescoes on a variety of themes and a marble-faced synagogue.

We go down to Talmudi St. which opens across from the center of The Palace. Crossing a narrow street, we reach the steps which descend to the main street of the Quarter, opposite an exceptional house with ornate windows built by the Davidoff family. One can recognize it from afar by its double pagoda-style shingled roof. To appreciate the architectural innovation involved, recall that this house predates World War I and contrasts sharply with its Jerusalem contemporaries. Note the layout of the street which is one of the Quarter's most notable features. The Bukharan Quarter is easily identified on a city map by its grid of perpendicular streets. This layout, reminiscent of New York, disregards Jerusalem's hilly nature, which is more conducive to the city's characteristic twisting alleyways. Observe the width of the streets. They were laid out more than 90 years ago when the city's broadest thoroughfares were no more than one third as wide. Such features are illustrative of just how exceptional the Quarter was in its buildings and design.

We turn left and follow Bukharan St. two blocks to David Hahazzan St. To our right and to the front stands the largest building in the Quarter in overall area — more than an acre and a quarter including interior courtyards! This is the **Mosheioff House**, erected in 1906. In order to see its typical inner court and imagine the Quarter's original glory, we shall turn right and follow the base of the building. The welder's shop we see there (note the lifelike head carved into its lintel), occupies what used to be the opulent main entrance. We shall enter through the narrow doorway at the edge of the building (No. 15) into the courtyard. Note the circumferential ground floor arcade and the upstairs balcony gallery. Dilapidated though it may be today, this courtyard still radiates something of its special character. You should be aware that there are people living in this house today.

We leave the Mosheioff courtyard and return by Adoniahu Hacohen St., which begins across from the narrow, low gate. It takes us to a special part of this Quarter which belongs to the Mashad sect — Iranian Jews who were forced to convert to Islam but secretly kept and practiced Judaism. Fleeing their home town in Iran, they settled in the Bukharan Quarter. Notice the house at No. 28 (at the corner of Fischel St.), paying special attention to the Hebrew dedication engraved in the windowsills. Also worth a visit is the courtyard in the **Adoniahu Hacohen Synagogue** down the street (No. 16) — one of the loveliest and best kept courtyards in the neighborhood, graced with several fruit trees. The synagogue itself is on the second story (note the pseudo-Gothic windows and proliferation of Stars of David). Here too, is a remnant of the Turkish period: a manhole cover adorned with a crescent.

Reaching the next intersection (Adoniahu Hacohen and Yehezqel Sts.) glance at the great eucalyptus tree along the street to your left. It is the last of a row of trees which once graced the Quarter's streets. The Turks chopped down the others for firewood during World War I. Across the street to the left is a large, externally unattractive building. It's the **Hamam**, the Turkish bath built by the wealthy Jews of Bukhara which served Jerusalem until recently. Under ultra orthodox pressure it was closed down and converted into a *mikve* (a ritual bath).

Crossing Yehezqel St., we pass through the small and active Bukharan Quarter market until reaching a passage to the right, which leads between the shops into an interior courtyard. This courtyard, one of the largest in Jerusalem today, was built by the Bukharans as a communal housing project for compatriots who could not afford an entire house of their own. A few trees have survived, their size attesting to their age. No fewer than four synagogues line the court. As a rule, hardly any building in the Quarter is without its own house of prayer.

Our last stop in the Bukharan Quarter is a **synagogue** which bears the name of **Baba Tama**, its benefactor. It can be found at the outside corner of the large courtyard in which we are standing. Walk through the gloomy, half-hidden aperture beside the concrete wall to the right of the large trees, across from the direction from which we entered; turn right. If the synagogue is closed, appeal to the owner of the jewelry and souvenir shop across the way who may be able to open it.

Baba Tama is a **Sephardi** synagogue, indicating an affiliation with the heritage of the Jews of Spain and the Orient, as opposed to the Jewish heritage from elsewhere in Europe known as **Ashkenazi**. The major difference in synagogues is their interior layout. In a Sepharadi synagogue such as Baba Tama, the chairs face a raised central platform which accommodates the prayer leader as if he were conducting a study group. In an Ashkenazi synagogue, by contrast, worshippers sit in rows facing the front, where the reader conducts services while facing ahead as well, his back to the congregation. While visiting Baba Tama, ask someone to open the Holy Ark where you can see ancient Bukharan Torah scrolls as well as newer ones. Sephardi Torah scrolls are encased in solid cylinders of wood which open lengthwise on hinges, whereas Ashkenazi Jews protect their scrolls only with a cloth cover, recalling the High Priest's clothing. At the back of the synagogue is a small gallery which is reserved for women and is separated from the main prayer hall by a dense latticewood partition.

Return to Yehezqel St. either to walk or to catch a bus to the city center. Alternately, stay a while in the Quarter, exploring other Bukharan Quarter courtyards and discovering further remnants of a once-glorious, but now faded and extinguished era.

North of the Old City Walls

In this area there are two tours which you can make.

Tour 1

The Rockefeller Museum
This museum, also known as The Palestine Museum of Archeology, is a redundant step-sister of the Israel Museum in many ways. Its existence as an independent institution is largely due to the partitioning of Jerusalem between Israel and Jordan (1948-1967). The unification of the city may have worked out to this museum's disadvantage. A visit to the archeology wings of the Israel Museum may be enough for you. Just the same, several exhibits here certainly belong to the top echelon of Palestine archeological findings. If you're in the vicinity, it's worth a brief visit. It may be reached by buses 23 and 27. Open Sun.-Thurs. 10am-5pm; Fri., Sat. and holidays 10am-2pm.

The Rockefeller Museum was funded by the famous American family and built by the British Mandatory Government. It stands on the hill from which the Crusaders breached the walls of Jerusalem in 1099. The handsome building was designed by British architect Austin St. Barbe Harrison as part of his intention (reflected also in the High Commissioner's Residence) to create a special Jerusalem building style. To achieve this, he opened a quarry which produced what is known as 'Harrison Stone' — a special stone used only for this building. The museum opened in 1938, though the dedication ceremony was canceled after British archeologist John Leslie Starkey, who had excavated Biblical Lachish, was murdered by Arabs while on his way to Jerusalem for the occasion.

The museum was run by an international committee until the 1948 war, after which agreements between Jordan and Israel stipulated Israeli participation in its administration. However, Jordan nationalized the facility to prevent this, thereby legitimizing Israel's post-1967 claim to the museum as an Israeli institution in every regard. Almost no new exhibits are on display here; its contents consist mainly of the original British collections. A few artifacts have been relocated to the Israel Museum.

The exhibition halls include two long galleries to the south and north, respectively, and two smaller halls to the east and west (the former of these is the entrance hall). Four square or octagonal rooms, at the four corners of the building, house many of the most important findings. We begin our tour by turning left at the entrance. In the first room to the left — the **South Octagon** — is a collection of monuments from Beit She'an dating from the **late Canaanite period** (15th-13th centuries BC). The black stela to the left dates from the time of Seti (14th century BC), in which the god Michal of Beit She'an is mentioned. From here we cross the southern gallery, devoted to the prehistoric and Canaanite eras (including findings from Jericho). The prehistoric exhibits include Carmelite Man, a rare species who dwelled only in Palestine (app. 40,000 years ago).

The **southern room** behind the gallery displays beautiful eighth century (early Muslim) carved wooden beams from the Al-Aksa Mosque, discovered while the mosque was being renovated. The next hall, too, is devoted to Muslim art. Included is a collection of very impressive findings from the lovely Umayyad Hisham Palace in Jericho.

The **northern interior room** is reserved for **Crusader antiquities**. Here we find the two lintels (dating from the latter half of the 12th century) which were removed from the entrances of the Church of the Holy Sepulchre. These may well be the most important examples of Crusader sculpture ever found in Palestine. One of them depicts five scenes from the life of Jesus, the other, images of man, animals and mythological creatures on a backdrop of flora. Notice, too, the 17th-18th century model of the Church of the Holy Sepulchre made of wood and embedded with mother of pearl.

To our right, in the **northern gallery**, are displays from the **Israelite** and **subsequent periods**, including figure-like sarcophagi and ritual objects. At the edge of the room is a reconstruction of a Canaanite burial cave in Jericho. The next octagonal room houses Jewish artifacts from the Temple period and afterwards, including a seven-branched *menora* (candelabrum) and mosaic floors from various synagogues. Two interesting inscriptions from the Second Temple period are on display in the passage leading back to the entrance hall. One inscription refers to Theodotus, a priest and head of a synagogue, proving that the Temple and synagogues existed simultaneously. A fragment of another inscription notes the border of the Second Temple area which was approachable by non-Jews (a similar inscription, recovered intact, is kept in Istanbul).

From here we return to the entrance hall, where the exhibits are changed from time to time. One may proceed to the courtyard to find a number of massive exhibits: sarcophagi; capitals of columns, and the like; arranged around a goldfish pool. The marks in the walls, by the way, are from bullets fired during the Six Day War.

The Area along the Northern Old City Wall
In addition to the Rockefeller Museum, the area north of the Damascus Gate offers several interesting sites.

Cave lovers will find interest in the **Cave of Zedekiah**, about 500 yards east of the Damascus Gate. (open daily 9am-5pm.) Legend reports that King Zedekiah of Judah fled from the Babylonians through this cave, emerging at the outskirts of Jericho. The site is also known as **Solomon's Quarries**, perhaps because it served as a rock quarry during and after the First Temple period. The grotto is about 300 yards long, it has electric lighting and is easy to explore. Another cave — **Jeremiah's Grotto** or **the Court of the Prison** (Heb. *Hatzar Hamatara*) is near the bus terminal, on the other side of the road.

Another site of interest, especially for Protestants, is the **Garden Tomb**, which Protestant tradition regards as the site of Jesus' burial. Open Mon.-Sat. 8am-noon, 2:30-5pm. Closed Sun. The narrow lane which leads to it, branching to the right of Derech Shechem, is named for 19th-century Jerusalem scholar and architect Conrad Schick. The Protestants, in a controversy stemming from one of the most famous archeological disputes in Jerusalem history, reject the traditional view that Jesus was entombed inside the Church of the Holy Sepulchre, in today's Old City. Since the Jews buried their dead outside the city wall, Jesus, could not have been buried inside. The controversy therefore concerns the location of that wall in the time of Jesus. The Protestants believe that it followed a path approximating that of today's wall, which leaves the Church of the Holy Sepulchre inside the walls. In 1867, General Gordon of England suggested that the sepulchre and Calvary (Golgotha) be sought on the hill opposite the Damascus Gate, since its shape resembles a skull — *golgoltha* in Aramaic (as seen when viewing it from the wall). A burial cave was found on that hill and caused much excitement as the Protestants were convinced that the true Holy Sepulchre was before them. It's usually possible to find someone there who will explain at length why this, and only this, is the correct view. However, the grotto evidently dates from the First Temple period, and not from Jesus' time. In any event, it is worth visiting for the well-tended, handsome garden surrounding the grotto.

A site off the beaten track is the lovely **Armenian Mosaic** in the **Chapel of St. Polyeuctus** (open daily 7am-5:30pm). To find it, follow Ha-Nevi'im St. about 300 yards from the Damascus Gate and look on your right for a half-submerged house somewhat off the street before the first intersection; the entrance is between

NORTH OF THE OLD CITY WALLS

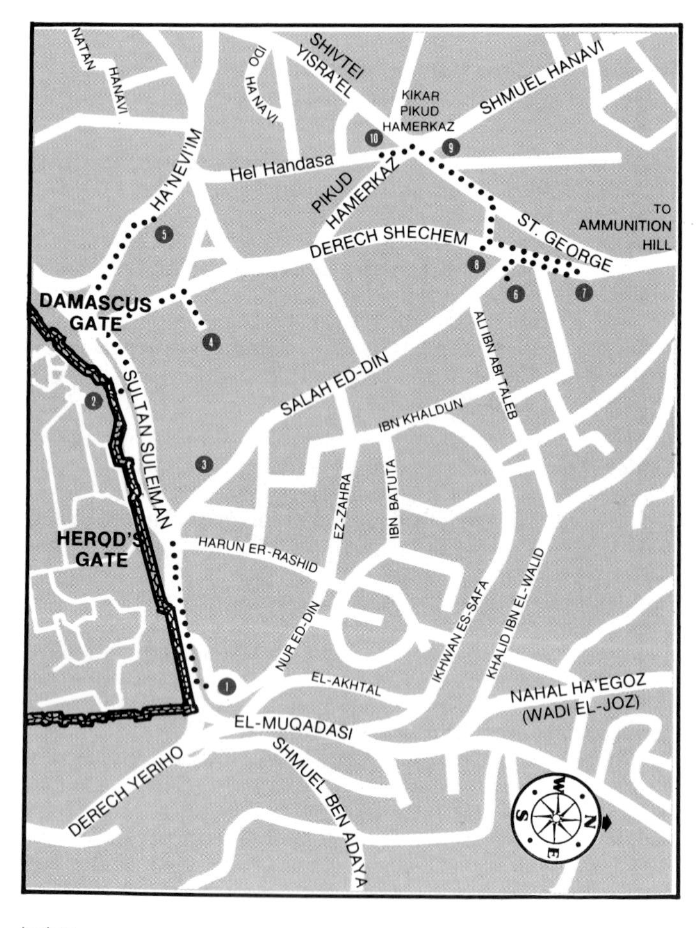

Index
1. The Rockefeller Museum
2. Cave of Zedekiah
3. Jermiah's Grotto
4. Garden Tomb
5. Armenian Mosaic
6. Tombs of the Kings
7. American Colony
8. Cathedral of St. George
9. Mandelbaum Gate
10. Tourjeman-Post Museum

Crowd at the north of the City walls

two other houses. Inside is the Armenian mosaic, known as the *Mosaic of the Birds*. Its characteristic fourth-sixth century style is similar to other mosaics discovered in Palestine. The main pattern, with its plaited fringes, depicts 45 birds, baskets of fruit and a bird in a cage, amidst medallions portrayed in a grapevine which grows out of a magnificent pitcher. Though the birds are arranged symmetrically around a central axis, the artist allowed himself to deviate slightly from this symmetry with regard to the depiction of the birds themselves. Note the quality of the work — the details of the vine leaves, tendrils and grapes, for example. The Armenian inscription at the apse apparently marks the tomb of a group of Armenians whose names were unknown, perhaps pilgrims who died before reaching their destination. It reads: *To the memory and salvation of the souls of all the Armenians whose names are known to God.* Armenian tradition attributes this half-chapel half-tomb to St. Polyeuctus, an Armenian officer in the army of Rome who was martyred for being a Christian. There is no proof, however, that this floor belonged to the monastery which bears his name.

Tour 2

To reach the area take bus line 27.

The Tombs of the Kings

About half a mile north of the Damascus Gate, at the intersection of Nablus Rd. and Salah ed-Din St., is an interesting archeological site known as the Tombs of the Kings. Open Mon.-Sat. 8am-12:30pm, 2-5pm. Closed Sun. Flashlight recommended. For ages this burial complex has aroused the excitement of visitors, including a Franciscan monk who argued that it should become the Eighth Wonder of the World. Though both its name, and the sign (put up by the French who own it) allude to the Kings of Judah, no such association actually exists. It is related to an extraordinary event from the late Second Temple period. In Persia there was a kingdom called Hadaieb (Adiabene in Greek) which apparently had a significant Jewish community. Between 35-40 AD, the Queen of Adiabene, Helene, decided to convert to Judaism together with her sons. This done, she made a pilgrimage to Jerusalem. Arriving during a famine, she was of great assistance in having food imported from Cyprus and Egypt. In addition to the palaces she built in southern Jerusalem and a contribution she made to the Temple, Helene established an opulent burial crypt in the city. The latter endeavor earned her praise in a classic description of the eastern Mediterranean area, which gives two tombs special mention: that of Mausolus in Halicarnassus (Asia Minor), and that of Helene in Jerusalem.

Over time, however, the place was abandoned and its history was forgotten. Various traditions persisted, one of which associated the site with the Kings of Judah. A French-Jewish family bought the 'Tombs of the Kings' in the 1870s and subsequently transfered ownership to the Government of France.

Bring a flashlight or candles with you (sometimes the watchman has candles). Our starting point is the broad staircase which leads to the tombs. At one time, three large pyramids stood here. The stairs which we descend made an excellent surface for collecting rainwater, and are in fact equipped with two channels which drain the water into cisterns. The steps, like the court to which they lead and the entire burial vault, are quarried out of the rock: about 20,000 tons of stone were hauled out during construction, by hand. Note the arched portal carved from the rock at the bottom of the staircase. We pass through this portal into the square court, about 35 ft. in depth; preceding the burial cave. Above the entrance to the cave is a frieze originally supported by columns which no longer exist.

The aperture leading to the cave, hollowed out of the rock floor to the left, was once concealed with a slab of stone against graverobbers. The ancient sources speak of a secret door with a special operating mechanism and a self-closing feature, but graverobbers managed to break in anyway. The only surviving piece of this mechanism is the stone which was rolled in front of the opening to seal the tomb.

From here we enter a large cave, on two levels, divided into several rooms which house a total of 48 graves. Note the fine stonework, the *arcosolia* (round niches above the benches where the sarcophagi were laid), and the special small niches meant for lamps. Again, every stone removed to create this vast cavern was taken out via the single entrance! One room, however, eluded the graverobbers' grasp. In the mid-19th century a sarcophagus was discovered, bearing an inscription — *Zadan Malketa*, or Queen Zadan. This is unquestionably a grand and memorable burial cave, one of the most impressive ever discovered in the Holy Land.

The American Colony

Not far away from the Tombs of the Kings are two buildings associated with the history of New Jerusalem. We exit the Tombs, turn right onto Nablus Rd., and take another right to reach the American Colony. Now a hotel, the American Colony was founded in 1881 by a group of Presbyterians from Chicago, led by Mr. and Mrs. Stafford who decided to engage in public activity in Jerusalem following the deaths of their four daughters. The Colony's residents were often at odds with the American Consulate.

At a later date, a group of Swedes with their own particular religious persuasion joined them. Their arrival and their lives here are described in *Jerusalem* by Selma Lagerlof, winner of the 1909 Nobel Prize for Literature, who lived in Jerusalem around the turn of the century. The Colony resided in the former home of a wealthy Muslim dignitary, a mansion reflecting the finest style and grandeur of that time. Visit the second story guest room and observe its special wooden ceiling. When you leave, you will see a mosque to the right (north); the Sheikh Jarrah mosque.

The Cathedral of St. George

Across from the Tombs of the Kings on Salah ed-Din St. is the Anglican Cathedral of St. George (look for the four spires at the top of its steeple). Development of the complex, using the colleges of Oxford as a model, began in the 1890s. Like the Russian Church on the Mount of Olives or the Italian Hospital, this structure 'imports' a European building style. Such designs were specifically used in order to demonstrate a presence in Jerusalem, and should be understood as part of the power struggle for influence and footholds in the city. Inside the church, in the wing to the left, is the British royal coat of arms. Originally at the British Governor's residence during the Mandate years, it was brought to the Cathedral when the British left the country on May 14, 1948. There is also a memorial plaque for members of the British Palestine Police who lost their lives in the country.

The Tourjeman Post Museum

In order to get to this museum at 1 Hel Handasa St. — walk south on St. George street to Pikud Merkaz Square, bear left to the second street on the left. The museum is devoted to a special and interesting facet of 20th-century Jerusalem: the period of the partitioning of Jerusalem between Israel and Jordan (1948-1967) is documented in an exhibit entitled *Jerusalem — a Divided City Reunited.* Open Sun.-Thurs. 9am-3pm. Bus lines 1, 11, 29 and 99.

The building itself, as its name indicates, was a fortified Israeli border position, adjacent to the Mandelbaum Gate through which traffic between the city's two sectors passed. The display — photos, maps, documents and an audio-visual show — describes Jerusalem history since Israel's War of Independence in 1948. Among the items there is a notice printed during the Arab siege of 1948 which explains to the Jews of Jerusalem how to get by on ten liters of water per day (compared with today's daily per capita consumption of some 140 liters); a map on which Moshe Dayan of Israel and Abdallah el-Tal of Jordan sketched the city's partition lines; photos depicting life in the divided city — a reality of coexistence under high tension; and the story of the **Mandelbaum Gate**. A rooftop observation point overlooks Old and New Jerusalem.

Ammunition Hill

Another site associated with Jerusalem's wartime history is Ammunition Hill, about three quarters of a mile north of the American Colony, left (west) of Nablus Rd. Ammunition Hill was the site of the fiercest and most famous battle of the Six Day War (June 1967) in Jerusalem and remains a symbol of that war. Now a public park, the site preserves the trenches and fortifications and houses a small museum primarily devoted to the Six Day War.

Culture and Democracy — The Israel Museum and the Knesset

Unlike the stark, stone buildings prevalent in so much of the city, this part of Jerusalem abounds in greenery and park land.

The Israel Museum

Located on the hill adjacent to the Knesset (Israel's Parliament) and overlooking the Valley of the Cross, is the Israel Museum. Israeli architects Alfred Mansfeld and Dora Gad designed the museum building in a manner reminiscent of a typical Middle Eastern village — white buildings, in harmony with the landscape, strewn across a hilltop. The Israel Museum, opened to the public in 1965, incorporates four major divisions: the **Bezalel National Museum for the Fine Arts** (Jewish art), the **Samuel Bronfman Biblical and Archeological Museum**, the **Shrine of the Book**, and the **Billy Rose Art Garden**. The **Ruth Youth Wing** offers a wide variety of activities.

Entering the museum court, right in front of you is the new Weisbord Exhibition Pavillion that houses a small but impressive art collection, as well as changing exhibitions. If you turn right you first pass Israeli sculptor Yaacov Agam's statue *Eighteen Levels* and come to the **Shrine of the Book** immediately to your right. If time is short, we recommend this as the best part of the museum. The Shrine shelters and displays the **Dead Sea Scrolls**, a collection of ancient documents of unique and revolutionary importance, which were discovered in 1947 and subsequent years in the Judea Desert and Dead Sea areas. Designed by American architects F.J. Kiesler and A.P. Bartos, its white dome and black wall are symbolic of the struggle between the Sons of Light and the Sons of Darkness, a central theme in the scrolls.

The entrance foyer houses an exhibit of documents from the time of Bar-Kokhba (or Bar-Kosiba, the name by which they refer to him) — the leader of the Jewish insurrection against Rome in Judea in 132-135 AD. Before these documents were discovered, contemporary accounts of this rebellion (which was repressed by Hadrian) and its leader were few and scanty. This explains the importance of the new findings. The exhibit includes 15 letters written by Bar-Kokhba himself, and documents from the archives of Babata, a wealthy woman who took part in the rebellion, married twice and left behind a sizeable collection of writings.

The Dead Sea scrolls themselves — part of a large collection of Hebrew documents from the first centuries BC and AD — are kept in the central hall. Their discovery was one of the major archeological events in Palestine and in the field of Biblical studies in general. The first seven were discovered by Bedouins in caves near Qumran in the Judea Desert, where the exceptionally arid climate prevented their deterioration. Israeli archeologist E.L. Sukenik bought three of them just before Israel's War of Independence from a trader in antiquities from Bethlehem. Four more surfaced in the United States where, in 1955, they were purchased and reunited with the others in Israel. Systematic exploration in the Qumran area and the Judea Desert brought up additional complete scrolls and thousands of fragments. Another important collection was found at Masada.

There are two major types of documents. The first category is Biblical manuscripts, which precede any previously known by about 1000 years. More than 100 copies of canonized books have been found here, including the entire canon except for the *Scroll of Esther*. The second category comprises the writings of the people of Qumran. Many scholars identify this community, known as 'the Judean Desert Sect', with the Essenes who are described by Josephus. By either name, this was a separatist and, by its own definition, 'chosen' sect. It was a community with strong internal discipline, special religious beliefs and a clear eschatological view on death, judgement and immortality.

The major scrolls displayed here (in the following order, if you turn right at the entrance are: 1) *The Scroll of Serech Hayahad*, the community's manual of discipline; 2) *The Scroll of the War between the Sons of Light against the Sons of Darkness* — an eschatological composition which describes in great military detail a future 40-year war between the Judea Desert sect, the Sons of Light — and the forces of evil, known as the Sons of Darkness. The scroll predicts that the Sons of Light will triumph in the end; 3) a commentary on the *Book of Habakkuk*, from the perspective particular to this community and its view of history; 4) *The Psalms Scrolls*, a compendium of 41 Psalm-like poems related to the sect's religious precepts; and 5) the *Book of Isaiah*, in a version which closely resembles the version read today. This is the oldest known version of any complete Biblical book. A facsimile of the entire scroll (about 25 ft. long) may be viewed in a display case in the center of the Shrine. Other findings from the Bar-Kokhba years (the Cave of the Letters) may be viewed in the Shrine's lower story.

We leave the Shrine of the Book and turn right, up the hill, to

THE KNESSET, ISRAEL MUSEUM AND AREA

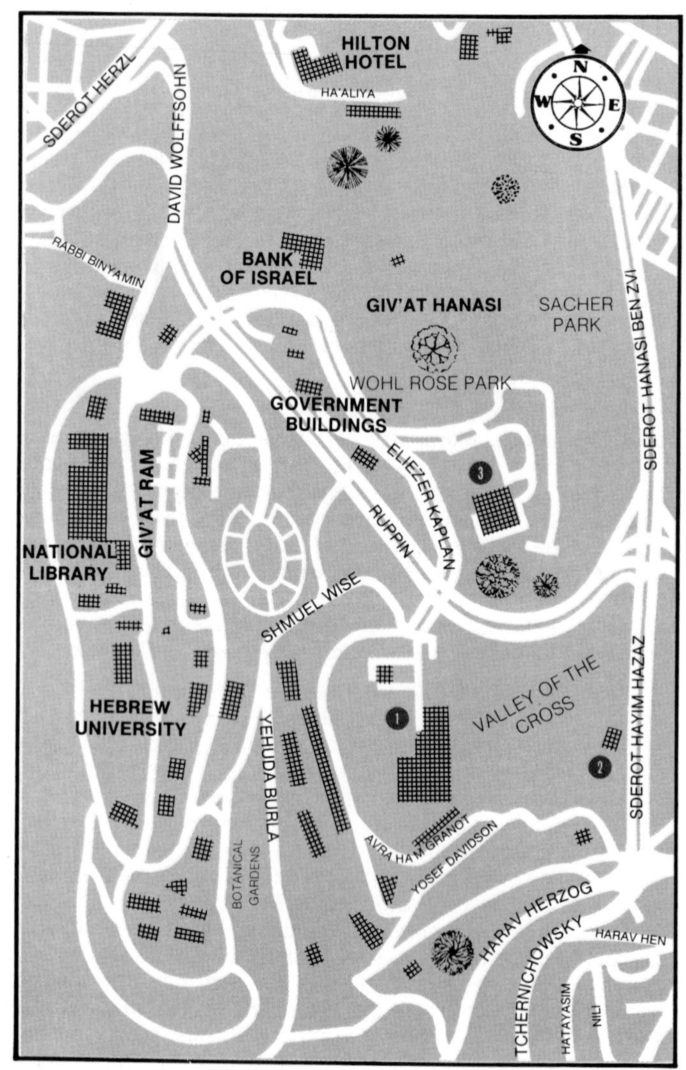

Index
1. The Israel Museum
2. Monastery of the Cross
3. The Knesset

the main museum building. Note the **sculpture garden** on your right. Japanese-American architect Isamu Noguchi, its designer, produced terraces of natural stone which are used as pedastals for statues dating from the 19th and 20th centuries. The display includes works by Picasso, Rodin, Vasarely, Henry Moore and others, with works of Israeli sculptors alongside. The plaza at the museum entrance offers a fine view of New Jerusalem (Rehavia) and the **Monastery of the Cross** in the valley just below.

On the entrance floor to the right (across from the hat-check room) is the entrance hall to the **museum's library** devoted to special exhibits. The Adjacent hall is also for temporary exhibitions. Other major exhibits are on the bottom floor. There we reach another hall which houses temporary exhibitions, and from here we enter the two wings which house the museum's truly special displays — the Archeology Wing on the left, and the Jewish Wing straight ahead. Exhibits on other themes are alongside the latter.

The Archeology Wing: Almost all the archeological findings displayed here were discovered in the Holy Land. We should bear this in mind when comparing the Israel Museum to counterparts such as the Louvre or the British Museum, where most archeology on display was unearthed in other countries (including the Holy Land). The exhibits, laid out in chronological order, are described clearly in Hebrew and English. Its official name is the Biblical and Archeological Museum. Take special note of exhibits which are marked as *News in Antiquities*; from recent discoveries in Israel.

The first hall is devoted to **prehistory**, and its findings are not unique to Palestine. The exhibits include prehistoric human remains, tools of flint and clay, a wall mask and a hand-sculpted skull from the seventh millennium BC, and Neolithic fertility idols. From the Chalcolithic period (fourth millennium BC) there are several exhibits worth noting: a woman with a churn and a man with cornets, in clay, and statuettes in a style named after the 'Ivories of Beersheva', in ivory. To the right is a collection of clay ossuaries engraved with human features. Follow the corridor to the right, to a spectacular find of the Chalcolithic period — the treasures found in a cave in the Mishmar wadi in the Judea Desert: 429 artifacts, which were wrapped in a straw mat. A few of them are made of ivory or stone; most though, are copper — clubheads, slender staffs, ritual masts, crowns and other objects. These implements attest to a high level of coppersmithing skill. The straw mat itself is here, as are certain organic findings — grainstalks, grains, seeds, etc. These attest to the astounding preservation which the special

Judea Desert climate affords. Another Chalcolithic-era exhibit is the largest flint tool discovered in the Near East, (30 inches long) which was unearthed in the northwestern Negev.

The next hall takes us into the **Early Bronze Age** (3150-2200 BC), and to the **Middle Bronze Age** (2200-1500 BC). The Middle Bronze Age commences the Biblical period (the time of the Patriarchs). The Bronze Age corresponds to the Canaanite period. Observe the fish-like implements, the gold treasure from Gezer, (a very rare find) and a stone mould which was used for casting figurines of the fertility goddess Astarte. From the **Late Bronze Age** (1500-1200 BC), the reconstructed Shrine of the Stelae from Hazor deserves special mention: it is conspicuous in its design of black stones on sand. On the middle pillar a pair of hands can be seen which reach for the crescent and wheel above. Other interesting findings are the anthropoid clay sarcophagi from the 13th century BC discovered in the Gaza area, which reflect Egyptian influence.

The **Israelite Period** (corresponding to the Iron Age) — from the initial Israelite settlements to the destruction of the First Temple — is represented in the following halls. First seen is a large group of ritual artifacts from the 11th-10th centuries BC. In a black display case on the right-hand wall is an especially important exhibit: a collection of 'Samarian ivories' unearthed in the Samaria (Sebastia) excavations. They depict gods, animals and plants in Oriental and Egyptian style. The ivory carvings were embedded in the wooden furniture in the palaces of Samaria when Kings Ahab and Jeroboam II ruled (9th-8th centuries BC). They may also be associated with the 'ivory house' mentioned in I Kings and the prophecy of Amos with regard to these kings. Ivory art was a Phoenician skill 'imported' from Tyre, possibly under the influence of Isabel, daughter of the Phoenician king of Tyre, who married King Ahab of Israel.

Still in the **Period of Kings**, we find a reconstruction of a fortress gate from Ahab's time (9th century BC) discovered in Hazor. Note nearby the column capitals of the proto-Acolic (or proto-Ionic) type which preceded the classical Ionic capital. In the next hall, to the left, is a reconstruction of the Holy of Holies in a temple from the Kings' Period discovered in Arad, displayed with various items from its interior. Several exhibits are devoted to Sennacherib of Assyria's march of conquest in 701 BC. One wall bears a replica of a relief from his palace in Nineveh, depicting the Assyrian siege on the Judean town of Lachish. A particularly interesting find is an Assyrian prism from the time of Sennacherib. The cuneiform inscription, dated 691 BC, describes his campaign. The siege of Jerusalem is described thus: *'I shut him up like a bird in a cage.'* His account tallies with that in the Scriptures, according to which Sennacherib, after having taken many cities in Judah, beseiged Jerusalem but failed to take it. The left side of the hall has a display of signet rings unearthed in excavations in the City of David in Jerusalem.

The rooms beyond the staircase are devoted to the **Second Temple Period** (6th century BC-70 AD), and to writing and inscriptions. Among the inscriptions displayed here, is one in Aramaic concerning King Uzziah's reinterment: *'Hither were brought the bones of Uzziah King of Judah; do not open.'*

An inscription from the Second Temple, found in the Temple Mount excavations, is inscribed: 'Place of Trumpeting'. This apparently comes from a tower at one corner of the Temple Mount, from which the *shofar* (ram's horn) was sounded at the beginning and end of the Sabbath. Another room to the left houses a display which charts the development of writing. Here one can see signet rings, some belonging to Biblical figures — such as Barukh ben-Nerya the Scribe, a confidant of the Prophet Jeremiah; ostraca (documents inscribed on clay slabs); papyrus missives and more. The collection includes replicas (the originals are located elsewhere) of famous inscriptions from the Biblical period such as the detailed account found in Hezekiah's tunnel describing its construction (an event familiar to us from the Bible); The Mesha Stele (Slab), on which the King of Moab describes his victory over the Kings of Israel (completing the Biblical account) and the Gezer calendar — a 10th century BC listing of the months and the agricultural cycle.

Exhibits from the Second Temple period in this wing include a collection of ossuaries, the permanent resting places of the bones of people who had initially been buried elsewhere. One of these, labeled 'Simon, Builder of the Sanctuary', evidently commemorates a builder or benefactor involved in construction of the Temple. Part of the hall is reserved for findings from the affluent Herodian residential neighborhood unearthed in the Jewish Quarter excavations. These include mosaic flooring, stone implements and one-legged tables. An especially important find is an engraving of a seven-branched *menora* (candelabrum) from the mid-1st century BC. This object of Jewish ritual, which subsequently became a Jewish symbol, is portrayed in several instances. The best-known is in a relief in the Arch of Titus in Rome, which depicts the booty the Romans hauled out of Jerusalem after conquering the city. At the end of the hall is an inscription from Caesarea which mentions Roman Procurator Pontius Pilate, known from the account of Jesus' crucifixion.

In the next room, there are findings from the **Roman Period**. The most conspicuous find here is a statue of Hadrian, the only surviving bronze likeness of this Emperor and a work of exceptional artistic quality. The next hall houses **Byzantine** artifacts. Do not miss the mosaic floor on the wall to the left, taken from a synagogue in Beit She'an; it depicts the Holy Ark and Jewish ritual objects (including *menoras*). Other items on display here include lead coffins, and an inscription discovered in the Jewish Quarter of Jerusalem describing the construction of the Nea Church by Emperor Justinian. Farther on is a collection of oil lamps, mostly of clay. From here, a corridor takes us past several displays of more recent vintage to an archeological collection of exhibits from Israel's neighbors.

We return to the center of the museum (the hall with the temporary exhibits, situated under the steps leading from the entrance hall). In the second wing of the museum is the Jewish Art and Ethnography exhibit. To reach it, walk through the glass pavilion which links the Roman Hall with the room devoted to the Time of the Patriarchs. There is also an exhibit of glass artifacts dating from the mid-second millennium BC to our time.

Jewish Art and Ethnography, divided into two wings; The New William Margulies Galleries and Sala wing for Israel Communities. In the entrance of this wing are two Jewish items of similar form but different function: a seven-branched stone *menora* from the synagogue at the Tiberias Hot Springs of Roman times (the *menora* had originally been part of the Temple rite), and an eight-branched *Hanukka menora* from 18th century Poland, used during the eight day 'Festival of Lights' which falls roughly in mid-December.

In the first room is a display of **ceremonial objects**. To the left are Torah scrolls and various Torah ornaments: finger-shaped pointers used by Torah readers, the headpieces (Heb. *rimmonim*, or pomegranates) which embellish the scrolls' protruding wooden supports, and cloth Torah covers. The collection includes items of this nature from various periods and communities throughout the Jewish Diaspora. Differences may be discerned between the mantle-like Torah covers used in the Jewish communities of Central Europe and the cylindrical wooden Torah cases favored by Oriental or Sephardi Jews. A 16-panel door from Fustat (ancient Cairo), built into the wall opposite the entrance, once belonged to the Ibn-Ezra Synagogue which Maimonides frequented.

We now proceed to the **Sabbath section** of the exhibit, devoted to various implements which serve Jews on their holy day. These include Sabbath candelabra, *kiddush* (Sabbath sanctification) goblets, and items used during *havdala* (the ceremony marking

The Monastery of the Cross

the end of the Sabbath and the return to the working week). Especially interesting among these are the spice containers or 'spice towers' on display to the right. The prevalence of the tapering 'tower' shape may reflect the fact that spices were often locked up in city towers due to their high value.

Continue to the **Jewish Holidays room**. On the left are *shofars* (ram's horns) which are used on *Rosh Hashana*, the Jewish New Year, which falls in early autumn. Beside them are four Torah ark curtains. There is also a large collection of *Hanukka menoras* from all over the world, dating from the medieval period to the present. They are made of various materials and reflect diverse styles. The next exhibit is a collection of illustrated manuscripts. There are specimens of the *ketuba*, the Jewish marriage contract which a groom hands his bride just before the nuptials (its provisions ensure her a secure future if the marriage fails). Here too, are volumes of the Pentateuch and the *haggada* (the Passover story recited during the *seder* feast), the *Scroll of Esther* (read on Purim) and other texts. Especially worth noting are the *'Birds' Head' Haggada* from the 14th century, so called because the people depicted in it are given heads of birds; the *De Castro Pentateuch*, also from the 14th century; and the *Rothschild Manuscript*. *Seder* plates too, are on display here.

A small collection of **Muslim art** is located further down and to the left. Jerusalem has a separate museum devoted to Islamic art (see Museum of Islam)

Be careful here so as not to miss the right turn to the museum's two reconstructed synagogues. On your right is the **Vittorio Venetto Synagogue** from that community in northern Italy dating from 1701. It is built in the customary Italian and Oriental Jewish manner with the congregation seated around a raised readers' platform toward the rear. To the left is an **18th century wooden synagogue from Horb, Germany** (near Bamberg). Its lovely wooden ceiling has been preserved; note the barrel vault and its embellished figures of animals (real and mythical) and plants. The synagogue's walls have not survived. Note 'Elijah's Chair', used during the *brit mila* ceremony — the circumcision of Jewish boys at the age of eight days.

We now reach the museum wing devoted to **Jewish Community and Ethnography**. Exhibits here include reconstructions of the dress, implements and residential rooms of various Oriental and Occidental Jewish communities. The sequence of displays depicts the Jewish life cycle and the attire and accessories required at each stage: birth, circumcision, childhood, schooling, *bar mitzva* (roughly corresponding to confirmation, when a 13 year old boy must undertake to observe the commandments), engagement and marriage, *henna* (a rite associated with marriage in certain communities), immersion (an essential ritual for married women), dowries, death and bereavement. Another room is reserved for distinctive Jewish clothing and its religious significance. Examples are head coverings, (*kipa*), *tzitzit* — (the Torah ordained fringes which Jewish men attach to their prayer shawls) and/or special vests worn throughout the day.

We now approach the wing devoted to **19th and 20th century art**. Its exhibits include works by Vincent van Gogh, Paul Cezanne, Maurice Utrillo, Pierre August Renoir and Claude Monet of the 19th century, and Oskar Kokoschka, Paul Klee, Pablo Picasso, Rene Magritte and Salvador Dali of the 20th. Another new wing exhibits ethnic art.

Nearby sites of interest

A new *Museum for Biblical Lands* is being completed adjacent to the Israel Museum and is due to open in recent future.

Further planning is to transform the whole area into a 'City of Museums', including a Natural History Museum etc.

Below the hill of the Israel Museum, in the valley is the **Monastery of the Cross** (open Tues.-Sat. 9am-4pm) which you can reach by taking the path between the olive trees, to the right of the museum exit. Here, according to tradition, the wood for Jesus' cross was taken. Though the fortress-like monastery (recall that until about 100 years ago this valley was a no-man's-land, far from town!) belongs to the Greek Orthodox Church today. It was a Georgian monastery until the 17th century. Here, Shota Rustaveli, the Georgian national poet, resided and wrote his masterpiece *Clad in Tiger's Skin* .

The Knesset

The Knesset building, home of Israel's Parliament, stands atop the hill across the road from the Israel Museum. It is open Sun. and Thurs. 8:30am-2:30pm, with guided tours by Knesset personnel. Bring your passport or ID and check bags and cameras at the entrance. Visitors may also observe public Knesset sessions.

The Knesset comprising 120 elected members, is the legislative body of Israel. The executive body is the Cabinet or Government which is chosen by a coalition of parties which, together, have won a majority in the Knesset. In recent years, the two major parties have been the Labor Alignment, representing Israel's left, and the Likud, the principal party of the right. Though the Cabinet tries to operate as autonomously as it can, the real source of power in Israeli politics is the Knesset.

The monumental structure, with its facing of reddish Jerusalem stone, is built largely in a neoclassical style — a choice regarded by many as in poor taste for a Jewish parliament building. From 1949 until 1966, when the building, funded by the Rothschild family, was dedicated, the Knesset met in today's Tourist Ministry (and Government Tourist Information Office) building on King George St. The present Knesset building and its court are graced with various *objets d'art*. Included in the reception area are three tapestries and a mosaic by Jewish-French artist Marc Chagall. Opposite the entrance stands a *menora* (candelabra) by Benno Elkan whose base and branches depict various events in Jewish history. West of the *menora* is a large garden with a mosaic from the Byzantine period which was transferred here from northern Israel. The buildings across the way, comprise the **David Ben-Gurion Government Center** (Heb. *Hakirya*).

Other sites of interest

If the Knesset and the Israel Museum are considered as two points of a triangle, the third is the hill to the west known as **Giv'at Ram**. Here is one of the **Hebrew University's** two campuses. It began serving the University after 1948 when the original Mt. Scopus campus, established in the 1920s, was cut off from Israeli Jerusalem. University activity returned to Mt. Scopus with the unification of the city. The Giv'at Ram campus primarily houses

The Knesset — Israel's Parliament

the **Natural Sciences Departments** and is home to the **National and University Library**. It is the largest library in the Middle East, boasting more than two million volumes. It houses an especially extensive collection of works on topics related to Judaism and the Land of Israel, including extremely rare books. On the second floor of the Library is one of Jerusalem's two famous **stained glass works** (the other being the Chagall windows at Hadassah Hospital). Created by Mordechai Ardon the windows portray the Prophet Isaiah's vision of the End of Days. Its left side depicts paths crowded with pilgrims streaming to Jerusalem, accompanied by an excerpt written in various languages from Isaiah 2:3: '*...Come ye, and let us go up to the mountain of the Lord...*'. The center depicts Jerusalem, with the wall designed according to a description found in the *Scroll of Isaiah*, one of the Dead-Sea scrolls. At the right side is the fulfilment of the vision in Isaiah 2:4 '*...And they shall beat their swords into plowshares, and their spears into pruning hooks; Nation shall not lift up sword against nation, Neither shall they learn war any more*'. (Open Sun—Wed. 9am—7pm, Thurs. 9am—3pm, Fri. 9am—12pm).

From here, we are but a short hop from the Talbiyeh and Rehavia neighborhoods.

Talbiyeh and Rehavia neighborhoods are considered among Jerusalem's most prestigious, although their population is not neccessarily wealthy. Talbiyeh, originally built by affluent

The Menora — seven-branched candlestick

Christian Arabs, is known today for its exceptional buildings. Rehavia, with its high-quality housing, was established in the 1920s by Jewish intellectuals.

A hill in the center of **Talbiyeh** (buses 15, 15a, 99) is home to several public institutions. The most important of these is the **residence of the President of Israel**, just off Hanassi St. (Hebrew: President). Its interior is a showcase of Israeli art. The position of President, who is elected by the Knesset for one five-year term (extendable only once), is largely ceremonial. Nearby are the **National Academy for the Sciences** and the impressive structure which houses the **Jerusalem Center for Stage Arts** (the Jerusalem Theater). Further along the street (Chopin St.) is *Jan's Tea House*, a nice place to rest for a while.

If you turn left from the President's Residence and follow the street as it takes an S-curve, you reach the **L.A. Mayer Museum of Islamic Art** at 2 Palmach St. Open Sun.-Thurs. 10am-1pm, 3:30-6pm; Sat. 10am-noon. Closed Fri. The Museum houses a collection of 5000 *objets d'art* from Islamic countries, demonstrating associations between these countries and Europe in matters of art. On display are a generous selection of Muslim ceramics; a lovely collection of glass and metal objects, incense containers, jewelry, fine ornaments, a collection of medieval chessmen and pieces of other games, Turkish silhouette pieces, Arabic calligraphy and *firmans* (government edicts) and so on. At one time the Museum also had a famous collection of rare ancient clocks, for which the institution earned some publicity when the most expensive and important specimens were stolen in a daring and still unsolved robbery a few years ago.

To compare Talbiyeh's buildings with Rehavia's, exit the Museum of Islamic Art, turn left twice and walk straight as far as Gaza Rd. (Derech Aza). Cross it, and you're in **Rehavia**. Apart from its houses and gardens, there is a small archeological site at 10 Alfasi St. It is the **Tomb of Jason**, a Hasmonean-era burial crypt. A reconstructed pyramid stands atop the tomb. A number of etchings and paintings were discovered on the interior walls, including a *menora*, ships, and an inscription mentioning a man named Jason. Also recommended is a visit to the *Tahana* (Windmill), a 19th century windmill which has been preserved by incorporating it into a new modern and exclusive shopping centre.

Western Heights — Yad Vashem and Other Sites

This tour covers several sites in the western section of New Jerusalem and its fringes. The sites are in fact unrelated, and are not even very close to one another. The major site in this Tour is the Holocaust Museum of Yad Vashem. The tour may be combined with a visit to the Second Temple Jerusalem model at the Holyland Hotel (see 'Ancient Jerusalem at its Peak — A Model').

Yad Vashem

Bus 99 goes to Yad Vashem, and the following buses stop on the main road at Mount Herzl, five minutes away by foot: 13, 17, 18, 20, 23, 24, 26 and 27. Open Sun.-Thurs. 9am-5pm, Fri. 9am-2pm. Admission free.

Yad Vashem, on Memorial Hill, is a government institute established by legislation in Israel for the purpose of studying and commemorating the Holocaust — the annihilation of six million Jews during World War II by the Nazis. The institution's name originates in an expression in Isaiah 26:5 which means 'an everlasting memorial'. Although a visit here is a harsh, unpleasurable experience it is a highly recommended one which should not be foregone. Yad Vashem is like no other museum: it stands as an everlasting memorial to one of history's most horrifying events — a Jewish national trauma, without which today's Jewish temperament cannot be understood.

Entering the museum we face the **Wall of Holocaust and Heroism**, created by sculptor Naftali Bezem. It is composed of four sections. The first on the left, symbolizes the Holocaust; the extermination of European Jewry. It depicts a factory with incinerator ovens, under which is a Jewish woman using Sabbath candles to burn her breasts. To her right is a butchered fish, symbolizing silent sacrifice. The second section depicts heroic resistance to the Nazi oppressor — houses in flames, hands clutching weapons, and a ladder, a symbol of hope. The third section portrays a boat being brought ashore on an angel's wing, a symbol of the Jews' return to the Land of Israel. The last section depicts a lion who confronts the memory of the Holocaust. Above the lion is a flourishing *sabra* — Hebrew for prickly pear, and a nickname for native Israelis. There are also Sabbath candles, turned upward and lit, unlike those on the left-hand side of the sculpture.

Another two sculptures outside the building are works of Nathan Rapaport, himself a Holocaust survivor. To the right: the last march to annihilation; to the left: the ghetto rebellion. Note the juxtaposition of the stooped Jews being led to the camps and the proud posture of those in the ghetto insurrection. Also note that the Nazis are faceless — nothing more than steel helmets and bayonets.

In the museum itself is a permanent documentary exhibition entitled **For a Sign and a Testimony**, which records the Holocaust in chronological sequence. By means of photographs, documents, newspaper clippings and pamphlets together with commentary, it charts the Nazis' rise to power in Germany, their prewar and wartime assaults on the Jews, the annihilation of European Jewry, the extermination campaign and the concentration camps, the Jewish rebellions — and the rescue operations. No visitor can walk away unmoved.

The **Tent of Rememberance**, a tent-shaped concrete structure on a base of basalt, commemorates the annihilated Jewish communities. The names of 22 Nazi extermination camps are engraved here and the ashes of victims are buried in the ground. Memorial candles are lit every day at 11am. The names of more than two million of the six million victims are recorded in a special **Room of Names**. The others are absent because many communities were destroyed to the last individual, together with their records, and have been wholly obliterated from history. Special ceremonies are held in Yad Vashem on Israel's annual Holocaust Remembrance Day.

Outside is the spacious **Janusz Korczak Park**, named for the Polish educator who willingly went to his death in a concentration camp together with the children under his care rather than abandon them. The **Pillar of Heroism** (65 ft. high) looms overhead, visible for miles around. Behind it is the Garden of Children who perished in the Holocaust and the Memorial for one and a half million children who perished. The site is built as a gloomy cave with thousands of lights glinting in the darkness. In the background a voice tells the names, birthplace and dying place of the children. Note the **Avenue of Righteous Gentiles** which leads to the museum. Its rows of trees were planted in honor of those non-Jews who endangered their lives in attempt to save Jews during the Nazi years. A sign beside each tree bears the name of the Righteous Gentile whom it commemorates.

Yad Vashem is also a documentation and research institute.

Yad Vashem — Janusz Korczak and his children

Its **Central Archives for Holocaust Studies** contain documents, personal accounts, anti-semitic material related to the Holocaust, and an extensive library. Material collected here has served as a basis for evidence against Nazi criminals, including Adolf Eichmann, who was tried in Jerusalem in 1961. Yad Vashem publishes studies and books, holds workshops and seminars, and instructs schoolchildren in Holocaust history.

Other sites of interest

As you leave Yad Vashem, look right when you reach the hilltop. There you'll see a conspicuous, massive red sculpture entitled **Homage to Jerusalem**. It was created by sculptor Alexander Calder, inventor of the mobile, who calls a work of this type a 'stabile'.

Now follow the road to the summit of **Mount Herzl**, named for Theodor (Benjamin Ze'ev) Herzl, the 'prophet of the Jewish state'. Herzl was among the first to actively advocate Jewish national independence — establishing political Zionism. In 1896, he published a pamphlet entitled *Der Judenstaat*, (*The Jewish State*) the blueprint for subsequent Zionist thought. In 1897 he convened the First Zionist Congress in Basel, Switzerland, as the first international conference of Jews on a national, non-religious basis. Herzl died in 1904, and on August 17, 1949 (shortly after the State of Israel was born) his remains were reinterred here.

The Herzl Museum on Mt. Herzl (open Sun.-Thurs. 9am-4:45pm, Fri. 9am-1pm) has a collection of Herzl's photographs, books and personal artifacts. Near Herzl's tomb and the museum is a national cemetery, where both pre-State and Israeli leaders (e.g., Presidents Izhak Ben-Zvi and Zalman Shazar, and Prime Ministers Levi Eshkol and Golda Meir) are buried. A separate section of the mount is set aside as a military cemetery, including monuments to Unknown Soldiers.

From Mt. Herzl, a side road snakes down to **Ein Kerem** (buses 17, 17a). In a valley between the mountains is a picturesque village, surrounded by greenery, whose special rural character has been kept despite the encroaching city. Though Ein Kerem has few sites of particular importance, it is a most pleasurable place for a stroll. The original Arab village was abandoned in 1948, and has evolved into a Jewish residential neighborhood with a considerable influx of artists. While Ein Kerem holds no special importance in Jewish tradition (though it does appear in the Old Testament), it is significant as the birthplace of John the Baptist. This accounts for the monasteries and churches built here during the Byzantine period and thereafter.

Foremost of Ein Kerem's churches (situated near the road from Mt. Herzl) is the **Church of St. John the Baptist**. Open weekdays 8am-noon, 2:30-5pm; summer 2:30-6pm; Sun. 9am-noon, 2:30-4pm; daily Mass 7:15am. According to tradition, St. John was born in a cave which may be reached by going down the stairs on the left aisle of the church. Although the building has been held since 1674 by the Franciscans, the first church structures here were from Byzantine and Crusader periods, and remains can still be seen. Sections of the stylized mosaic floor of the Byzantine church were discovered in the northern chapel. The design includes birds, flowers and an inscription in Greek: *'Hail Martyrs of God'*.

From the Church of St. John, we walk downhill to the center of the village, cross the road and continue straight to the spring which bubbles from a cave and surfaces beside an abandoned mosque. It is known as the **Spring of the Virgin** because of its association with Mary, mother of Jesus, who reportedly drank of its waters. A path to the right of the spring leads to **Visitatio Maria** (Church of the Visitation). Open 9am-noon, 2:30-5pm; summer 3-6pm. It marks the site where Zecharias and Elizabeth, parents of John the Baptist, had their home. According to Luke I, Mary stayed with Elizabeth, a relative, for three months after the Angel Gabriel gave the Annunciation of the future birth of Jesus. The new church, designed by Italian architect Barluzzi, was built in 1955.

Nearby, on the rise to the left of the spring, is the **Russian Church** (or the 'Muscovites', as the Arabs call them). The Russian Convent, with its conspicuous red turret, is named 'Mar Zechariah' for John the Baptist's father and is staffed by Pravoslav nuns. The site is usually closed, unless one of the nuns is favorably disposed and agrees to open it. On the hill is a large church whose construction came to a halt at the start of the Russian Revolution, and has not been resumed.

Another convent, on a hill to the left of the path which leads from the spring back to the main road, belongs to the **Soeurs de Sion** (Sisters of Zion) and was established by Alphonse Ratisbonne, a French Jew who became a Christian. You may recall Ratisbonne, who is entombed in the convent court, from the Soeurs de Sion monastery on Via Dolorosa.

We return to Mt. Herzl and turn right at the main street, to the **Hadassah Hospital** and the famous **Chagall windows** (bus lines 19 and 27; signs lead from their last stop to a tourist center). On the way, note to your left a huge playground sculpture — a three tongued monster by Niki de Saint Phalle; each tongue is used as a slide for children. From there, the road continues down

Ein Kerem — The Church of St. John the Baptist

a mountain ridge, through lovely scenery and a beautiful view of Ein Karem, to Hadassah.

The original Hadassah Hospital was built on Mt. Scopus but was evacuated after the War of Independence, when Mt. Scopus became an Israeli enclave in Jordanian territory. Until 1961, when this medical center was dedicated, the hospital's departments were scattered in various buildings around town. Since the renovated Mt. Scopus facility reopened after the Six Day War, the hospital we are about to see has become **Hadassah Ein Kerem**. Our interest here, again, is to view the 12 stained glass windows created by Marc Chagall for the hospital's synagogue. Open Sun.-Thurs. 8am-3:45pm, Fri. 8:30am-12:30pm; guided tours until 12:30. Chagall used Jacob's succinct blessings of his twelve sons in Genesis 49 to create emblematic compositions; thus, for example, Jacob's description of Reuven (Genesis: 49:4) as "*unstable as water*" led the artist to incorporate fish into his own rendering.

A sign-posted road which turns left on the way to Hadassah Hospital leads to the **Kennedy Memorial** (about two miles away). Built in 1966 in memory of John F. Kennedy, the monument is in the form of a felled tree trunk — a symbol of Kenedy's life which was cut off in its prime. The site of the monument is pleasant, and the view of Jerusalem and Hebron is beautiful.

Ancient Jerusalem at its Peak — A Model

To reach this area in Bayit Vegan, at the end of Uzi'el St., take bus 21, 21A or 99. Open daily, 8am-4pm.

This model of Jerusalem, as it appeared at the end of the Second Temple period, presents a unique tangible picture of Jerusalem at the peak of its history. It was during this period, nearly 2,000 years ago, that Jerusalem attained an unsurpassed level of development and status in both the Holy Land and the Jewish world altogether. The model represents Jerusalem of 66 AD, just prior to Roman destruction. Its cityscape is dominated by the Herod's unequalled public works — particularly the Temple. Herod's Jerusalem was also that of Jesus. This is how it looked when Jesus reached the Mount of Olives, beheld the city's beauty and lamented its impending destruction.

The model is built on a scale of 1:50. To imagine this better, an average person reduced to the model's size would be about two inc. tall; a structure one ft. high in the model actually soared to a height of 50 ft. The landscape surrounding Jerusalem, however, is not portrayed in precise scale. If it were, deep and precipitous wadis to the "city's" east and west would have surrounded the model, blocking the view of the city. The model's orientation, though, is accurate; north is true north. Its building materials, too, are as 'real' as can be.

Credit for the model's design and construction belongs to the late Professor of Archeology Michael Avi Yonah. His sources were in part written — the Mishna, the Talmud, and the detailed accounts of Josephus and other historians, and in part archeological, digs and findings. Equivalent Roman examples from the same period, elsewhere in Palestine, and the Roman world made reconstruction of several of the structures possible.

Construction of the model was completed in 1969. At this time, the extensive excavations in the Old City (which became possible after the Six Day War) were barely underway. In this light, Prof. Avi Yonah's genius should be appreciated all the more, for the ancient city was correctly recreated without this vital information, though it now serves as a basis for periodic modifications. The model also incorporates structures whose exact locations were not known but whose existence is important for understanding the nature of the city.

The model is described in a counterclockwise direction. We begin near the three towers which protrude from an area approximating that of today's Jaffa Gate, the Jerusalem Citadel and David's Tower. The wall is actually bordering the slopes of the Valley of Hinnom which does not appear in the model. From here it is easy to see that Jerusalem had two important centers: one spiritual/religious — the Temple Mount — and the other governmental — the hill with the three towers and **Herod's palace**. The latter is the long building to the right of the towers (note the magnificent courtyard and pillars). Few remains of the palace have been discovered at this site and reconstruction is based on an equivalent structure in Jericho. Since the gentle topography of Jerusalem's north made this direction 'the city's soft underbelly', Herod had special fortifications built in this direction. North (left) of the Temple Mount and protecting it is the **Citadel of Antonia** (identifiable by its four square towers). To the north of Herod's palace are the three towers which were probably among Jerusalem's most impressive buildings at the time. The square **Phasael Tower** (named for Herod's brother) is five feet high in the model, corresponding to 250ft — or a 25-story skyscraper. Its design imitates that of Alexandria's Lighthouse, one of the Seven Wonders of the Ancient World. The other two towers bear the names of **Hippicus** (a commanding officer in Herod's army) and **Miriamne**, Herod's wife, whom he had murdered in one of his fits of jealousy... Though the model depicts them in a triangular array, they apparently stood beside one another in a single row, forming Jerusalem's strongest fortification. So formidable were they that the Jewish rebels who hid here during the insurrection against Rome held out for a whole month after the Temple Mount had been stormed and burned.

From the towers, the city wall sets out southward (to the right) encircling the city. Three walls - the First, Second and Third by Josephus' account — defended northern Jerusalem. The **First Wall** leads from the towers directly to the Temple Mount; the **Second** turns left inside the city, and the **Third** encircles the city at its extremity. All this was necessary because northern Jerusalem's gentle hills, though they allowed the city easy expansion, were devoid of natural defences. The precise route of the **Second Wall** is disputed, with the authenticity of Golgotha (Calvary) as site of Jesus' crucifixion in question. Since Jesus was crucified and interred outside city limits, as defined by the Second Wall, the question is where the wall ran relative to Golgotha. The model places Golgotha outside the wall, lending credence to the doctrine of Catholic and Eastern Churches. Again, though, there are other opinions. The remote **Third Wall**, in any event, was completed in 66 AD, just before the Jewish rebellion against Rome.

Now look for a red arrow on the right side of the **western wall of the Temple Mount**, facing us. It marks the Western Wall of today, which is but a short section of a Second Temple retaining wall which reached a length of about a quarter of a mile.

The slope descending from the three towers to the Temple Mount is known as the **Western Hill** or the **Upper City**. Here the affluent people of Jerusalem lived, priests, those of the Royal Court and so on. Note the large, spacious houses with interior courtyards which Prof. Avi Yonah reconstructed from examples found on the Greek island of Delos. When he produced several houses with floor space in excess of 400 square feet, many thought he had exaggerated. Subsequent excavations in the Jewish Quarter however, revealed homes of even greater dimensions. One noteworthy building is the semicircular **Roman Theater** located on the Western Hill. Although its precise location is not known, its very presence in the Jewish holy city, as an imported typical Roman institution is both important and interesting. Its existence, described in written sources, was verified when 'season tickets' of bone, including row and seat numbers, were found in the excavations. Walk downhill (i.e., south) and note a building with a pyramidal roof to the left. It marks the **Tomb of David**, whose location was apparently known in Second Temple Jerusalem, but is not today.

At the very edge and lowest extremity of town, we find the **King's Garden** at the confluence of the three streams which shaped the layout of ancient Jerusalem. One branch is known as the **Valley of Hinnom** (Hebrew: *Gai Ben-Hinnom*), the second is the Tyropoeon which bisects the city into two ridges, and the third is **Brook of Kidron**. From the city's southernmost point a low hill rises toward the Temple Mount. Several structures conspicuous for their reddish hue and special style stand here. These are the **palaces of Helene, Queen of Adiabene**, who converted to Judaism together with her people in about 35 AD. The palaces, whose precise location is unknown, as well as a magnificent complex of tombs were built in the wake of her subsequent visit to Jerusalem. The hill on which these palaces stand is the **City of David**, where Jerusalem's development began. To its left, in the valley, is **Hezekiah's Pool**.

Before reaching the Temple Mount, study the hill to its west and note the three towers which punctuate it, where our tour began. Here we observe the homes of the wealthy of this area, in juxtaposition to the houses of the less affluent down the slope. The contrast, somewhat exaggerated in the model, aims

Ancient Jerusalem at its peak

to illustrate the social disparities and polarization which typified the period (and which may have served as a social backdrop for Jesus' teachings). It is no coincidence that when the revolt against the Romans began, the people at first attacked not the Romans, but the archives where their debts were recorded.

This angle affords a second look at the **theater** and a view of another typical Roman place of amusement — the **Hippodrome**, where horseraces took place on its clearly visible colonnaded oval track. Since no remains of the Hippodrome have been discovered, the reconstruction is based on a similar structure in Barcelona, Spain. Its location in the model, — south of the Temple Mount in an area bustling with traffic — does not reflect any real findings and appears wholly out of place. The designers' intent was to emphasize the fact that Roman influences such as the theater and the hippodrome had penentrated Jerusalem, the world Jewish center at the time.

We have reached the **Temple Mount** from the south, facing the City of David. This is its "front" facade. Calculating once again, we find that the facade here was about 170 ft. high! Note the two apertures in the southern wall. These are the **Hulda Gates**, through which worshippers entered the Temple Mount. Structures on the Mount were divided into two wings — the major one reserved for religious activity, the other set aside for secular affairs. The **Royal Stoa**, or the Basilica, which was the secular center, is the lengthy colonnaded structure atop the southern wall. This wing had its own entrance from the west, comprising a staircase and bridge borne by a massive structure known today as **Robinson's Arch**. The two wings were kept totally separate. Those seeking to enter the consecrated zone passed through the Hulda Gates and followed an underground passageway (which still exists today) to the Temple without coming into contact with the other wing. The Temple Mount entrance area and its surrounding plazas, which may be viewed today, are familiar to us from the archeological excavations.

Virtually nothing remains of the **Temple** and the other structures on the Mount; they were reconstructed here on the basis of copious written sources such as tractates of Mishna and Talmud devoted to the laws governing the Temple's use. The major surviving remnant is the **Temple Mount Podium - or plateau.** Herod's engineers created this totally flat area by raising four walls around the natural hill, filling in or covering up the spaces between the wall and the hill, and paving the resulting plateau with stone. The **Western Wall** is a section of one of these retaining walls.

The most impressive fact about the Temple Mount is the size of the Temple area. Including the adjacent plazas, it was the largest holy compound in the ancient world. Why did Herod consider this necessary? The answer lies essentially in the nature of Temple activity. Whereas other peoples worshipped their gods in various temples throughout the year, the Jews served one God in one Temple, and — in the sense of mass participation — pursued the major activity during the three 'pilgrimage festivals' — Succot, Shavuot and, in particular, Passover. On these occasions throngs of Jews from all over the country and from other parts of the world flocked to Jerusalem. It is estimated that the city's own population of 100,000 doubled during the Passover holiday. The vast plaza was necessary for the masses of guests and locals during the holy ceremonies. An additional reason was Herod's audacity. Here, as in many other building enterprises in Palestine, he felt obliged to invest tremendous energy and to overcome natural difficulties to produce works of tremendous dimensions.

Let's examine the **Temple** and its courts. The projections on the roof, according to Josephus, were meant to keep birds from landing there and dirtying the roof. Among the gates leading into the Temple, pay special attention to the conspicuous 'green gate'. It is known as **Nikanor's Gate**. Nikanor, according to a Talmudic legend, a wealthy merchant from Alexandria, decided to donate a pair of gates to the Temple. He built a set of copper portals, plated them with gold and silver, adorning them with embedded gems and loaded them onto a ship. A storm broke out en route to Palestine, and one of the gates was washed overboard. Reaching shore, Nikanor lamented the loss whereupon the sea, pitying him, coughed up the portal — but without its precious coating. The Gates of Nikanor were installed in this unembellished form to commemorate the miracle. So goes the legend. As for its veracity, a burial vault was found during excavations on Mt. Scopus with the inscription *Nikanor, Installer of the Sanctuary Gates.*

In the very heart of the Temple, behind two curtains, was the Holy of Holies. The bare chamber was accessible only to the High Priest, and only once a year on the Day of Atonement. Though unverified, its probable location was the rock at the center of today's Dome of the Rock.

The consecrated area of the Temple Mount was surrounded by a low fence equipped with signs prohibiting entry to non-Jews. Fragments of these signs have been found and one is on display in the Rockefeller Museum. Between the Temple proper and the Royal Stoa (to the left) are the openings of the tunnels leading from the Hulda Gates. The Stoa, a building no less impressive and dominating than the Temple, housed secular facilities including courts of law and the stands of the moneychangers. The latter were situated here because donations to the Temple Priests were payable in only one of the many currencies in use in the region, the strong and stable shekel of Tyre.

As we continue to circle the city, we find a prominent fortress to the north on the Temple Mount: the **Citadel of Antonia** where, according to tradition, Jesus' walk of afflictions began. The reconstruction here appears to be inaccurate as the Antonia Citadel had a single high tower rather than the four symmetrical towers shown here. By capturing the citadel in 70 AD, the Romans cleared the way for a march on the Temple and essentially secured their victory in Jerusalem. Note the pools north of the Temple Mount. The double pool is known as Bethesda (Heb. *Beit Hisda*) where Jesus reportedly healed the sick, the blind and the lame.

Second Temple Jerusalem, as we see, was much larger than today's Old City. This is especially evident in the northern part of town, where we complete our tour of the model. The northernmost point in today's Old City wall, the Damascus Gate, sits roughly where the gate in the Second Wall appears in the model. Past it is a vast area of scattered development which extends as far as today's Russian Compound. The circumferential wall encasing the entire city, as stated, was completed just before the Rebellion. In 70 AD the Romans crushed the rebellion and managed to almost completely destroy the unique and impressive city recreated in the model.

One Day Excursions

Though Jerusalem is Israel's heart and undoubtedly its richest site, Israel abounds in a fascinating amount of attractions for such a small country. The marvels of central Israel are easily reached in day trips from Jerusalem. We survey a few of these briefly, but add that they deserve further reading. They are arranged into five tours which can each be done comfortably in one day. While you are in the country, we also highly recommend a few longer tours in Israel — **Galilee** and the **Golan Heights** to the north (rich in interesting sites and beautiful hiking trails), the steep wadis of the **Judea Desert** to the east (visit only with someone who knows them!); **the Negev** to the south (an extraordinary desert whose landscapes include crater-like canyons), and **Eilat**, Israel's southernmost point, with its famous beach and some of the world's best scuba diving.

Tour One: Bethlehem, Solomon's Pools and Herodion

Bethlehem

Bethlehem, the birthplace of Jesus Christ, is about six miles south of Jerusalem. Today it is an Arab city, its population half Christian, half Muslim. Although King David was born here, the city never acquired any sanctity in Judaism. New Testament tradition places Jesus' birth in Bethlehem (though his family was based in Nazareth, in Galilee), establishing a certain parallel to David's birthplace and to Micah 5:1: '*...From Bethlehem one shall come forth unto Me that is to be ruler in Israel*' The birth of Jesus — celebrated as the most important holiday in Christianity (Christmas) — turned Bethlehem into one of the holiest sites in the Christian faith.

The major site in Bethlehem is the **Church of the Nativity**. It was first built by Constantine the Great over a cave where, according to tradition, Jesus was born. Before Constantine, pagan rites had been practiced here. Constantine's edifice was destroyed in the sixth century, whereupon Justinian built a new church which, in general lines, survives to this day. During the Crusader period (12th century) the building was revitalized, elevated to cathedral rank, and used for the coronation of the kings of Crusader Jerusalem. Under Muslim rule the church was neglected, plundered and partially demolished.

The holiest site in the complex is the cave where Jesus was born. It is marked with the Star of the Nativity. Above it is a mosaic-embellished 12th century altar. The manger itself (where Jesus was born) is downstairs; opposite it is a chapel dedicated to the Three Wise Men. Most of the other mosaics and ornamentation around the Church are of Crusader vintage and a few are Byzantine.

Another Bethlehem site worth noting is the **Milk Grotto** over which a Church was built. Tradition attributes its whitish coloration to a drop of Mary's milk which fell to the floor. Nearby too, (on the main road into town) is **Rachel's Tomb**. Though its authenticity is disputed, it is a popular attraction for pilgrims.

Solomon's Pools

South of Bethlehem, a few minutes by car on the road to Hebron, are Solomon's Pools, part of the system which provided Jerusalem with water from sources to the south. The complex includes three vast pools, one below the other, fed by two aqueducts from the Hebron hills. Two aqueducts — the 'lower' and the 'upper' — set out from here northwards for Jerusalem. This impressive engineering feat originated during the Second Temple period. The name 'Solomon's Pools' is a later invention with no historical association.

The present condition of the pools reflects extensive renovations during the British Mandate period. The structure alongside is an abandoned Turkish fortress built to defend them. While the aqueducts are no longer in service, the pools do fill up in part and, together with the surrounding foliage, combine into an especially impressive sight in the otherwise barren mountain landscape.

From here one may continue south to Hebron, or enjoy a highly recommended side trip down a narrow road to **Artas**, a picturesque village with an early 20th century monastery overlooking a lovely cultivated valley.

Herodion

Southeast of Bethlehem is another interesting site — **Herodion**, or Herod's mountain. Its unmistakable volcano-like cone comes into view from the main highway. Herodion is a complex of palaces, fortifications and other structures built by Herod in 25-15 BC. Herod himself, according to Josephus, is buried here.

The road approaches the mountaintop, and the last stretch

is an easily negotiated footpath. Upon closer observation, the whole mountain proves to be semi-artificial. After finishing their work, the builders threw the excavated earth down the mountainside and created a hollowed-out cone. The fortress and palace complex is encased in two impressive peripheral walls punctuated by four towers. Inside this mantle is Herod's palace, including a magnificent Roman bath. Here, as in Massada, the Herodian structures served Jews in their rebellion against Rome (66-73 AD). They turned the palace hall into a synagogue (one of the earliest known) which may be viewed today. The mountaintop affords a lovely view. Inside the hill there is a labyrinthine system of tunnels utilized by Bar-Kokhba forces during his rebellion of 132-135 AD. They have recently opened to visitors. Extensive archeological digs continue below the mountain (we may speculate about finding Herod's grave here). In this area, there is a massive pool with a round structure and several columns in its center. This was once a building which people would swim to or paddle boats around.

Tour Two: Sorek Cave, Scrolls of Fire, Beit Guvrin

The Sorek Cave

A 45 minute drive to the west of Jerusalem takes you to a handsome, multi-colored stalactite cavern — the Sorek Cave, or Absalom's Cave. One way of reaching it is from Ein Karem at the edge of Jerusalem, along a beautiful scenic route down the Brook of Sorek. The road crosses the railroad, climbs to the settlement of Nes Harim and descends to the cave (the way is marked). The cave may also be reached from the town of Beit Shemesh to the south. The cave, discovered quite by chance during a quarrying operation in 1968, is a small stalactite cave which is distinctive for its exceptional variety of features. The authorities went to great lengths in preparing it for public access while leaving its natural treasures unharmed. Open daily 8:30am-3:45pm; Fri. and holiday eve until 12:45pm. Photography permitted Fri. only; the visit consists of a 45 minute guided tour, including a film show. There is an admission charge.

The Scroll of Fire

Another worthwhile visit on the way back to Jerusalem is the Scroll of Fire. To reach this monument, travel a little north of Beit-Shemesh and turn right (east) on a road which reaches Jerusalem via Kesalon and Ramat Raziel. The site (marked) is next to Kesalon. The impressive monument, produced by sculptor Nathan Rapaport, depicts Jewish history in the form of two scrolls of stone — 30ft in height. One scroll is dedicated to the Holocaust and resistance; the second symbolizes the Jewish national rebirth in its homeland. From here, enjoy the excellent view of the western Jerusalem hills.

Beit Guvrin Caves and Tel Maresha

This is a good point to begin a somewhat adventurous, off-the-beaten-track tour, custom-made for cave and mystery lovers. Twelve miles south of Beit Shemesh is the **Beit Guvrin** area, renowned for its hundreds of caves of various types. Most were hewn by man into soft stone for reasons mostly unknown to us. Some have been equipped for visitors, many of the caves, however, are difficult and even dangerous to visit.

To reach the most accessible ones, take the first left after Kibbutz Beit Guvrin (note the ruins of a handsome Crusader church along the road). When you reach a fork in the road, a left turn brings you to a large cluster of interconnected **'bell' caves** (narrow roof openings, broad interiors) which may be explored. Some claim that these caves were lime quarries from which construction materials were extracted.

Nearby is **Maresha hill** with a system of unusual caves at its base. Especially famous is the **Columbarium Cave** — a lovely hall with hundreds of niches cut out from the stone in a cave shaped like a double cross. The exact function of these niches is not known. They may have contained the ashes of the dead, or perhaps they were simply dovecotes. Further on is a burial crypt which houses the remains of Sidonian dignitaries from Maresha.

Tour Three: The Judea Desert

This tour combines a unique natural phenomenon — **the Dead Sea** - with one of the most famous locations in Jewish history — **Masada**. One immediate **warning**: it is an exceptionally hot area, particularly in the summer. Be sure to bring with you a head covering and an ample supply of water.

The Dead Sea

Geologically part of the Afro-Syrian Rift, the Dead Sea is the lowest point on earth. Still seismically active, the forces which shaped it are responsible for its depth and the steepness of the escarpments descending to it. Though the Dead Sea surface fluctuates in elevation according to its water level, the norm is about **1,200 ft. below sea level**. The Dead Sea holds another world record as well — 32% salinity (compared with 3% in the Mediterranean). It is known in Hebrew as "the Salt Sea" (Hebrew: *Yam Hamelach*). Its English name reflects the fact that virtually no animal life can cope with such a concentration of salt.

As the saltiest body of water on earth, the Dead Sea is extremely buoyant. Give it a try! Cooking salt, and other minerals are extracted from it, and its entire southern end is really one great artificial evaporation pond. The eastern shore belongs to Jordan.

Interesting sites on the western (Israeli) side include **Ein Fesh'ha** and **Ein Gedi**, freshwater springs spilling into the Dead Sea (wonderful for bathing), the salt formation known as the **Mountain of Sodom** (with interesting caves and other phenomena) and of course, **Qumran**.

Qumran

The Qumran Ruins became world-famous when the **Dead Sea Scrolls** were found here by Bedouins. Dating from the Second Temple period, the scrolls were preserved in caves here by virtue of the astonishingly arid Judea Desert climate. Their contents are tremendously important for the study of Bible history and Hebrew language, since they include Biblical manuscripts about a thousand years older than any previously known. Some of these documents describe in detail the faith and way of life of an ascetic Jewish sect which dwelled here — the 'Dead Sea Sect', which may be identified with the Essenes who appear in literary sources. These findings are also tremendously important for study of the early years of Christianity. The settlement where the sect lived has been excavated, and its character was evidently dictated by the peculiar life style of the people living in it.

Ein Gedi

The **desert oasis** and **nature reserve** at Ein Gedi are among Israel's loveliest natural treasures. The location, climate and abundant water have created an extraordinary nook of tropical vegetation and wildlife. Two streams — David and Arugot — plunge through pitched canyons in gorgeous waterfalls. As you explore the area, you'll see wild ibexes and rock rabbits at close range. From a distance a leopard may even be glimpsed. Ruins of ancient settlements are found nearby as well. A field school run by the Israel Nature Preservation Society can provide further information and guidance.

Masada

One of Israel's most interesting archeological sites, its fascinating history, known in detail, has made it a cornerstone in Jewish history and one of its most famous symbols. Its archeological digs unearthed an abundance of well-preserved ruins, making a visit here an interesting and impressive experience. One can get here by car, on a tour or by regular bus service.

Masada, about 16 miles south of Ein Gedi, stands atop a conspicuous butte towering above the Dead Sea basin. If you haven't the time or the athletic inclination to climb it by the one hour **Snake Path** (try to time this for daybreak), a **cablecar** makes the ascent from the east. One may also climb Masada by the much easier and shorter (30 minute) western route. Its base, however, is reached by a lengthy detour via Arad. Again, beware of the heat in this desert location, especially during the early afternoon!

The Masada excavations focused on two major periods which we may call 'body' and 'soul'. The 'body' of Masada was the well-appointed fortress built here by Herod. It includes magnificent **palaces** (the **Northern Palace** juts over the abyss with tremendous engineering audacity), a **Roman bath**, a **water storage system** and **fortifications**. Beautiful architectural details such as mosaics and wall murals survive in some cases. Despite the time and effort invested in building the Masada fortress, Herod made little use of it.

The second period can be referred to as the 'soul' of Masada. It was at the end of the Great Rebellion against Rome (during which the Temple fell) when the site served as a refuge for a Jewish faction known as the Zealots. The Roman siege of Masada, in 72-73 AD, was the last battle of that insurrection and of the Zealots. The Zealots, inspired by a dramatic speech by their commander, took the decision to put themselves to death, rather than fall into enemy hands. Though they burned the buildings beforehand, they left some of their food supplies intact to let the Romans know they had not succumbed to hunger. The tragic drama turned Masada into a symbol. The Zealots, who spent only a brief time on the mountain, left remarkably simple and functional traces compared to Herod's grand palaces. The Zealots used these structures for housing and command headquarters.

The most important Jewish ruin here is the synagogue (where several scrolls were found). Ritual baths (*mikves*) were also found. An especially fascinating find was a group of 25 skeletons in a cave. In addition, skeletons of a man, woman and child were discovered in the northern palace; the woman's scalp, hair and sandals were found intact. This apparently had been the family of one of Masada's commanders because remains of magnificent armor were discovered nearby. The skeletons were buried in 1969, with full Israeli military honors, west of Masada.

If you look down you will be able to see the well-preserved remains of the Roman siege system around the base of the cliff. An audio-visual show is held on some summer evenings, giving an impressive presentation of the history of the site.

Tour Four: Jericho and Wadi Kelt

Jericho

Jericho, one of the oldest settled urban sites on earth, occupies a large oasis which stands out in contrast to the arid Jordan Valley. The ancient city, **Tel a-Sultan**, is next to the **Spring of Elisha**, to which Jericho has owed its existence from the beginning. In addition to the greenery, the trees and the market, Jericho and its vicinity offer several especially interesting places to visit.

Hisham Palace, or **Hirbet al-Mafjer**, an eighth century Umayyad Muslim palace, about one and a quarter miles north of Jericho, is one of Israel's most impressive archeological sites. Its buildings are noteworthy for their elaborate ornamentation. In addition to the palace, special mention should be made of the bathhouse, the largest ever discovered in the Muslim world. Apart from its dimensions and its domes, note the mosaics, among the most vast to have survived from the ancient world. Notice, too, the *diwan* (reception room for guests), decorated with an uncommonly beautiful mosaic which depicts a lion attacking deer at the base of a large tree. Some of the Hisham Palace findings are exhibited in Jerusalem's Rockefeller Museum.

Talul Abu al-'Alaiek,Second-Temple period palaces, at an archeological site at the mouth of Wadi Kelt, has yielded ruins of Hasmonoean and Herodian (second Temple period) royal winter palaces. The large structures are surrounded by an unusual concentration of waterworks, such as pools and baths. The location, along the course of Wadi Kelt, kept them filled and made them especially attractive when water flowed. Though the findings here are impressive, the most interesting things in this vast area are hard to find without a guide. Be sure to bring an ample supply of water with you.

Na'aran

Follow the Jericho-Ramallah highway about two miles to a restaurant transversed by a flowing stream (Casino al-'Amara) — a pleasant place to spend part of an afternoon in any case. From here, a short walk along an aqueduct takes you to the ancient **Na'aran Synagogue**. Note the handsome mosaic floor

— a partially defaced Zodiac, some animals, and two seven-branched *menoras* (candelabra) with inscriptions alongside.

The Quarantal Monastery or The Monastery of Temptation

The athletically inclined may leave the Jericho-Ramallah highway for an easy climb to a Greek Orthodox monastery which clings to the cliffs of the Mount of Temptation. A visit is a unique experience: you will see a monastery which incorporates caves into half its area, and an unsurpassable view of the Jericho Valley. The monastery is built into the rock face of the mountain where, according to tradition, Satan tempted Jesus for 40 days. Its name, Quarantal, originates in the word *quarante* — forty. Apart from its mountain caves and rooms hewn out of the rock, the Greek monastery makes use of buildings erected on a narrow stone terrace.

Wadi Kelt

Traveling from Jerusalem toward Jericho, we pass through the Arab village of **El-Azariyya** (ancient Bethany). Here Jesus resurrected Lazarus, as the name of the village, though somewhat corrupted, attests. Several ancient ruins and churches may be seen here.

Closer to Jericho, Wadi Kelt runs north of the highway and crosses the Judea Desert from east to west. The traveler, equipped with more detailed information, may stop at any of three pleasurable **springs,** a **Greek Orthodox monastery** pinned to the mountain face, canyon abysses, rich vegetation and archeological ruins. The easiest place to tour is the monastery. A section of an older road branches to the left about 12 miles outside of Jerusalem. Follow it about two miles until you come to a parking lot. From here, make your descent into the watercourse and come up on the other side to the monastery. The entire side trip may take about 90 minutes. The picturesque monastery, known as **Deir Mar Giris**, is identified by tradition with the site of the cave where the Prophet Elijah, taking refuge, was brought bread and meat by ravens (Kings I, 17:4, 6). For a longer visit of Wadi Kelt one can walk along the valley between the springs or on the aqueduct.

Nebi Mussa

The ancient, dome-embellished walled structure about one mile south of the Jericho-Jerusalem highway is known in Muslim tradition as the **site of Moses' grave**. It was apparently erected by the Mameluke Sultan Baybars in 1265. The annual Easter-time pilgrimage to the tomb is determined by the solar Christian calendar, not by the lunar Calendar by which the other Muslim holidays are calculated. The decision indicates a Muslim intent to create a counterweight to the intense Christian pilgrim traffic in Jerusalem at Easter. A hospice and other structures were built around the tomb. The number of pilgrims dwindled after Israel's War of Independence and the site is inactive today.

Tour Five — Tel Aviv

Though Jerusalem is Israel's capital and represents 3,000 years of history, the country's major city and economic, diplomatic, cultural and communications hub is Tel Aviv. Some 50 miles from Jerusalem, Tel Aviv sometimes seems world's apart in its lifestyle and character. Insiders claim that Tel Avivians wake up when Jerusalemites go to bed. Perhaps a bit of an exaggeration, but there may be something to it. The city offers the visitor a chance to relax and just have fun. Explore Tel Aviv's shops and markets, take in the concerts and theater, sun at the beach, enjoy the night (and day) life in the many outdoor cafes, nightclubs, restaurants and other attractions.

Less than 80 years ago, what is now Tel Aviv, was nothing more than desolate sand-dunes. The only settlement was in Jaffa, then a small Arab town. In 1909, an area north of Jaffa was purchased with the intention of building a new neighborhood. The new neighborhood was named Tel Aviv — Hill of Spring. Development of the area accelerated after British occupation (1917): Jewish immigration during this period increased and many newcomers settled in Tel Aviv.

Tel Aviv has more to offer than beaches. Apart from entertainment and shopping centers, it has a few 'musts'. Perhaps the most important of these is **Beth Hatefutsoth**, or **The Museum of the Jewish Diaspora**, a modern museum on the campus of **Tel Aviv University**. (Open daily 10am-5pm, Wed. 10am-7pm. Closed Fri.-Sat. Bus lines 13, 24, 25, 27, 74 and 79). The fascinating exhibit brings to life the history of Jewish communities around the world during their 2,000-year exile. Located nearby is the **Ha'aretz Museum** which is, in fact, a cluster of museums — ceramics, glass, coins, writing, ethnography and folklore, science, technology, and a modern planetarium. Open daily 9am-1pm, Tues. 4-7pm, Sat. 10am-1pm. Bus lines 13, 24, 25, 27, 74 and 79).

In the center of town one can find the **Dizengoff Center**, the **Mann Auditorium**, the **Habima Theater** (Israel's national theater) and the **Tel Aviv Museum** (27 King Saul Blvd.), the city's most important trove of art. Open Sun.-Wed. 10am-5pm., Thurs. 10am-10pm, Sat. 10am-3pm, Fri. closed.

Another, literally outstanding spot is **the Shalom Meir Tower**, at 9 Ahad ha-Am St., the tallest building in the Middle East.

A few blocks from the Shalom Tower is Tel Aviv's largest open air market, the **Carmel Market** (Heb. *Shuk Hacarmel*).

South of Tel Aviv is **Jaffa,** whose old city offers a few attractions. Besides the old port, reminiscent of more glorious days, Old Jaffa accommodates nightclubs, restaurants, cafes, a small park, jewelry and antique shops, and number of art galleries. The narrow alleyways, little houses and picturesque shops create a pleasant and special atmosphere worthy of a visit. A special feature is the 'Israel Experience', a one-hour multimedia show which takes you through the history of Palestine/Israel from the Biblical period to our time (open daily; screenings in English, French, German and Hebrew. Tel. 03-813205). Another attraction is Jaffa's **Flea Market** (Heb. *Shuk Hapishpashim*) near the Clock Tower (buses: 18, 19, 25, 46).

Check the *Jerusalem Post* for up-to-date information regarding various events in Tel Aviv.

"MUSTS"

Here is a list of "musts", sites which without viewing, no visit to Jerusalem could be considered complete. Each site has a corresponding tour route in the book.

View from the Mount of Olives: A spectacular and unforgettable view of an unparalleled city. Bus 99. (See "From the Mount of Olives to the City of David".)

The Holy Sepulchre: The most sacred site in the eyes of millions of Christians. Open 4:30am-7pm, summer till 8pm. Buses 3, 13, 19, 20 or 30 to Jaffa Gate. (See "The Church of the Holy Sepulchre").

The Temple Mount: Landmarks of Muslim architecture on Islam's third most holy site. The most famous sites are the Dome of the Rock and the Al-Aksa Mosque. Best access is to enter the Old City at Jaffa Gate and follow David St. to Shalshelet St. until the Gate of the Chain. (See "The Temple Mount").

The Western Wall: The last remnant of the Jewish Temple, symbol of Jewish hope and aspiration. Most interesting on Friday evenings and Saturday mornings or on Jewish holidays. Buses 1, 38 and 99. (See "Past and Present").

The Israel Museum: Incomparable collections of antiquities from the Holy Land, and of Jewish art and ethnography. Open Sun.-Thurs. 10am-5pm, Tues. 4-10pm, Fri. and Sat. 10am-2pm (for Sat. buy tickets in advance). Buses 9, 24 and 99. (See "Culture and Democracy").

Yad Vashem: A unique museum and memorial devoted to the Jewish Holocaust. Open Sun.-Thurs. 9am-5pm, Fri. 9am-2pm. Bus 99, 13, 17, 18, 20 and 23. (See "Western Heights")

Highly Recommended

Brook of Kidron: Dramatic topography, beautiful churches and ancient tombs. This can be reached from the Mt. of Olives observation point. Bus 99. (See "From the Mt. of Olives to the City of David".)

Hezekiah's Tunnel: Walk in water through this astonishing engineering feat of the 7th century BC. Open Sun.-Thurs. 9am-4pm and Fri. 9am-1pm. (See "From the Mt. of Olives to the City of David".)

JERUSALEM

Via Dolorosa: The path of Jesus' afflictions through the Old City. Procession every Friday at 3pm. Buses 1 and 99. (See "The Via Dolorosa").

Rampart Walk: A stroll on top of the Old City's Wall, with unusual views. This walk begins at Damascus Gate. Gate and wall open daily 9am-5pm. (See "Walls and Ramparts.")

The Jewish Quarter: The reconstructed Jewish Quarter, retaining the atmosphere of yesteryear. Best access is via Jaffa Gate. Buses 3, 13, 19, 20 or 30. (See "The Armenian and Jewish Quarters").

Old City Market: A buzzing Oriental market. Shops in Moslem Quarter closed Fridays. Access through Jaffa Gate. Buses 2, 13, 19, 20 or 30. (See "The Armenian and Jewish Quarters".)

Me'a She'arim: A unique glance into the ultra-Orthodox Jewish world, unchanged by the 20th century. Not advisable to visit here on Friday evenings or on Saturdays. (See "A Unique Ethnic Experience").

Second Temple Model: A tangible record of Jerusalem at its peak. On the grounds of the Holyland Hotel. Buses 21, 21A and 99. (See "Ancient Jerusalem at its Peak").

Making the Most of Your Stay

Wining and Dining

Although Jerusalem is not renowned for its hectic nightlife, there are several clubs and theaters, and plenty of restaurants where one can spend a pleasant evening.

The most popular local food, eaten at any hour of the day, is *felafel* (fried rissoles made of chickpeas), served in *pita* bread with *hummus* (ground chickpeas), *tehina* (ground sesame sauce) and salad. Many pavement cafes also serve *shwarma* which consists of delicious pieces of veal or lamb sliced off a rotisserie and served with pita, salad and chips. *Knafe* are sweet pastries soaked in syrup, sometimes with a filling of chopped nuts and spices, which are sold all over the Arab market in the Old City.

Those who want to eat traditional Jewish food such as *gefilte fish*, can try one of the more traditional restaurants, but Jerusalem also has many restaurants specializing in more exotic cuisine. If you wish to dine in a more elegant restaurant, and enjoy a good meal after a full day's touring, it is best to make reservations.

The list below covers several good restaurants in various categories according to style and cuisine. Remember, not every restaurant accepts credit cards — ask first.

Middle Eastern

Au Sahara — 17 Jaffa Rd., tel. 233-239.
Ruchama — 3 Yavets St. off 49 Jaffa Rd., tel. 246-565. Typical Yemenite cuisine.
The Roof Top Garden — National Palace Hotel, 4 Ez Zahra St., East Jerusalem. tel. 282-246. Sumptuous cuisine and a magnificent view of Mt. Scopus and Mt. of Olives.
Imah — 189 Agrippas St., tel. 246-860. Very popular with the locals.

Popular Middle Eastern

Abu Shukri — Hagai St., Old City.
Rahmu -2 Ha'eshkol St., tel. 234-595. Outstanding *hummus.*
Rimon — 4 Lunz St., tel. 222-772.
Shemesh — 21 Ben Yehuda St., tel. 223-232
Sima — 82 Agrippas St., near Mahane Yehuda market.

Ta'ami — 3 Shamai St., tel. 223-644. Unquestionably the best *hummus* of all.

Top of the Town
American Colony Hotel — Nablus Rd., Old City. tel. 282-421. Recommended for its buffet.
Chez Simon — 15 Shamai St., tel. 225-302. Highly recommended.
Cow on the Roof — Sheraton Plaza Hotel, 47 King George St., tel. 228-133 ext. 3129. Elegant French cuisine.
Fat Henry's — 3 Yanai St., tel. 228-898.
Hungarian Goulash — Ein Karem. tel. 419-214.
Seven Arches Hotel — Mt. of Olives. tel. 282-551. Outstanding buffet.
Jozi's Courtyard — 38 Emek Refa'im St., tel. 664-323. Superb Romanian grills.
Katy's House — 16 Rivlin St., tel. 234-621.
Mishkenot Sha'anannim — Yemin Moshe St., tel. 233-424. Patronised by visiting artists and the local who's who.
Windows on Jerusalem — 29 Nablus Rd., East Jerusalem. tel. 282-375. Superb panoramic view of Jerusalem. Excellent lunch buffet on Sundays.

Chinese
Mandarin — 2 Shlomzion Hamalka St., tel. 222-890.
Mandy Tachi — 3 Horkenos St., tel. 248-233.
Teppanyika — King Solomon Hotel, 32 King David St., tel. 241-433 (ext. 3). Japanese fare.
Yo-Si Peking — 5 Shimon Ben Shettah St., tel. 226-893.

Italian
Alla Gondola — 14 King George St., tel. 225-944.
Mama Mia — 18 Rabbi Akiva St., tel. 248-080.
Mamma Leone — 5 Hillel St., tel. 242-767.
Richies — 7 King George St., tel. 244-130. Delicious pizzas, fast food style. Very popular with foreign students.

Mexican
Cactus — 36 Keren Hayesod St., tel. 667-719.

Traditional Jewish
Feferbergs — 53 Jaffa Rd., tel. 224-841.
Heppner's Deli — 4 Lunz St., tel. 221-703.

Seafood
Beni — Mesilat Yesharim St., Menora Square, tel. 222-403. Highly recommended.
Elat Hayam — 3 Ben Sira St., tel. 246-122. Fish and grill restaurant.

Sea Dolphin — Al Rashid St., East Jerusalem. tel. 282-788.
La petit Differance — 9 Diskin Kiryat Wolfsohn tel. 636-848. French.

Dairy
Home Plus — Heleni Hamalka St., tel. 222-612. Young and dynamic atmosphere.
Magdalena — 22 Shlomo Hamelekh., tel. 224-710. Restaurant with a gallery.
Of Course — Emile Botta St., Yemin Moshe., tel. 245-206. Lovely view.
Leyad Hakikar — 6 Yo'el Salomon St., tel. 242-549.
Poondak Hakhalav — 17 Bezal'el St., tel. 231-888.
Poire et Pomme — 2 Remez Square near Khan Theater. tel. 719-602. Serves delicious blintzes.

Light Meals
Bagel Nash — 14 Ben Yehuda St. (Pedestrian Mall). American style.
Chocolate Soup — 6 Rivlin St., off Jaffa Rd. Village style atmosphere.
Khan — 2 Kikkar Remez. tel. 718-283.
Pie House — 5 Horkenos St., tel. 242-478.
Tea and Pie — 33 Jaffa Rd. Delicious homemade pies.

Coffee Shops

Atara — 7 Ben Yehuda St., tel. 225-088. Also serves the best onion soup in the city.
Jan's Tea House — Chopin St. Under Jerusalem Theater.
Sefer-Ve-Sefel — 2 Yabez St., tel. 248-237. A coffee house inside a bookstore.
Ticho House — 9 Harav Kook St., tel. 244-186. Set in the beautiful garden of the Ticho House Museum.
Kamin — 4 Rabbi Akiva St., tel. 234-819. Wonderful to sit outside in a nice weather.

Galleries

A short list of some of the best known gallerie in Jerusalem follows:

Arta — 4 Rabbi Akiva St., tel. 227-829
Engel — 13 Shelomzion Hamalka St., tel. 223-523
Gimmel — 4 King Salomon St., tel. 227-636
Nora — 9 Ben Maimon Bd., tel. 632-849
Safrai — 19 King David St., tel. 224-885

There are also a number of galleries and artists studios in Yemin

Moshe, Ein Karem and the Jewish quarter in the Old City.

Art and Craft Centers

Armenian ceramics — available in various shops in the Old City. The shop on the Via Dolorosa is recommended.
Hutzot Hayotzer Art and Craft Center — near Jaffa Gate, outside the old city.
Kuzari — 10 Rehovot Habukharim St., tel. 826-632. Specializing in traditional embroidery of the Middle East.
Maskit — 12 Harav Kook St.
Ot Hamutzar center — 12 Derech Hebron
WIZO — 34 Jaffa Rd., tel. 233-955

Culture and entertainment

Though Tel Aviv is Israel's nightlife center, Jerusalem offers some nightlife for the visitor. Jerusalemites seem to prefer rather straight-laced amusements; cultural events rather than discotheques. The culture menu is rich, largely due to various festivals which the city hosts each year.

Two regular festivals take place at the same time. The more important of them is the Spring Festival with dozens of performances of high quality. The second is a film festival, with rare films.

Concerts and theater: *Binyanei Ha-Uma*, near the entrance to town between the Hilton and the Central Bus Station, is Jerusalem's largest and most important performance center. It hosts important fairs and conferences as well. *Sultan's Pool*, between Jaffa Gate and Yemin Moshe, stages large musical performances under the stars. The *Jerusalem Theater* and the adjacent *Crown Auditorium* (20 Marcus St.) have concerts and dramas, as does the *Gerard Bechar Center* on 11 Bezal'el St.

Smaller halls host various chamber performances. They include the *Khan Theater* at 2 David Remez Sq., and the *Pargod Theater*, 94 Bezalel St. The latter specializes in jazz, by the best performers in Israel.

Various churches around town offer a variety of concerts, especially Church music. One example is the *Lutheran Church of the Redeemer* in the Old City.

Cinema: Jerusalem has 20 movie houses, mostly located downtown. Films are shown in their original languages, with Hebrew sub-titles. There is usually no need to buy tickets in advance; get them at the theater box office just before the show begins.

The highly popular **Jerusalem Cinematheque** screens several films every evening. A certain theme is usually pursued for a given period of time — an actor, stage director, or cinema genre. The cinematheque is located in a lovely building on Derech Hebron. Lovers of French cinema will want to visit *Maison Alliance Francaise* on Agron St., where French films are screened every evening.

Bars and discotheques: Though these are not traditionally the preferred mode of amusement in Jerusalem, they have begun to catch on in recent years. The bar and discotheque 'district' is the area off Yoel Moshe Salomon St. and Zion Sq., an alley branching from 31 Jaffa Rd., and adjacent to Rivlin St.

The Ben-Yehuda pedestrian mall bustles day and night with its cafes, of which *Atara* and *La Riviera* are recommended. Street entertainment is on hand during the summer.

Advance purchase of tickets for various events, secures your place and saves a lengthy and irritating wait in line. Jerusalem has three ticket offices:

Ben-Naim: 38 Jaffa Rd., tel. 224-008.
Cahana: 1 Dorot Rishonim St., tel. 222-831.
Kartison: 8 Shamai St., tel. 224-273.

Holidays and Festivals

One needs to scan the calendar minutely to detect a day which is not holy to one of the religious groups in Jerusalem. Moreover, enumerating the holy days in Jerusalem is made more complex by the fact that different groups go according to different calendars.

Of the Christian holidays, Christmas and Easter are the most important. In both cases, one can encounter interesting activities in many churches, especially the Holy Sepulchre. The holy week of Easter is noteworthy for the Palm Sunday procession which leaves from the Mt. of Olives. Note that the various denominations celebrate those holidays on different days, especially if you are interested in seeing Eastern Orthodox festivities. The Greek Orthodox, for example, celebrate Christmas on January 6th. There is also a weekly procession along the Via Dolorosa every Friday (see 'Via Dolorosa'). For specific details contact the Christian Information Center. tel. 287-647.

Few Jewish holidays are interesting to the outsider. The Jewish year begins around September with New Year celebrations and the Day of Atonement, but there is not much to see then. More attractive is *Succoth*, a few days later, when Jews build tabernacles with foliage roofs outside their houses, and are expected to live in them for a week. Especially interesting is the area of Me'a She'arim, where every balcony and courtyard has a tabernacle.

Around December, Jews celebrate *Hannukah*, the Festival of Lights, in which you can see beautiful *hanukiot* (candelabra) on windowsills, especially in Me'a She'arim and other religious neighborhoods. On Passover (around April, approximately the same time as Easter) Jews have a special ceremonial meal, the *seder*, which might prove interesting if you receive an invitation. During Passover week Jews eat *matzot* (unleavened bread). A different type of celebration is the Day of Independence, around May, in which multitudes fill the streets, dancing and just having fun. The previous day is Memorial Day for those that have fallen in Israel's wars.

One cannot see much of Muslim festivities. Most holy days are celebrated in the Temple Mount, and at those times entrance is prohibited. One month every year, the *Ramadan*, the Moslems fast during the day and eat after a special cannon signals sunset. Since the Muslim year is shorter by about two weeks than the Christian year, the *Ramadan* does not correspond to the same Christian month each year.

Important Addresses and Phone Numbers

Emergencies

Ambulance (*Magen David Adom*): tel. 101.
Fire: tel. 102.
Police: tel. 100.
Information: tel. 144.
International Operator: tel. 188.
American Consulate: 18 Agron St. West Jerusalem. tel. 234-271.
British Consulate: 19 Nashashibi, East Jerusalem. tel. 828-281.

Airlines

El Al: 12 Hillel St., tel. 233-333.
Air France: King David Hotel. tel. 222-655.
Alitalia: 33 Jaffa Rd., tel. 228-652.
British Airways: 33 Jaffa Rd., tel. 233-112.
K.L.M.: 33 Jaffa Rd., tel. 232-881.
Olympic: 33 Jaffa Rd., tel. 234-538.
Sabena: King David Hotel. tel. 234-971.
S.A.S.: 25 Jaffa Rd., tel. 233-192.
Swissair: 30 Jaffa Rd., tel. 225-233.
T.W.A.: King David Hotel. tel. 221-516.

INDEX

INDEX

INDEX

NOTES

NOTES

NOTES